# Indonesian Muslims in a Global World

# Indonesian Muslims in a Global World:

## *Identity Narratives of Young Muslims in Australian Society*

By

Teuku Zulfikar

**Cambridge**
**Scholars**
Publishing

Indonesian Muslims in a Global World:
Identity Narratives of Young Muslims in Australian Society

By Teuku Zulfikar

This book first published 2017

Cambridge Scholars Publishing

Lady Stephenson Library, Newcastle upon Tyne, NE6 2PA, UK

British Library Cataloguing in Publication Data
A catalogue record for this book is available from the British Library

ISBN (10): 1-4438-7941-X
ISBN (13): 978-1-4438-7941-5

# CONTENTS

# ACKNOWLEDGMENTS

Completing this project requires hard-work and commitment, and thus I am indebted to many individuals for their support in encouraging me during these four years of tedious work. I would first thank *Allāh* the Almighty for giving me patience, strength and persistence in completing this difficult, yet interesting project. This project would not have been completed without the help of several important scholars, Dr. Cynthia Joseph and Dr. Fida Sandjakdar for their close supervision on my work.

My biggest thanks go to my parents and family whose support has taken me on this beautiful academic journey. I also would like to thank Dr. Margaret Gearon, Dr. Elizabeth Tudball, and Dr. Joel Windle for their comments and feedback during my fieldwork. My thanks also go to Ms. Rosemary Viete for guiding me during my writing process. I wish to thank Monash University, especially the Faculty of Education and the TLC for providing me the spaces and venues to widen and broaden my knowledge. Thanks also go to MERC for providing me with some important programs that allowed me to improve my research and presentation skills. I am extremely grateful to the 12 young Muslims who willingly participated in this project. They have given time to me during my fieldwork, and much information was generated from our interaction within the Muslim community in diaspora. I thank them for their time and generosity in sitting in my series of interviews and for their willingness to write their personal narratives.

To the Muslim parents, I also express my gratitude for the times they spent at interviews and for allowing me to interview their children, welcoming me into their homes, and serving me with light meals during my interviews with them and their children.

In completing this project, I am also indebted to Indonesian Muslim community leaders for their total support and for introducing me to Indonesian community members who later on participated in this important academic endeavour. I also thank them for giving me very useful and important information regarding the Indonesian Muslim community in Victoria and a brief history on their migration process. They allowed me to use the Indonesian Muslim community centre for posting my invitation and most importantly gave me permission to interview and observe the participants in the mosque.

I also appreciate Cambridge Scholars Publishing for being interested in publishing this piece of work and I have a strong confidence that the book will reach a wide international audience.

# CHAPTER ONE

# RATIONALES AND REFLEXIVITY: WHY STUDY YOUNG MUSLIMS?

I would start this book through reflecting on my experience being Muslim in multiple settings. This is important to provide the basis of thinking and inquiry toward the exploration of Indonesian Muslim youth's ways of being Muslim in Australian Society. This is also because throughout the book my focus will be on narratives of young Muslims living within their fluid and hyphenated identities.

I am an Indonesian Muslim living in Indonesia, one of the largest Muslim communities in the world. I have been exposed to Islamic values through parental guidance, community, and schooling experiences. I perceive my parents' teaching of Islamic values, my exposure with Muslim communities, and my education in Islamic institutions from primary up to the tertiary level as having been significant in the construction of my Muslim identity. My life is shaped by the teaching of Islam; thus my commitment to observing the five pillars of Islam such as the *salāt* (praying) and the *sawm* (fasting), and my embracing of Islamic conduct such as respecting elders and not drinking alcohol are reflections of these lifelong influences. This positioning definitely shapes my understanding of being Muslim, and in this book, I will highlight my research positioning. It is important to state research positioning as it influences the way I perceive things as the researcher.

I realize that during my studies in Australia, I find my positioning shifting from being an "insider" in the Muslim-majority of Indonesia to somewhat of an "outsider" as part of the Muslim minorities in Australia. I use the term "outsider" or 'Insignificant Other' (Halstead 1995b) to refer to my status as a part of the Muslim minority within Australian society. Since arriving in Australia, I have developed close relationships with the Indonesian Muslims through my involvement with the community in Melbourne, which has enabled me to observe the social dynamics within the Indonesian-Muslim community and the broader Muslim communities in Melbourne.

I have observed in my interaction with Indonesian Muslim families in Australia that most of these first generation Indonesian Muslims are committed to the Islamic teachings. In fact, they attempt to increase their Islamic knowledge through religious programs held in the Indonesian Muslim community centre and also within Muslim families. In contrast, their children negotiate their religious identity in different ways from their parents. Some young Indonesian Muslims do not show a great interest in being in the mosque[1]. This lack of interest may be the result of multiple reasons, which are revealed in this book. Similar observations are seen in many other Muslim communities in the West, such as in North America and in Europe (Alghorani 2003; Küçükcan 2004; McGown 1999).

Many studies on Muslims, such as those by Hussain (2004), Saeed (2003), and Zine (2007), indicate that the majority of Muslim parents in non-Muslim countries are concerned with enhancing their children's understanding of Islamic teaching and helping them to become devoted Muslims. Some Indonesian Muslim parents living in Victoria, for example, are found to engage in similar attempts[2] to shape their children's Muslim identity, and they frequently consult Muslim scholars to generate the best possible ways to teach their children about Islam. However, their children do not live in a vacuum; they have friends to interact with, either in schools or in their neighbourhoods. During their interactions with their friends, and the broader community, Muslim youth engage with different values and attitudes, which may be in conflict with the Islamic values as advocated in the Islamic religious texts and doctrines (Doogue & Kirkwood 2005).[3]

For example, Akhtar (2007b) and Bayoumi (2010) found in their studies a certain degree of generational conflicts within Muslim communities in the West. Akhtar (2007b), for example highlighted some major behavioural issues suffered by Muslim youth in the United States. He found that some young Muslims in his study did not show any interest in discussing religious issues. He also identified that most young Muslims he interviewed indicated that dating and the living together of different sexes without marriage are considered as acceptable forms of social life. These young Muslims also perceive that alcohol and smoking are individual choices.

---

[1] This fact was observed during my presence in religious programs in the mosque and in Muslims' houses.

[2] An example of this is that some Indonesian Muslim parents invite their children to Friday praying, weekend school, religious congregations in the mosque and other events that may instil religious principles.

[3] Visit this website http://www.aihw.gov.au/publications/phe/sdua00/sdua00.pdf for more detail about this issue.

Such ways of thinking are assumed to be in conflict with the teaching of Islam as stipulated in the religious texts (Akhtar 2007b). In addition, the other striking issue revealed is a cultural conflict between the younger and older generations (Akhtar 2007b). Akhtar suggests that generational conflicts emerge in terms of educational and career choices, and the other frequent conflict concerns parents' over-protection of their daughters' relationships with friends of different sexes.

The study by Bayoumi (2010), however, uncovered a rather different reality from that of Akhtar's (2007b) study. Bayoumi revealed that some young Muslims were found to be more religiously devoted than their parents. In his study of young Muslims of Arab background in Brooklyn USA, he found that these young Muslims, unlike their parents, realized that they were vanguards of Islam and they were required to represent it well in the wider American society (Bayoumi 2010). This kind of generational conflict also occurred in terms of religious attire. The feasibility of wearing the veil in public is increasing in the contemporary global world, and young female Muslims in research conducted by Ali (2005) and Mishra and Shirazi (2010), for example, choose to take on the veil. However, their decision to wear the veil may be opposed by their family members. Parents of these young Muslims in this study felt a sense of insecurity when their daughters were wearing the veil while living in a non-Muslim country such as the USA (Ali 2005; Mishra & Shirazi 2010).

Given these generational conflicts within the Muslim family and the *ummah* (Muslim community), I intend to understand whether such generational conflicts emerge within the Indonesian Muslim families and communities in Melbourne. Understanding young Muslims' ways of constructing and negotiating their Muslim identity at home and the religious spaces is an important aspect of inquiry in this study. Studies examining the construction of Muslim identity have been increasing in recent times. These studies adopt different concerns, settings, and methodologies. For example, there are studies on the contestation of Islamic values and the resistance of some Muslim parents of Somali background toward the school system in Canada (see Collet 2007; McGown 1999). Another such study is by Marranci (2007), which examines the process through which Muslim women in Northern Ireland construct their identity. A study that took place in Britain explores how young Muslims conceptualize their identity and citizenship (Basit 2009). In addition, studies on Muslims in Australia have been abundant. For example, Mansouri and Kamp (2007) investigate factors affecting the social and schooling experience of Muslim students of Arab-speaking background. This book adds a particular focus on young Muslims of

Indonesian heritage in Australia and also enriches the literature on Muslims and their construction of identity.

Studies indicate that ways of being Muslim, especially in a 'western context' are complicated. There are different ways of practising Islam and being Muslim, shaped by various social factors, such as culture, race, ethnicity, geographical location, and socio-cultural location (Kabir 2010; Sirin & Fine 2008). A study by Masquelier (2010), for example, indicates that while young Muslims in Nigeria claim themselves to be Muslim, they do not necessarily show their religious conviction through the performance of rituals. The complexity of being Muslim is also indicated by Zine (2006), who suggests that while some young Canadian female Muslims in her study take their religious markers through wearing Islamic outfit, they are challenged by stereotypical sentiments in their host countries. This study aims to add to the body of literature that sheds further light on the complex ways of being young Muslims.

In addition, this book sees Muslim families and the Muslim *Ummah* as important social and educational sites, through which the identities of young Muslims are moulded and shaped. This book, therefore, aims at investigating how Indonesian Muslim family dynamics shape the identity of young Indonesian Muslims. It also examines how religious programs in Islamic spaces such as the *madrasah* (the religious weekend school) and the *Masjid* (the mosque) shape young Muslims' identity. Given there are various discourses of being Muslim operating within families and the *Ummah*, and different ways of interpreting religious texts within these spaces, the book aims to investigate how young Indonesian Muslims negotiate these different discourses and create their own ways of being Muslim.

The data in this book is important because it provides researchers with insights into the ways in which the younger generation of Muslim youth in a 'western' context such as Australia construct their '*Muslimness*', that is, their ways of being Muslim. It also provides an understanding into the complex identity practices these young Indonesian-Muslims in Australia engage with through the discourses of religion and culture with their family and within the immediate religious community and the broader Australian context.

The data presented throughout this book is also significant in its attempt to understand the roles of religious spaces, such as the *madrasah* (religious weekend school) and the *masjid* (the mosque) in shaping the Muslim identity of young Indonesian Muslims. The book thus hopes to enable readers to understand the significance of the existence of the religious spaces for the Muslim community. In addition, the research outcomes will also give insights to Muslim community leaders in their attempts to safeguard Muslim identity through Islamic programs held in the *madrasah* and in the *Masjid*. The findings of the study will add on to the important body of literature on Muslim youth in these new times and contexts.

Previous studies have discovered the importance of family practices (Becher 2008) and the mosque as educational sites in which Muslim identity construction takes place (Lotfi 2001). This study explores further how young Muslims negotiate their ways of being Muslim within the family and the *ummah* spaces, providing important information to the broader society through the voices of Muslim parents on their aspirations for their children, and through their children's own accounts of their developing ways of being Muslim in a non-Muslim country. This study is expected to bridge the gap between Muslim communities and the mainstream Australian society. The following section briefly discusses Muslims in the West, especially those living in Australia.

# Muslims in the West

## *Muslims' ways of engagement in non-Muslim countries*

In recent times, Muslims have migrated to many parts of the world. There are Muslims in France (see Keaton 2005); Britain (see Anwar 2008; Küçükcan 2004); Canada (see McGown 1999; Zine, 2008); the USA (see Curtis 2009; Kaya 2003; Sirin & Fine 2008); Australia (see Mansouri & Wood 2008; Saeed 2003) and in other parts of the world.

Muslims who migrated to the West live as minorities within their host countries. In spite of their minority status, their ways of engagement in their host countries differ from country to country (Esposito 2010; Raedt 2004; Schmidt 2004; Spalek & Imtoul 2007). Particular Muslim immigrant communities may experience different challenges in negotiating their ways of being Muslim while living in western countries. For example, immigrants' adaptation to life in certain host countries is relatively easy. Anwar (2008) revealed that Muslims in Western Europe encounter many more difficult situations compared to those living in Britain. Raedt (2004) also found in his study that Belgian Muslims of Turkish and Moroccan background experience different ways of engagement in their host countries. This difference occurs because of quite different migration histories. Raedt (2004) notes:

> The Turks (naturalized or not) seem to have adopted more cautiously than the Moroccans... They [the Turks] migrated more in a chain, and recruited

more partners from their home region, and therefore have a stronger sense of community. The Moroccan pattern evolves toward internal fragmentation (Raedt 2004, 23).

This comment indicates that Turkish Muslims develop a strong connection with their family in their home and this strong bond to their home country becomes a barrier in their integration process. At the other end of the spectrum of integration, Muslim communities of Moroccan background, by contrast, have been more rapidly assimilated into the mainstream society, lacking a strongly 'present' community. Raedt (2004) also found that "the students belonging to the Moroccan communities succeed better in the Belgian educational system than the students from the Turkish communities" (p. 23). This information suggests that Muslims in the West as minority communities engage differently in their host countries. Their different engagement is also likely to have been shaped by their different attitudes toward their host countries.

A further example of this diversity is the relative ease with which Muslims in the USA, for example, engage in the American society (Esposito 2010) if compared to those living in different western countries such as in France and Belgium (Raedt 2004; Samers 2003). Such different experiences may be contingent on conditions of migration and can certainly shape different ways of being Muslim within these multiple social settings. Esposito notes:

> The identity of Muslim immigrants has been shaped by their religious-ethnic, and cultural backgrounds as well as their experiences in the West … Muslim integration into society in Europe is more difficult than in America. In contrast to immigrant American Muslims, many of whom came with education and skills, Muslims came to Europe under very different circumstances, primarily as labourers … Many Muslims in, for example, Britain, France, Germany, and Holland are trapped in social ghettos … (Esposito, 2010, 23-25)

This suggests that ways of being Muslim are not only shaped by religious and ethnic values but also shaped by the social and political contexts of Muslims' host countries. This fact leads to my inquiry in this research on the extent to which Australian societies influence Indonesian Muslim parents' ways of exercising their parenting roles at home. It also explores how young Muslims construct and negotiate their Muslim identity within their family and their religious spaces.

In one of his recent books, Esposito (2010) suggests that Muslim communities in the West are divided in their attitudes toward their host countries. First, Esposito (2010) found that Muslim leaders discourage

Muslims living in the western countries from integration into their host countries. These Muslim communities rely on their connection with the wider Muslim world. They obtain financial aid from Muslim countries such as Saudi Arabia and Egypt and other Gulf states. Through the financial aid, they build mosques and schools and most of the time they hire from these countries religious clerics (*Imam*) who have little knowledge about their host country. As a result, the way they teach Islam and engage in their host countries reflects the attitudes of their home countries. As a consequence, this attitude impedes their ways of integration (Esposito 2010).

The second attitudinal response, according to Esposito (2010), is that Muslim leaders encourage Muslim communities in the West to view themselves as an integral part of their host countries. For example, Esposito (2010) found that Muslims living in the United States view themselves as American Muslims. They do integrate within the American society and thus feel a connection to their host country through "common civic, religious and social values and interest" (Esposito 2010, 25).

Irrespective of these two different responses, most Muslim immigrants hold somewhat similar characteristics. They engage in transnational identity. This suggests that Muslims living in foreign lands are aware of their need to connect themselves with other Muslim communities in the global world. Vertovec (1998), for example, in a study of the Muslim communities in a small town Keighley, found that they engage with issues facing Muslims in transnational settings. In fact, their feeling of sympathy for the problems of Muslim's *ummah* is realized through conducting rallies, such as the rally against the war in Iraq, and also the rally against Israel's aggressive invasion of Palestinian land. Vertovec provides the further example of Muslims being involved in a series of demonstrations regarding Rushdie's satanic verses affair. In these various rallies, young Muslims and the old generations are both involved.

Although Muslims have a long presence in many parts of non-Muslim worlds, such as Australia, some Muslim immigrants do not necessarily integrate well within their host societies as noted earlier. In fact, their settlement in and engagement with mainstream societies have not been easy for several reasons, one of which is because of their minority status (Kusat, 2001). As minority communities, Muslims living in the West may suffer from prejudice. This kind of prejudice emerges because mainstream societies fail to understand the values preserved by these Muslim minority communities (Kusat, 2001). Kusat, for example, states:

> Minority groups categorised by race, nationality, and religion generally suffer from the prejudices of majority groups and especially from political

authorities. Minority groups feel distressed and insecurity even though
their rights may be protected firmly by law (Kusat, 2001, 364)

Different cultural values between those of the mainstream non-Muslim
societies and those of Muslim minority communities are seen as the
reasons for the emergence of tensions (Azmi 1997; Nielsen 2000).
Mainstream communities do not possess a full understanding of Muslims'
daily practices. In addition, scholars discuss how the distinct cultural
values brought by Muslim immigrant communities aggravate the level of
stress upon gaining a settlement in the host societies. Most Muslim
immigrant communities come from traditional cultures (Azmi 1997),
which provide norms and values distinct from those of mainstream
communities in the West. For example, Muslim immigrants of Pakistani
and Moroccan descent emphasise extended family values, and also on the
role of men as the main caretakers of family income, which differs from
Western values (Nielsen 2000). Thus, balancing the values of the home
country with those of the host country is a challenge in itself within the
Muslim immigrants (Azmi 1997).

For this reason, Moghissi (2006) states that Muslim immigrant
communities face a barrier in their process of integration into the
mainstream society. Some researchers such as Vertovec (1998), Johns and
Saeed (2002), Yasmeen (2010) and Anwar (2008) found in their studies
that some Muslim immigrant communities still encounter difficulties in
their process of settlement and engagement within the mainstream
societies. For example, some Muslims face difficulties finding a proper job
because of their commitment to religious attire, such as wearing the veil.
However, a study by Dizboni (2008) and Kabir (2006) suggest otherwise.
They found that Muslims have succeeded in their process of integration
into their host societies.

In addition to facing the challenges within Muslims' lives in their host
countries, some young Muslims have been found by a number of scholars
to face substantive challenges within their own Muslim minority
communities. Dwyer (1999a) and Vertovec (1998), for example, revealed
that young Muslims, especially the female Muslims in his study, while
feeling secure being within the Muslim community, felt discomfort at the
attitude of the community toward them. They found that their fellow
Muslims within their immediate communities engaged in what they
perceived to be excessive monitoring of their dress styles and their ways of
behaving in their daily lives.

This section has discussed Muslims' different ways of engagement
within their host countries, suggesting that these emerge because of
different attitudes while living in their host countries, different migration

stories, and different ways of perceiving their ways of being in their host countries. Some Muslims feel that integration into the host society is discouraged, while others perceive otherwise, seeing integration as strongly encouraged. In spite of these different ways of engaging in the host countries, they acquire similar characteristics, one of which involves taking on a transnational identity. Finally, I have shown that some young Muslims living within their immediate Muslim communities experience a sense of surveillance on their dress code and their ways of engaging with others in their Muslim communities.

## *Muslims in Australia*

Islam reached Australia in the 18th century upon the arrival of Macassan fishermen from today's Indonesia (Saeed 2003). A Muslim historian, Bilal Cleland recorded that those fishermen visited the coast of *Marege*, which is located from just east of Darwin to the Gulf of Carpentaria (Cleland, 2001). The harmonious relationship between the Maccasans and the Aborigines has been evident from the imprint of architectural symbols and language (Ganter 2008). Macassan fishermen have made fishing their business commodity. They collect *trepang* from the northern shores of Arnhem and the Kimberley coast (Ganter 2008). However, the expansion of colonialism in the late of the 19th century resulted in the decline of the *trepang* industry. Macassans were subject to customs duty and license fees by the South Australian government. Although Macassans' involvement was fleeting, these early Muslim traders were among the first to establish their enterprises on Australian shores.

Despite these early contacts, the first formal Muslim settlers in Australia were Afghan cameleers (Kabir 2004, 2005, 2007). Muslim cameleers from Afghanistan reached the number of roughly 2,000-4,000 in the mid- and late 19th century although there is no record of their exact number (Stevens 1993). Although Afghan cameleers played a significant role in transportation when Australia was under the British Penal Colony, their roles were marginalized (Cleland 2001). Afghan cameleers made a significant cultural and economic contribution to Australia, which, however, was not acknowledged by the British colony.

The British colony replaced the service of camels as the main means of transportation with railways. As a result, the need for Afghan cameleers declined (Cleland 2001). Later, after the introduction of the *Immigration Restriction Act* after 1901, the Muslim communities gradually vanished. In spite of various hardships faced in the new place, these pioneers attempted to maintain their religious values in the face of public discrimination (Johns & Saeed 2002; Kabir 2007; Monsour 2002), through building communities to share their faith and cultures.

In 2007, Australian Muslims were estimated to be approximately 1.2 to 2% of the Australian population (ABS 2007) and count as one of the fastest growing minority groups in Australia (Ho 2007). Muslims numbered fewer than 100,000 in 1981 and increased to more than 300.000 in 2006. The recent figure in fact suggests that Muslim population in Australia reach the level 2.2% (the 2011 census). The presence of Muslims in Australia and whether Muslims should assimilate with the local culture continue to be the focus of academic debates at local and national levels in Australia. As part of this debate, the metaphors of 'melting pot' or 'salad bowl' have been touted in the Australian public domain (Bone 2003).

Although Australian Muslims of Indonesian background represent only 2.5% among Australian Muslims, the first Muslim community that arrived in Australia were Indonesian Muslims working along the seashore in the 17th century (Kabir 2004; Tuncer 2000). The second wave of Muslim migrants from Indonesia to Australia were the Javanese cane cutters, who were employed in Queensland (Mulyana, 1995, 2000; Tuncer, 2000). The third group of Indonesian Muslims were students who pursued their study under the Colombo Plan scholarship schemes (Tuncer 2000). In addition, in the 1950s many Indonesian Muslims migrated who were radio broadcasters recruited to work in Radio Australia. The other group of Indonesian Muslims arriving in Australia were academics who were invited to teach Indonesian history in Australian universities. Their presence in Australia in the 1950s, as temporary residents, has contributed to the emergence and to the strengthening of the Australian-Indonesian Muslim community (Tuncer 2000). In addition, in the 1970s after the White Policy was officially dismantled, many Indonesian Muslims arrived in Australia, some of whom did so illegally but have since been naturalized. Most parents participating in this study had migrated to Australia in the 1970s-1990s and some others in 2000. Those Muslim families are the first generation Muslim families in Australia and their children are the second and 1.5 generations.

# An Ethnographic Study of Indonesian- Australian Muslims

## *Overview of methodology and theoretical frameworks*

This study takes place in Victoria, in an Indonesian Muslim community centre in Australia and in some Indonesian Muslim families in Victoria, and it explores the Muslim identity construction of twelve young Indonesian Muslims. Members of the second and 1.5 generation of Indonesian Muslims were recruited to voluntarily participate in this study. The second generation refers to children from immigrant communities who were born in Australia, while children of the 1.5 generation are those who were born overseas and moved to Australia before 5-7 years of age. In addition, nine Muslim parents whose children participated in my study were also interviewed to examine their roles as educators and their aspirations for their children. The community leader and a senior community member were also interviewed to identify and examine programs conducted within the Muslim community centre that they regard as helping shape the Muslim identity.

This is an ethnographic qualitative study, and thus in collecting the data, I adopted instruments and methods of the ethnographic inquiry. Identity narratives of young Muslim analysed in this book were collected through semi-structured in-depth interviews, personal written narratives, and observations. These various methods of data collection allowed me to understand how young Muslims living in a 'western' context construct their Muslim identity. The methods also enabled me to examine how Muslim family dynamics and the religious spaces of the *ummah* shaped the Muslim identity of the Indonesian Muslim youths.

Studies on Muslim identity have been conducted by scholars from various fields. For example, Clark (2007) examines the schooling experiences of Muslim refugees in the USA, using the work of Pierre Bourdieu on cultural capital. Another study on female Muslim youth, conducted by Basit (1995) referred to the work of Erikson (1950; 1956; 1968), while other studies, such as that by Imtoual (2006) referred to the concepts of Islamophobia and religious racism. In addition, a study by Khan (2009) used the concept of globalization to frame his investigation.

In this book, I draw on the religious texts of the *Qur`ān* and the *Hadith* and the works of some scholars, such as Mondal (2008), Ramadan (2004), and Yasmeen (2008) to conceptualize the notion of Muslim identity. I refer to these two religious texts since they provide essential characteristics and categorizations of behaviour to which Muslims are meant to adhere to. In addition, these two main sources of religious principles in Islam have given an essentialized understanding of Muslim identity, which is often seen as fixed rather than static. However, the *ayāt* of the *Qur`ān* and the contents of the *Hadith* are subject to various interpretations (Saeed 2006b).

The interpretation of the *Qur`ān* is also shaped by the political agendas of competing parties within the Islamic communities themselves (Saeed 2006a). The different approaches used by exegetes in interpreting certain verses in the *Qur`ān*, for example, have led to multiple ways of understanding things in Islam. For instance, the *Qur`ān* has commanded Muslims to fast and pray, and if some Muslims fail to completely observe these principles, the majority of exegetes regard them as still holding Muslim status. Nevertheless, some exegetes perceive these Muslims' religiosity as incomplete and as having committed one of the greatest sins. Other scholars have explored how different ways of constructing female and male Muslim identities result from such different approaches used in interpreting religious texts (Duderija 2008; Mernissi 1991).

The work of Muslim scholars, such as Samina Yasmeen (2008), Tariq Ramadan (2004), Ansuman Ahmed Mondal (2008), Jasmin Zine (2008) and Tehmina Naz Basit (1995) have also helped me to conceptualize Muslim identity. These scholars have examined the construction and negotiation of Muslim identity in the West, and have provided a deeper insight into the ways of being Muslim among those who were born in the West. The work of Yasmeen (2008), for example, provides typologies of Muslim identity; some Muslims tend to be orthodox, while others tend to prefer the moderate type of Muslim identity. These different preferences on different discourses regarding ways of being Muslim are shaped by multiple factors, which I will discuss in Chapter Two.

This book looks at the ways in which a group of Indonesian-Muslim youths in Australia construct their identities of being Muslims in the family and the *ummah*. The family and the *ummah* are important social and educational sites. As we shall see in Chapter Two, the essence of education in Islam lies in the perfection of one's mind, body, and soul, and the educational process toward this starts from home (Ekram & Beshir, 2009). This means that parents are seen as educators in Islamic perspectives, and thus the family is seen as an important educational site. The same applies to the notion of the *ummah*. Muslim communities are required by Islamic teaching to nurture the Muslim faith through religious spaces, such as the *masjid* and the *Qur`ānic* class. Mosques are then a significant educational setting in Islam.

## *Meeting the young Muslims*

Three groups of participants took part in my study. My main group of participants consisted of 12 Muslim youths of Indonesian background. These young Muslims at the time of the interview were enrolled in Australian public schools in Year 9 up to Year 12, and they were 14 to 17 years old when interviewed. Two students were 14 years old (Year 9); one student was 15 (Year 10), five students were 16 years old (Year 11), and the other four were 17 years old (Year 12). Twelve students took part in my study. Six of the Indonesian Muslim youths were second generation Muslims. Their parents or one of their parents were Indonesians but they were born and had grown up in Australia. The other six were recorded as being of the 1.5 generation. They were born in Indonesia but moved to Australia at an early age. Two young Muslims participating in my study came from a mixed family. Yani has an Indonesian mother and an Australian father, while Zaki has an Australian mother and an Indonesian father. The other young Muslims have Indonesian parents.

*Hanafi* is 17 years old, and by the time of the interview, he is in Year 11. Hanafi was born in Indonesia and moved to Australia when he was 5 five years old. Both his parents are Indonesians. His father is an accountant in a cosmetic company, while the mother works as a research assistant in an Australian university. He has two siblings, and Hanafi is the oldest in his family. *Hafnizar* is 15 years old, and by the time of the interview, he is in Year 9. Hafnizar is Hanafi's brother and was born in Indonesia but moved to Australia when he was four years old.

*Yani* is 17 years old and was born in Indonesia to a mixed-family background and moved to Australia when he was 2 years old. At the time of the interview, he is in Year 12. His mother is an Indonesian and the father is an 'Anglo' Australian. His father works for an oil company as an engineer.

*Ikhwan* and Salma are two young Muslims who were born in Indonesia to an Indonesian family and moved to Australia at the age of 5. Ikhwan is 16 years old and Salma is 17. Ikhwan is in Year 11 at the time of interview, while Salam is in Year 12. Their father holds a doctorate's degree from an Australian university and works as an adjunct professor at the Faculty of Economics and Commerce in an Australian university. His mother also holds a doctorate's degree and works at Botany Laboratory.

*Billah* is 16 years old. He was born in Australia to an Indonesian family. His father is a professional plumber, and the mother is a housewife. He lives with two other siblings, and he is the youngest child in the family. He is in Year 11 at the time of interview.

*Zaki* is 16 years old and was born in Australia to a family of a mixed family background. His father is an Indonesian and the mother is an Australian. His father works in a factory and the mother is the housewife. He is the only child in the family and he lives with his parents. At the time of the interview, Zaki is in Year 11. *Darni* is 17 years old and was born in Indonesia but moved to Australia in the age of three months old. Her father is a factory worker and the mother is a housewife. She was in Year 12 by the time of interview.

*Fatma* was born in Indonesia and moved to Australia when she was 5. She is 16 and sits in Year 11. Her father runs a business in Australia, and the mother holds a doctorate's degree from an Australian university and works as research assistant at the university. *Suci* was 15 and she was born in Australia to an Indonesian family. Her father is a factory worker and the mother is a housewife. He is in Year 10 at the time of interview.

*Imani* was 15 and she is in Year 9. She was born in Australia to Indonesian parents. Her father is a factory worker and the mother works in a hospital. *Hera* was 17 and sits in Year 12. She was born in Australia to Indonesian parents. Her father owns a private business and the mother was the housewife.

# CHAPTER TWO

# THEORIZING MUSLIM IDENTITY

To understand Muslim identity, I work with two bodies of literature in this book. Firstly, I draw on the interpretations of the Muslim religious texts, the *Qur'ān* (The Muslim Holy book) and the *Hadith* (The Prophet traditions) to understand the ways in which Muslim identity is represented in these religious texts. For Muslims, the *Qur'ān* is the main source of guidance in their lives, in which *Allāh* prescribes the Islamic principles (Guessoum 2008; Saeed 2008) to be adhered to by Muslims. In addition, the *Hadith*, the Prophet Muhammad's actions and remarks, is also seen as the main religious text that provides guidance in being Muslim, and thus the teaching of the *Qur'ān* and the *Hadith* shapes Muslim identity (Duderija 2010a).

In understanding ways of being Muslim as represented in the religious texts, I first identify some verses of the *Qur'ān* and some *Hadith* that provide an understanding of Muslim identity. I then draw on the works of *Ibn Kathir,* a *mufassir.* A *mufassir* is an Islamic exegete who knows and narrates the religious texts of *Qur'ān* and *Hadith. The* exegesis is a critical explanation or interpretation of a text, especially a religious text. There are many Islamic exegeses or *tafsir* for Muslims to refer to, such as *tafsir al-manār, tafsir al-misbah, tafsir Ibn Kathir* and other *tafsir* on the interpretation of the *Qur'ān*. The works of *Ibn Kathir* are commonly used in the Indonesian-Muslim community here in Australia and in Indonesia as well.

The second body of literature that I engage with relates to the social and cultural construction of Muslim identity since social settings shape Muslim identity and vice versa. I draw on the work of Muslim scholars studying Islam and Muslims in the west, such as Tariq Ramadan (2004), Jasmin Zine (2008), Alia Salem Imtoual (2006), Tehmina Naz Basit (1995), Samina Yasmeen (2008) and Ansuman Ahmed Mondal (2008). They argue that the conceptualization of Muslim identity is located in the interplay of discourses of religious texts, and the social and cultural lived experiences of young Muslims.

I provide a discussion on the roles of Muslim families and the *ummah* in shaping young Muslims' identity. In Islam, Muslim parents and the *ummah* have the responsibility to take on an educational role in developing their children's minds, bodies, and souls. Thus, Muslim families and the religious spaces within the *ummah* are considered as educational and social sites for the identity formation of Muslim youth.

## Muslim Identity

In this section, I explain two interrelated issues. First, I discuss the conception of Muslim identity as prescribed by the religious texts. This is one of the theoretical frameworks used in this study. In the second sub-section, I draw on the understanding of Muslim identity as conceptualized through agencies and discourses surrounding Muslim communities, and as conceptualized by some Muslim scholars whose work provides insights into Muslim communities in the West as well as their ways of being Muslim.

### *The Qur`ān, and the Hadith: The conceptions of Muslim identity*

Michel Foucault (1926-1984) is one of the theorists that problematises the notion of discourse in his work. Sara Mills who reviews Foucault's works suggests that various meanings of discourse are proposed by Foucault in a number of his different works. One of these meanings is that it constitutes the meaningful utterance that has an effect on something; another definition is seen as being a group of statements that provide a certain meaning (Mills 2003); discourse is also seen as practices, which are governed by unwritten rules (Mills 2003). These varied meanings convey a somewhat similar understanding of discourse, which is that it consists of unwritten rules and statements that individualize certain groups of people and regulate their practices.

According to Foucault, some religious texts such as the Bible in Christianity can be a source of rules that regulate discourses or statements, to which people, such as political figures frequently refer to back up their points. In my work, I consider the Muslim Holy Book, the *Qur`ān* as an important source of discourses of Muslim identity and practices, since it is the sacred book referred to by Muslims around the world (see also Saeed 2008). For many Muslims, the *Qur`ān* and the *Hadith* are important sources of Islamic discourses, which guide and frame ways of being

Muslim (Guessoum 2008). The religious texts of Islam, the *Qur'ān* [1] and the *Hadith* of the prophet Muhammad (PbuH[2]) provide important markers of Muslim identity. Some prominent themes of the *Qur'ān* are *Imān* (faith), *Akhlāq* (conduct) and *Ibadāt* (ritual), which characterize ways of being Muslim (Mir 2007).

The *Imān* is an expression of the Muslims' faith addressed in the first pillar of Islam, the *Shahāda*, and is the key component of Islamic identity (Esposito 2010; Marranci 2008; Ramadan 2004; Rippin 2005). It is a declaration that there is none worthy of worship but *Allāh* and that the Prophet Muhammad is His final messenger. The *Akhlāq* relates the approved forms of conduct of Muslims as prescribed by the *Qur'ān*. For example, it is stated in the Muslims' religious texts that Muslims should ensure that their conversations and actions do not harm others. It is also stated in the *Qur'ān* that Muslims are encouraged to respect their elders such as parents. Muslims are not to engage in derogatory acts toward other people, be they Muslims or non-Muslims alike.

The Prophet Muhammad (PbuH), as reported by *Al-Bukhāri* and also reported *by Hakim, Ahmad,* and *Ibn Asakir*[3], said that:

> Indeed, I was sent to the world to perfect and purify the conduct and the behaviour of the human being

This *Hadith* suggests that one of the main teachings of Islam is the perfection of one's behaviour. In fact, the Prophet as narrated by Abu Musa also asserted that:

> The best among you is the one who behaves best toward people (This *Hadith* is reported in *syahih Bukhāri*-the collection of *Bukhāri*, no.8, p.21)

---

[1] *Qur'ān* is the Arabic word for 'recitation' or 'reading'; various names are applied to the *Qur'ān*: "revelation (*tanzil*), the reminder (*dhikr*), the creation (*Furqan*) and the scripture (*kitab*)" (Saeed, 2008, p. 38). The *Qur'ān*, revealed to the Prophet Muhammad peace be upon him more than fourteen centuries ago, contains major issues ranging from theological and ritual to social issues (Saeed, 2008)

[2] PbuH stands for Peace be upon Him (the Prophet Muhammad); it is a noble title that should go with the prophet Muhammad. It means that all Muslims who mention the prophet's name should use this title; it is highly recommended for Muslims to do so.

[3] These persons are some of the collectors and preservers of the *Hadith*. This *Hadith* is reported in the collection of Al-Bukhāri, no 273, and reported by Al-Hakim in his book, no. 163/2, and by Ahmad, no. 318, and by Ibn Asakir, no. 8, p.21

In a similar tone, the *Qur`ān* states that:

You will never attain piety until you spend of what you love. And anything
you spend of, God has full knowledge of it (*Ali-Imran*, 92).

The *Hadith* and the *ayāt* also encourage Muslims to be respectful in
their interactions with fellow human beings. The other important
component of the *Qur`ānic* teaching is the *Ibadāt* (Ramadan 1999, 2001,
2002, 2004), the ritual. These include *salāt,* the five daily prayers; *sawm,*
fasting during the month *of Ramadhan*; *zakāt,* charity to the poor, and *hajj*
or pilgrimage to Mecca. The observance of these Islamic rituals can be a
framework to measure Muslims' religious piety (Hassan 2008) and it
marks the character of the believers (Rippin 2005). That *Ibadāt* as a
significant marker of Muslim identity has been stated in the *Qur`ān:*

Who performs the salāt and spends out of what We have provided them, it
is they who are the believers in truth (*Al-Anfaal*, 3-4)[4].

The requirement for Muslims to have faith in *Allāh*, the God Almighty,
to observe good conduct during personal and social interactions and to
worship faithfully has become the central identity marker for Muslims.
The discourses of religious texts identify that those who are considered
Muslims are those who possess these identity markers.

In addition, the *Qur`ān* covers the issue of modesty. It requires
believing men and women to cover certain private parts of their body. The
issue of modesty is more emphasized in respect for believing women than
it is for believing men. In spite of the controversy in the interpretation of
the messages of the *Qur`ān,* mainstream Muslim communities see these
messages as religious requirements, and thus as Muslim-specific markers.
The obligation to cover certain parts of the body is revealed in the
following two *ayāt.*

Say to believing women that they should lower their gaze and remain
chaste and not to reveal their adornments – save what is normally apparent
thereof, and they should fold their shawls over their bosoms (*An-Nur*, 31)

O Prophet! Tell your wives and your daughters and wives of the believers
that they should draw over themselves some of the outer garments [when
in public], so as to be recognized and not harmed (*Al-Ahzab*, 59)

---

[4] Taken from *tafsir ibn kathir*-this *tafsir* (the book on *Qur`ānic* interpretation) is
famous in the Muslim world as well as among Muslims in the West.

One of the most prominent Muslim scholars in the Islamic world, *Ibn Kathir* sees these two verses as the command to cover certain private parts of Muslim women's bodies. In his interpretation of these verses, *Ibn Kathir* views the veil as a marker that differentiates believing women from the non- believers.

As interpreted by *Ibn Kathir,* covering the private parts of women's bodies, popularly known as the *aurāt* in the Islamic literature, is a religious duty which is obligatory for all believing women. Because of this command, the veil in Islam becomes the specific marker of a Muslim woman as advocated by the Qur`ān. However, Zine (2006) suggests that there are many possible interpretations of these verses. According to some scholars, these verses do not indicate a particular sanction for un-veiled believing women (Zine 2006). This is so because the verses do not explicitly mandate the need for believing women to cover their hair. They rather refer to the encouragement for believing women to draw a veil to cover their bosoms. Some other modern Muslim thinkers, such as Fatema Mernissi, and Leila Ahmed also do not see covering hair as an obligation. In fact, a progressive Indonesian Muslim scholar, Musda Mulia, sees the imposition and the formalization of the veil in the public sphere as not Islamic.

In this section, I have described *essentialized* understandings of Muslim identity as represented in the interpretation of the religious texts: *Qur`ānic* verses and the messages of the *Hadith.* Markers of Muslim identity as represented in these religious texts include praying five times daily, fasting, alms giving and also the pilgrimage to Mecca. Although religious texts provide essentialized understandings of Muslim identity, ways of being Muslim are also shaped by social and cultural factors, and thus there are multiple and different ways of being Muslim. In the following discussion, I examine the work of some Muslim scholars on ways of being Muslim.

## *Social and cultural construction of Muslim identity*

While acknowledging that the construction of Muslim identity is rooted in religious doctrine (Ramadan 1999, 2004; Yasmeen 2008; Zine 2008), Muslim researchers and scholars also believe that Muslim identity is socially and culturally constructed (Bayat & Herrera 2010; Duderija 2008; Imtoual 2006; Mondal 2008). Zine (2008), for example, acknowledges:

This malleability of Islamic identity is a function of the disjuncture between how Islamic identification is socially mapped, enacted, and lived, on the one hand, and the religious conception of Islamic identity rooted within doctrinal texts, on the other. These two aspects of Islamic identity – the social and the religious – generate a dichotomy between the socially defined, ascriptive characteristics of Islamic identity and those which are divinely ordained and inscribed within the praxis of religious tenets, such as the Five Pillars of Islam (Zine, 2008, p. 143).

As shown in the quote, Zine (2008) indicates that the term 'Muslims' refers in society to those who declare their faith to Islam as their religion, regardless of their level of practice of the Islamic rituals such as the *salāt* and the *sawm* (Zine 1997). However, she also suggests that understanding Muslim identity cannot only be approached through discourses of religious texts but also needs to be based on the exploration of the political, social, cultural, and historical contexts, since they shape Muslim identity (Kabir 2010). Therefore, interrelated discourses such as those of home environments, educational institutions, and broader community contexts shaping Muslim identity also need to be considered (Duderija 2008, 2010a; Herrera & Bayat 2010b) in studying Indonesian young Muslims' ways of constructing their Muslim identity.

Given this fact, in this section, I describe social, political and cultural factors that are significant in shaping Muslim identity (Curtis 2009; Duderija 2010b; Esposito 2010; Werbner 2004). For example, the social contexts of particular countries where Islam has been rooted for centuries such as in some South-East Asian and Middle-Eastern countries shape certain ways of being Muslim. Muslims who live in a country such as Kazakhstan will view and practice the religion differently from those who live in Saudi Arabia, because Islam has yet to become the mainstream religion in the former country (Hassan 2002, 2008). Likewise, different cultural values and politics within Muslim families, Muslim communities, and educational institutions influence young people's ways of being Muslim. Furthermore, Muslims' commitment to religious principles, such as donning the veil and adherence to the five-times-daily prayers, is also shaped by the policies and politics of the countries in which they live (Ali 2005; Cole & Ahmadi 2003; Herrera & Bayat 2010b; Mishra & Shirazi 2010).

An additional factor that contributes to different ways of being Muslim is the fact that the religious texts are interpreted differently (Ramadan 2004; Zine 2008). Adis Duderija notes this issue in the following:

> any attempt to understand the religious identity construction among Western-born generation of Muslims needs to take … the structural-hermeneutical factor in religious identity construction. This phrase refers to

a particular approach to the interpretation of the primary source of the Islamic *Weltanschauung*, namely the Qur'an and the Sunnah. However, ... religious tradition and its source are subject to various interpretations based upon certain methodological and epistemological assumptions (Duderija 2008, p. 391).

As ways of understanding the messages of the religious texts are multiple, Muslims are divided into various types of Islamic groups. Some researchers, such as Yasmeen (2008), Peek (2005) and Saikal (2005) have come up with typologies of Muslims. Yasmeen (2008), in her study of examining the construction of Muslim identity in Australia, provides a useful categorization of different ways of being Muslim: practising and non-practising. The first category includes the 'orthodox' and the 'moderate/liberal' Muslims. The second group, the non-practising includes 'quiet observant' and 'exited' Muslims (Yasmeen 2008, p. 30).

I acknowledge that ways of being Muslim cannot be understood as neat categories as ways of being are shaped by contexts and other social dimensions. However, Yasmeen's (2008) categories provide a useful framework for understanding Muslim identity. I refer to this categorization as a tool to examine my participants' ways of being Muslim. I seek to understand in this study whether young Muslims participating in this research see themselves within certain categories as suggested by Yasmeen (2008).

In addition, Yasmeen (2008) argues that these different categories emerge due to different perceptions of what counts in being good Muslims. For example, the orthodox Muslims believe in the assumption that to be a good Muslim, one has to follow all the teachings of Islam, such as the rituals, and also to comply with the dress code as enjoined by Islam, and they firmly believe that only through commitment to religious rituals, can they reach the level of religious piety (Yasmeen 2008). In fact, they may view that some cultural practices in their host Western states, such as celebrating birthdays with a party as not Islamic, and thus discourage their children from participating in such parties, as we can see in the following narration of Yasmeen's (2008) participants:

He learnt about Islam and came to subscribe to orthodox understandings. He changed his dress code opting for what he identified as the *sunnah* (Prophetic tradition-[ways of life]. *sic*)...Her exposure to orthodox understandings has shaped her cultural practices. She does not send her children to birthday parties because, in her understanding, it is un-Islamic practice. She feels sad about not being able to slaughter sheep in the 'Islamic way' during Eid-ul-Adha (Yasmeen, 2008, pp. 32-33).

Although some Muslims do not call themselves orthodox, they believe that ways of being Muslim are based on fulfilling the religious commitment, which is the *ibadāt*. For example, in the study of young British Muslims, Mondal (2008) found that some young Muslims represent their ways of being Muslim through observing religious rituals. They believe that the rituals are considered as the source of inner comfort, and being devoted to performing the rituals is the essence of being Muslim (Marranci 2008). Muslims who hold such an idea, regard rituals as a way to keep the balance between their spiritual world and the worldly world.

This 'principled' group of Muslims takes Islam wholeheartedly and they do not believe there are any ways of being Muslim other than by observing the rituals (Mondal 2008). They also believe that being devoted or religious does not mean they have to live a one-sided life, in which there is no room to enjoy their lives or claim their 'youthfulness' (Bayat & Herrera 2010; Mondal 2008). Muslims in this group also work to the best of their ability to imitate the attitudes and physical attributes of the Prophet Muhammad (PbuH) such as growing a beard and wearing the skullcap, which may be considered as a sign of radicalism in some parts of western societies (Mondal 2008).

The moderate/liberal Muslims, on the other hand, do not take on all the attributes of Muslim identity as emphasized by the orthodox Muslims. They take not only Islam as their main marker of their identity but also other sources of identity markers. Mondal (2008) refers to this typology of Muslims as individualized Muslims. For them, Islam remains at the individual level. They believe that being good to others and helping out in the community are ways of being 'good' Muslims. One of Mondal's participants expresses his understanding of being a 'good' Muslim; Mondal (2008) notes:

> being a good Muslim is, fundamentally, about being good to others ... For me, Islam is about just quietly getting on with it, trying to improve myself in my everyday life, in my dealings with Muslims, with non-Muslims, the world, everyone (Mondal 2008, p. 39)

This quote reflects that for some Muslims being 'good' to others is the essence of a 'good' Muslim, and those who believe so will improve their ways of dealing with others.

The other study on Muslim youth in Nigeria carried out by Masquelier (2010) finds different ways of being Muslim, especially among young Muslims. He says that:

> For the large majority of youth, however, "being Muslim" is not about
> engaging in pious acts (daily prayers, fasting and so on) so much as it is
> about seeing the world through the lens of Islam. This does not mean that
> these youths do not consider themselves Muslim (Masquelier 2010, p. 225)

As shown in these studies above, ways of being Muslim are shaped by
different ways of understanding the message of Islam. Some Muslims who
see themselves as moderate Muslims relate being 'good' Muslim to being
'good' to others. Some other groups of Muslims may suggest that being
Muslim is merely related to believing in Islam, rather than to ritual
practices.

The two groups of Muslims, the orthodox and the moderate/liberal,
tend to perceive themselves as more Islamic. For example, the orthodox
group regards the other groups of Muslims as less Islamic, and at the same
time, the moderate/liberal Muslims see the orthodox as narrow-minded
and fundamental, overly focussed on the symbolism of the dress code and
other aspects of physical appearance considered to be the *sunnah* (ways of
life) of the prophet (Mondal 2008; Yasmeen 2008).

The second category of Muslims emerging in Yasmeen's (2008) study
are the non- practising Muslims, including the quiet observant, the secular
and the exited Islam (p. 30). The emergence of this last Muslim category is
shaped by many factors, one of which is a lack of exposure to the Islamic
teachings or the Islamic environment. Most members of this group in
Yasmeen's study stated that their reason for exiting Islam was their
disappointment with the reality of their religion. For example, they
perceived that believing in a certain religion such as Islam required them
to develop their sense of hatred toward other religions.

As noted earlier, these categories, however, remain not fixed; they are
constantly and continually shifting (Mondal 2008). Some Muslims may
regard themselves as orthodox at one time and then shift to the other end
of the spectrum. This shift could occur due to their exposure to the other
environments or their other circles of friends. In fact, some Muslims may
take both the orthodox and the moderate ways of being Muslim at the
same time. For example, some Muslim women may believe in the
obligation of putting on the veil and strictly follow the Islamic principles,
but at the same time, they may consider that participating in the western
environment is permissible in the Islamic teaching.

Other typologies of Muslim identity have been proposed. In a study of
young American Muslim identity, Peek (2005) categorizes Muslim
identity into three typological groupings: the first, *ascribed* religious
identity, the second, *chosen* religious identity and the third typology,
*declared* religious identity. Some Muslim youth in Peek's study express

their ascribed religious identity; children who were born and raised in a Muslim family will be urged to take for granted that Islam should figure prominently in their identity. At such a young age, these Muslim children lack the ability to reflect on such an ascribed identity. However, depending on their level of maturity, Muslim youth possess the capabilities to choose good or bad things for themselves.

This reflexivity on religious identity oftentimes occurs during their college year. At this stage, Muslim youth consider either to choose Islam as their identity or reject it. This kind of religious identity is described as *chosen* religious identity. The third religious identity as discussed in Peek's article is *declared* religious identity. It is an identity which is strongly declared by Muslims. Post 9/11 Muslim Americans have been placed under public suspicion and national and international spotlights. These treatments have forced Muslims to adhere more closely to their religion and declare Islam as their identity. In fact, under such surveillance, some Muslims are more determined to assert their *Muslimness* instead of denying it. In addition, Muslims have begun to return to their Islamic teachings through improving their knowledge on Islam as well as practising its teachings. The rapid growth of knowledge on Islam is needed to help combat suspicion against Islam and to respond to queries about it.

In a study of Muslims' attitudes, Saikal (2005) suggests four attitudes of Muslims in response to their issues in the West, especially in the aftermath of the event of 9/11. Saikal (2005) dubs the first attitudinal grouping of Muslims *moderate Islamists.* These Muslims are also referred to as secularist and liberalist. Avoiding violence in facing and solving the problems of the Islamic world is the main platform of this Muslim group. Those who fall into this group stand in between love and dislike of the Western community. On the one hand, they keenly accept Western education; on the other, they are critical of the 'unfair' treatment of Muslim communities by the West. The second attitudinal group is that of the *radical Islamist.* Unlike the former group of Islamists, this group is more assertive in expressing their identity. It is also puritanical in social and political behaviour. The radical Islamist neither totally rejects nor fully observes modernity; instead such Muslims are cautious in accepting modernity. In contrast to the moderate Islamist, the radical Islamist assumes the western world, especially the US and the UK, to be responsible for problems facing the wider Muslim community today, and thus this group considers violence as legitimate under certain circumstances.

The last two groups of Muslims in Saikal's (2005) study is the *neo-fundamentalist* and *societal Islam.* The former adheres to a strict and literal interpretation of the teachings of Islam. This group holds a particular school of thought and is more puritanical and assertive than the radical Islamists. This group, however, possess low levels of Islamic knowledge and only holds a very basic understanding of Islamic principles. The latter attitudinal group, societal Islam, is seen as belonging to ordinary Muslims who may be political or apolitical. The societal Muslims hold a very little understanding of Islamic teachings. Therefore, this group of Muslims may become radical and fundamental in their thought on Islamic principles.

The studies by Yasmeen (2008), Peek (2005), and Saikal (2005) have provided useful typologies of different ways of being Muslim. Although my participants may represent their ways of being Muslim differently again, these categorizations from Yasmeen (2008), Peek (2005), and Saikal (2005) provide a helpful framework for my efforts to understand my participants' ways of being Muslim.

In addition, ways of being Muslim are also influenced by Muslims' ethnic cultures. Muslim scholars and sociologists such as Bayat and Herrera (2010), Mondal (2008), Ramadan (2004), Yasmeen (2008) and Zine (2008) argue that as a result of the intersection between cultural and Islamic values, Islam is understood differently by different Muslim communities. These different ways of understanding Islam also shape their ways of engagement within the mainstream societies (Duderija 2008).

Due to the intersection of religious and ethnic values, it is difficult for most Muslims, whether they live in Muslim minority or majority countries, to see clear distinctions between cultural values and religious teaching (Ramadan 2004). This difficulty leads to the complexities in understanding the religion, especially for Western-born Muslim youth. Ramadan (2004) argues that Muslims living in non-Muslim western societies embrace ethno-religious identity located at the intersection of Islamic and ethnic values. Ramadan argues:

> The Muslim women and men who emigrated from, for example, Pakistan, Algeria, Morocco, Turkey or Guyana brought with them not only the memory of the universal principles of Islam but also, quite naturally, the way of life they followed in those countries. Moreover, to remain faithful to Islam meant, in the minds of first-generation immigrants, to perpetuate the customs of their countries of origin (Ramadan, 2004, p. 215)

As they tend to adopt the customs of their home in their host countries, the first generation Muslim immigrants perceive themselves (and are perceived) as Pakistani-Muslims, Bangladeshi-Muslims or Iranian-Muslims in the US or in Europe (Ramadan 2004). When the younger generations do not see themselves as parts of those ethnicities (i.e. Pakistani, Bangladeshi, Iranian) and do not take on their ethnic cultural practices, they seemed to be viewed as losing their religious identity (Ramadan 2004). In my study, I am interested in understanding how Indonesian Muslim parents perceive the identity of their children. Therefore, in my effort to understand the Indonesian family dynamics, I examine whether Indonesian Muslim parents relate the embracing (or not) of ethnic cultures with their children's sense of Muslim identity.

Nevertheless, it should be noted that, although Islamic and cultural values co-exist, Ramadan (2004) contends that Islam is not a culture; rather, it is a religion with *Tawhid* (the belief in the oneness of God) as its central principle (Marranci 2008). Therefore, he argues, Islam needs to be detached from the Muslims' ethnic cultures. Ramadan (2004) suggests that many second generation Muslims begin to realize the need to distance themselves from ethnic culture. He says:

> Many young Muslims by studying their religion, claim total allegiance to Islam while distancing themselves from their culture of origin. At the same time, more and more converts to Islam, who find themselves having to choose between "becoming" Pakistani or "becoming" Arab rather than Muslim, have slowly begun to be aware of this mistake: so there is a clear difference between Islam and the culture of origin! (Ramadan, 2004, p. 215)

Ramadan (2004) believes when Islam is detached from certain ethnic cultural values, it can be transferred to any part of the world; one can be a Muslim in Australia, the USA, the UK, European countries, and in other Muslim minority countries. When Muslims reside in these non-Muslim countries they could see themselves as Australian, American or European Muslims instead of addressing themselves as Muslims living in Australia and so forth. With this claim, Ramadan invites Muslim immigrants to see themselves as an integral part of those western states (Ramadan 2004).

This section has elaborated how Muslims' ways of engaging in the mainstream society are different. Sirin and Fine (2008) found that young Muslims integrate well with the mainstream society. They found that young American Muslims engage in multiple-shifting identity, referring to their many highly compatible identities. Muslim youth in their study are found to hold on to both identities: the Muslim and American identities. The two identities are not 'mutually exclusive'; instead they are equally important for these Muslim youth. This means that the possession of one identity does not necessarily mean the rejection of the other. Basit (2009) also provides a similar argument that the young Muslims in her study hold on to both British and Muslim identities which are found compatible, in that being a young Briton does not mean rejecting a Muslim identity.

However, the Muslim youth seem to realize that they encounter multiple challenges within their Muslim inner circle as well as from mainstream people in negotiating both markers of identity (Sirin & Fine 2008). In spite of the tremendous challenges experienced by Muslims, especially Muslim youth in the USA, these do not result in the rejection of their Muslim or American identities (Sirin & Fine 2008). This present study explores how young Indonesian Muslims engage in the Australian social contexts and how their family and the *ummah* dynamics play a part in their ways of constructing their Muslim identity.

## Summary

The conceptions of Muslim identity as described in this section indicate that Muslim identity is constructed through the interplay of various discourses: religious texts; the interpretations of the texts and Islamic traditions by religious clerics and members of the *ummah*; Muslims' ethnic cultures, and social, cultural, economic and political issues in the home and the host countries. Because of these various factors shaping Muslim identity formation, ways of being Muslim are also multiple, shifting and contextual. There are different ways in which Muslims negotiate the various markers of Islamic religious texts and markers of Muslim identity in different contexts. Some are devoted Muslims and hold on to particular 'scriptural hermeneutics' (Duderija 2008, p. 390), and see the only way of being Muslim as through practising the Islamic rituals, while others tend to follow the ideas prescribed by the liberal or moderate Muslims who value different and multiple ways of being Muslim. Some Muslims have a strong attachment to both their ethnicity and Islamic religious identity. There are also some migrant Muslims who take on the cultures of their host country in the process of negotiating their Islamic identity.

In the next section, I will discuss the concept of Muslim family as seen in the religious texts and their ways of negotiating Muslim identity in 'western' contexts.

## Muslim Family

In this section, I begin with the representation of Muslim family as prescribed in the religious texts. I discuss the roles of parents in Islam and their obligations within the family unit, an important social and educational site. I also look at studies on the Muslim family in the West in relation to Muslim family practices and parents' cultural and religious aspirations for their children.

## Muslim family: An Islamic perspective

The teaching of the *Qur`ān* and the *Hadith* has emphasized the need for Muslims to establish a family through Islamic legal binding in a form of marriage. For example, the *Qur`ān* says:

> And among His signs is this: He created for you spouses from yourselves that you might find rest in them, and he ordained between you love and mercy" (*Qur`ān*, Ar-Rum: 21).

*Allāh* has created spouses for all mankind, with whom they will establish family units and harvest happiness, and nurture their children. The Prophet Muhammad (PbuH) also recommends Muslims who are emotionally, physically and financially capable of establishing families, since it is seen as an important institution, in which human beings are raised and educated, and it is a "cornerstone of Muslim society" (Basit 1997, p. 426). As argued by the *Qur`ān,* men and women are created equal, moreover, there are no significant differences between husbands and wives in Muslim families. They bear similar responsibilities to ensure their children's physical, emotional and educational needs are sufficiently fulfilled.

In addition, as stipulated in Islamic teachings, Muslim parents are encouraged to teach their children about worship in Islam, such as abiding by the *ibadāt*; developing competence in reciting the *Qur`ān*; and keeping good conduct. In this case, they are to work cooperatively to ensure their children's capability in reciting the *Qur`ān* and having good conduct (Ekram & Beshir 2009). In exercising their teaching roles, they are encouraged to act as role models. In addition to assuring that their children are capable of reciting the Islamic Holy Book, Muslim parents are expected by Islam to set good examples for their children. For example, upon teaching their children about performing the *salāt* or the *sawm*, they are obliged to set the example through actions to enable their children to imitate their ways of performing the rituals and to help their children to get used to these *ibadāt*. This suggests that in Islam education starts from home.

This means parents are teachers and educators within their families (see Ekram & Beshir 2009; Stewart, et al. 2000). The *Qur`ān* briefly discusses educational contents that parents need to bear in mind. *Allāh* the

Almighty states in the *surā* of *Luqman*: In this chapter of the *Qur'ān*, there is an example of a quote where parents educate and nurture their children.

> And when Luqman said to his son when he was advising him, O my son, join not in worship others with *Allāh*...O my son! Lo! Though it is in the weight of a grain of mustard-seed, and though it is a rock, or in the heavens or in the earth, *Allāh* will bring it forth. For *Allāh* is Subtle, aware. O my son! Establish prayer, enjoin goodness, forbid iniquity and bear with patience whatever may befall you. For that is the steadfast heart of things. Turn not your cheek in scorn towards people, nor walk the earth with pretences, for *Allāh* loves not each braggart boaster. Be modest in your bearing and subdue your voice for Lo! The harshest of all voices is the voice of the ass (*surā* 31: 13-19).

*Ibn Kathir* explains that Luqman is a righteous person who is used as an example of parents in Islam. These verses indicate that Muslim parents are invited to teach their children some important educational content as explained in these verses. Having faith in the oneness of *Allāh* is the first and the foremost teaching component to teach. In addition, honesty is another important trait to be instilled in Muslim children besides other important principles noted in these verses. These educational principles represent the comprehensiveness of Islamic teaching. This means that being Muslim is not only limited to performing the obligatory rituals, such as prayers five times daily and the fasting in the month of *Ramadhan*. In fact, it reaches beyond the boundaries of performing these rituals. Being Muslim includes being good with people in one's social life. For example, as noted in the verses, the command to teach Muslim children to be modest in their daily routines, such as avoiding pretentious acts while interacting with people, represents the encouragement for Muslim parents to shape their children's attitudes, and having good attitudes is one of the important components of being Muslim.

As the essence of being Muslim covers both social and spiritual spectrums, Muslim parents are encouraged to shape their children's spiritual being by regarding the rituals and guiding their children to live their social lives in accordance with Islamic teachings. For instance, Muslim children are taught to prevent themselves from acting pretentiously in public in ways that may harm others. They are also encouraged to be just in their actions. These teachings reflect the essence of being Muslim, which is to balance their spiritual and social lives.

As Islam stipulates that Muslim parents should shape their children's spiritual, intellectual, and emotional maturity, as noted in these verses, to achieve these goals they need to go beyond ordinary instructional methods commonly used in schooling. Thus, in their attempt to play their role as educators, Muslim parents are required to understand the essence of education in Islam. The concept of education in Islam is represented through three interrelated Arabic terms conveying a common message: *Tarbiya, Ta'dib* and *Ta'lim* (Al-Attas 1977; Douglass & Shaikh 2004; Halstead 1995a, 2004; Hussain 2004; Muhaimin 2006). Each of these terms represents a different meaning, and yet leads to a similar goal, which is to produce Muslims who are spiritually, intellectually and emotionally mature.

*Tarbiya* is an Arabic word derived from the root word *rabā*, meaning to grow or to increase people's potential and shape them to be 'good' Muslims as prescribed by *Allāh* (Halstead 2004). *Tarbiya* aims at perfecting Muslim children's soul. Ekram and Beshir (2009) note that the two main goals of the *tarbiya* are producing Muslim children's righteousness and happiness. To achieve these main goals, they argue that Muslim parents need to boost their children's self-worth. In doing so, the first and the foremost approach that parents need to consider is to understand their children's personalities. This understanding enables Muslim parents to play an important role in developing their children's potential. However, these goals can be achieved through avoiding some attitudes, such as over-perfection, overprotection, humiliation, being authoritarian or over controlling. These attributes are assumed to inhibit parents' ability to play their parenting roles within their families.

Ekram and Beshir (2009) note several key procedures in the process of *tarbiya*. They perceive that a positive family atmosphere is important in empowering children's soul and potential. As the home is children's first socialization (Poole 2007), they tend to imitate what they observe in this first environment. For this reason, parents are responsible for showing positive attitudes when dealing with their children. For example, Muslim parents need to show their politeness in communicating and in their ways of solving family problems. Parents are responsible for making home a family unit, in which love toward one another is nurtured. The second important factor that affects children's personalities is children's position at home. Parents are discouraged to show their preference for a particular child. It is the responsibility of Muslim parents to make their children feel that they hold similar places at home. A Muslim family is a place where children are expected to cooperate, providing mutual help, and where loving siblings are encouraged and nurtured. Therefore, Muslim parents are invited to provide spaces that allow these positive traits to emerge within the family.

The second important term used in Islamic educational concept is *ta'dib*. It derives from its root *aduba* meaning "to be refined, disciplined, cultured" (Halstead 2004, p. 522), which functions to shape students' moral discipline. The goal of *ta'dib* can be achieved through parents' persistent and consistent efforts. These efforts can be done through modelling. Parents, for example, act as the role model for their children. Upon asking their children to behave modestly, which is recommended by Islam, Muslim parents themselves should first act modestly. Providing good models, which can be imitated by their children, is the most important approach to implement the *ta'dib*. In addition, some other Muslim parents promote dialogue with their children.

The last term, *ta'lim*, from the root word *alima* means "to know, be informed, perceive, discern" (Halstead 2004, p. 522), which refers to the process of transferring knowledge. In addition to transferring and the acquiring knowledge, the process of *ta'lim* also enables students to reach the stage of spiritual consciousness and intellectual empowerment, which leads the student to *imān* (faith), *amāl sālih* (virtuous acts), and *yāqin* (certainty about their faith). *Ta'lim* commonly resembles a particular instructional method used in the schooling setting. However, there are also some differences. While it aims at transferring knowledge to Muslim children, it also sets out to foster spiritual awareness. For this reason, the *ta'lim* in the Islamic concept of education is embedded with far richer dimensions. It seeks not only to make Muslims knowledgeable but also to produce religious Muslims. Some Muslim parents delegate the process of *ta'lim* to the Muslim clerics. They send their children to Islamic schools and also other religious spaces, such as the mosques and the Islamic weekend schools.

*Tarbiyah, ta'dib* and *ta'lim* are three educational concepts advocated in the religious texts and are intended to perfect Muslim children's soul, body and mind. Muslim parents are encouraged to put into practice these concepts in their roles as parents. Muslim parents therefore, as educators are required to nurture and fulfil their children's and their own intellectual, corporeal, spiritual, and emotional needs (Cook 1999; Halstead 2004). For this reason alone, Islam conceives home environments and religious spaces as the venue of students' spiritual, corporeal, and intellectual empowerment, which does not merely function to prepare mankind to reach happiness in this world but also helps them to reach a certain level of spirituality that leads to eternal happiness in the *akhirāt* or life in the hereafter (Alavi 2008; Cook 1999; Douglass & Shaikh 2004; Hussain 2004). Acquiring both intellectual and spiritual knowledge will enable mankind to perform their role as *khalifāt Allah fi al-ardy* (*Allāh*'s vicegerents on earth).

As the family unit is considered the cornerstone of Muslim society (Basit 1997), in which educational processes are taking place, parents as educators are encouraged to play the roles of *murabbi, muaddib,* and *Muallim* (all of these terms referring to teachers and educators) at home (Halstead 2004). As noted earlier in this section, in terms of teaching methods, Islam suggests that while parents are required to understand their children's emotional and physical conditions and expectations prior to engaging in instructional processes, Muslim children are recommended to respect their parents as learned and wise individuals (Alavi 2008). Alavi also suggests that Muslims educating their children within the family are encouraged to nurture their children's intellect and personality in ways that empower them in their daily lives as young Muslims.

In addition, Islam requires Muslim parents to encourage their children to pursue knowledge. This does not refer to religious knowledge only but to other forms of knowledge as well. Some *Hadith* convey this message: For example, the Prophet Muhammad asserts that 'seeking knowledge is an obligation for all Muslim men and Muslim women' (this *Hadith* is narrated by ibn Majah). The prophet Muhammad (PbuH) also requires the adherents of Islam to seek knowledge constantly from the cradle to the grave (Hilgendorf 2003). This indicates that the pursuit of knowledge in Islam is a life-long journey. Muslims are expected to be knowledgeable and educated in many branches of knowledge, Islamic or general knowledge. In addition, the main source of Muslim faith, the Holy *Qur`ān* esteems *ilm* (knowledge) and places great value on learned people. Islam suggests that *ilm* correlates with the *imān*, since to have a strong faith, Muslims are expected to acquire the foundation of deep knowledge. This suggests that Islam expects its adherents to seek knowledge as reflected in the first verse revealed to the Prophet Muhammad (PbuH). *Allāh* said in Surah *Al-Alāq*:

> Read! In the Name of your Lord Who created. He has created man from a clot. Read! And your Lord is the Most Generous. Who has taught by the pen. He has taught man that which he knew not (*Qur`ān*, 96: 1-5).

These *ayāt* indicate that Islam requires Muslims to engage in constant reading to gain not only *ilm* (knowledge) but also *hikmā* (wisdom). In another instance, *Allāh* states that those who have knowledge are of great value in the eyes of Allah. The *Qur`ān* says that:

> Allah will exalt in degrees those of you who believe, and those who have been granted knowledge. And Allah is Well-Acquainted with what you do (*Qur`ān*, 58: 11).

As this *ayāt* suggests, the position of the knowledgeable is exalted by *Allāh,* and Muslim parents are stipulated by Islam to take responsibilities for their children's education.

In addition to parents' obligation to their children, Muslim children are also strongly advised to treat their parents with respect and avoid speaking harshly to their parents and elders, since being disrespectful is considered as one of the greatest sins in the Islamic principles. The *Qur'ān* gives clear guidelines on the obligation of children toward their parents. *Allāh* said in *surā* 17: 23-35 that:

> Your Lord has decreed that you worship none but Him, and that (you show) kindness to parents. Should one or both of them attain to old age with you, Say not "Fie" unto them nor repulse them, but speak unto them a gracious word. And lower unto them the wing of submission through mercy and say: My Lord! Have mercy on them both as they did care for me when I was little. Your Lord is best aware of what is in yourselves. If you are righteous, then Lo! He was ever forgiving unto those who turn unto Him (17: 23-25).

These *ayāt* discourage Muslims to say even a single harsh word that may hurt their elders such as parents, grandparents or other close relatives. In addition, Islam suggests that great rewards will be given by *Allāh* to children who take on the responsibility of looking after their parents when these parents have reached an advanced age. For this reason, in Muslim families, there is family support for elders (Basit 1997).

Upon examining how Islamic teaching conceptualizes Muslim identity, we understand that there are specific markers of being Muslim within Muslim families. Respecting elders, loving, nurturing the young, and transferring religious principles are some features of Muslim families as prescribed in the religious texts. For example, Muslims are expected and strongly encouraged by Islam to serve their parents well, and when they themselves grow up and establish a family, they are required to teach their children about *ibadāt* and ensure that their children are committed to these *ibadāt*. These norms shape young Muslim identity. The main responsibility of Muslim families is to prepare Muslim children with strong *imān*, noble *akhlāq*, and perfect *ibadāt*. One of the inquiries in this study is to understand how Muslim parents of Indonesian background play their roles as teachers and educators of their children, especially in regard to Islamic knowledge. Reviewing the concept of Islamic education enables me to frame this inquiry.

This section suggests that the *Qur'ān* and the *Hadith* provide guidelines on perceived 'ideal' ways of bringing up children within

Muslim families, and such teachings shape their Muslim identity (Ekram & Beshir 2009). However, Muslim families living in non-Muslim countries may encounter some challenges that hinder them in raising their children in accordance with the Islamic principles as prescribed in Islamic religious texts (Akhtar 2007a). Cultural values of the host countries and their policies may be in conflict with cultural and religious values brought by Muslim immigrants, and thus create some difficulties in Muslim parents' ways of acting upon these Islamic principles (Akhtar 2007b; Ekram & Beshir 2009). In this study, I attempt to understand the construction and negotiation of Muslim identity of young Indonesians living in Australia. The interaction of parents and their young children at home as a social and educational space is worth researching, and understanding Muslim families' principles as prescribed by the *Qur`ān* can be a tool to frame this inquiry.

The religious texts explain that Islamic principles as prescribed in these texts dictate somewhat 'fixed' ways of being Muslim, which is through total observance of religious principles. In addition, they give a considerable amount of information on how Muslim identity may be constructed within multiple contexts. Islam requires parents to take responsibility for constructing the Muslim identity of their children across settings. In home environments, Muslim parents are required to teach their children about Islam and guide their children's Muslim identity. Therefore, essentialized understandings of good Muslim children are those who respect parents and observe the *ibadāt* in Islam. In their lived experience in the community, Muslims are recommended to interact with decent attitudes and spread peace to all mankind. The religious texts have emphasized that the possession of noble *akhlāq* is one of the essentialized markers of Muslim identity.

However, ways of being Muslim are shaped by multiple factors such as historical, cultural and political issues, which will be explained in the following section.

In the following sub section, I describe the role of Muslim family as the venue that nurtures Muslim children's intellect and personality.

## *Muslim family: Important social and educational sites*

In the previous sections, I have discussed the roles of parents as educators within the family unit. As I have elaborated in the previous sections, Muslim parents teach their children about the *tawhid*, which is the belief in the oneness of *Allāh*. This is the first educational component in Islam, which all parents are obliged to introduce to their children.

Within the Muslim family, the teaching of the *tawhid* starts from an early age. In fact, it starts when the child is still in his/her mother's womb. For example, during their pregnancy period, Muslim women are encouraged to read the *Qur'ān* more often, to listen to the Islamic sermons and to frequently visit the mosques.

These encouragements are seen as the attempt to provide the first exposure to Islam for a Muslim child. In addition, as has been exemplified by the Prophet Muhammad (PbuH) and thus required in Islam, Muslim parents are expected to call the *adzan* (the call for prayer) to the right ear of their children as soon as they were born. This also functions to introduce the Islamic faith to Muslim children. The Prophet Muhammad PbuH said as reported by his companion, Abu Rafi':

> I saw Prophet Muhammad PbuH, called the *adzan* to Hassan ibn Ali when his mother Fatema gave birth to him (This Hadith is narrated by Abu Dawud, Kitabul Adab no.5105 and by Tirmidzi, Kitabul Adhaahi, no. 1514)

The calling for *adzan* functions to introduce a new-born baby to spirituality. The *adzan* contains the declaration of faith, such as the declaration on the oneness of God and the proclamation that the Prophet Muhammad (PbuH) is the messenger of God.

In the earlier discussion in this chapter, *tarbiya, ta'dib* and *also ta'lim* are seen as important methods of teaching Muslim children about the *imān, ibadāt* and *akhlāq*. Asking Muslim youth to perform the rituals is indeed challenging for most Muslim parents. Therefore, parents are required to take extra care and attention to succeed in their attempt to invite their children to perform the rituals. First, they need to be consistent and persistent in their requests. For example, upon asking them to pray, the parents need to do so with a strong commitment. For example, Becher (2008) found in his study that South Asian Muslim families assign a particular time, which they called the 'sacred time' for religious purposes, such as for the performance of the *salāt*. All members of the families as indicated in Becher's (2008) study need to pay attention for these 'sacred time', in which they have to retreat from the daily routine of their work to perform the *salāt*, which is done five times a day. Likewise, the religious spaces within the *Ummah* also regularly give notice about the time for the *salāt* through the calling of *adhan* (the call for prayer). Observing these 'sacred times' is an avenue to create the discipline in Muslims to attend to their religious duties and this itself is an educational process.

Second, upon asking their children to fulfil the religious duties, the parents themselves teach their children through a modelling approach. For example, the parents show their commitment to performing the *ibadāt*. The other approach the parents may adopt in teaching their children is through training them to perform the *ibadāt* from an early age. Islam, for instance, requires Muslim parents to encourage their children to pray from the time they reach the age of seven. When young Muslims reach the age of fifteen, the parents are required to ask their children's commitment and persistence in fulfilling the religious rituals. Their commitment is shown through their degree of 'being there' for their children (Becher 2008). Islam also stipulates that Muslim parents train their children about fasting from a young age. Muslim children may start fasting for half a day and then gradually increase their fasting period. This command indicates the need to provide the habit that enables Muslim children to fulfil their religious duties.

Another instance is concerned with consuming certain types of food. Muslims are taught to consume only *halal* food. The awareness of what constitutes *halal* food also starts from the earlier age. In terms of teaching children about this type of food, the parents introduce the meaning of *halal* food and explain why certain types of food are permissible by Islam, while others are prohibited. For Muslim families living in the West, the type of food to consume is one of their main concerns. Parents' encouragement for their children to consume *halal* food is also seen as an educational process. In addition, as noted earlier in this chapter, *Allāh* exalts knowledgeable Muslims some degrees higher than ignorant Muslims. Parents become the educators and transform their family units as educational sites, and thus parents are also asked to encourage their children to pursue knowledge, such as learning to recite the *Qur`ān* and other Islamic knowledge.

In addition to shaping their children's commitment to fulfilling the religious rituals, as noted earlier, Muslim parents are commanded to shape the attitudes of their children. One of the most important components of being Muslim is having a good *akhlāq*. The family unit and the religious spaces are two important venues in which children's moral conduct is perfected. Parents need to introduce modest attitudes in children's interactions with others and most importantly when interacting with parents. For example, The *Qur`ān* prescribes young Muslims to pay respect to their elders. This prescription shapes the identity of young Muslims.

Parents' role as educators in teaching their children about the *imān, ibadāt* and *akhlāq,* show the important role of a family unit as social and educational sites. This also indicates that the Muslim family is the first site of socialization for young Muslims, determining their ways of being Muslim within their home and beyond. Because of the important role of parents in the construction of their children's Muslim identity, the Prophet

Muhammad (PbuH) reminds Muslim parents to pay extra attention to the process of identity construction of their children. Indeed, Muslim parents are seen as accountable for their family's physical and spiritual wellbeing.

Ekram and Beshir (2009) suggests effective methods in the process of *tarbiya* and in the attempt to introduce Islam to Muslim children. First, they suggest that Muslim parents should raise their children's awareness about the existence of *Allāh*. For example, it is important that parents introduce *Allāh* as the caretaker, and as loving and protecting. Therefore, when they invite their children to perform the rituals, they also need to make the argument that *Allāh* loves them for fulfilling their religious duties. Presenting God as loving and caring shapes children's positive view about *Allāh*. The second important method of teaching as suggested by Ekram and Beshir (2009) is showing mercy.

The Prophet Muhammad (PbuH) throughout his life-time showed a great mercy to all God's creatures. In fact, the *Qur`ān* says that: "We have not sent you, but as a mercy to all creatures" (Al-Anbiyā':107). The prophet showed his greatest mercy to children through smiling to them, hugging and also kissing them upon interacting with these children. As the prophet is the best role model for Muslims, Muslim parents are expected by Islam to follow the prophet's actions and perform them in their daily routines. Ekram and Beshir (2009) suggest that in the process of *Tarbiya*, it is important for Muslim parents to work cooperatively to shape their children's upbringing. The Prophet Muhammad PbuH himself shares responsibilities with the family as he said:

> The best of you is the one who is best with his family and among you I am the best to my family

In addition, the Muslim parents are encouraged to show the same level of mercy and firmness in teaching their children about Islam. For example, upon asking them to fast and to behave well, they need to be firm with that request. This means that when their children fail to observe the regulation, Muslim parents should remind them wisely but also show some level of firmness in their request. Firmness suggests parents' commitment and persistence in asking their children to fulfil their religious duties as required (Ekram & Beshir 2009).

In addition, Ekram and Beshir (2009) suggest that in the process of *Tarbiya*, parents are discouraged from using harsh words; instead, they should act kindly and gently in teaching their children regarding the Islamic principles. For example, when asking their children to perform a particular *ibadāt*, they need to choose appropriate wording and show their love to their children. The prophet, for example, tends to use the term 'oh my dear son' when giving advice to young Muslims. This type of expression not only nurtures the love between parents and their children but also provides fertile ground for successful parenting.

All Muslim family practices as discussed in this section reflect an educational process, and thus the family unit is one of the most important educational venues for children. As Muslim children spend most of the time at home, as noted earlier, the parents are required to provide an educational environment reflecting Islamic values at home. Parents need to use good ways of communication within the family unit, reflecting gentleness and politeness. This research attempts to understand Indonesian Muslim parenting styles and parents' ways of nurturing their children.

In this section, referring to the teaching of Islam, I have identified the Muslim family unit as an important social and educational site. In the following discussion, I examine Muslim family dynamics and their roles in shaping their children's Muslim identity in the West.

## Muslim family in the West

The previous sections draw on Islamic teaching about the types of roles parents play in their family. These sections have also discussed important teaching approaches that Muslim parents use in their efforts to shape their children's Muslim identity. This section moves beyond the discussion of the Muslim family in reference to Islamic teachings, reviewing the complexities that Muslim families in the West face in shaping their children's Muslim identity. It also examines how young Muslims construct and negotiate their ways of being Muslim within their home environment.

Shazia Irfan, a Muslim scholar in Britain, captures the importance of family units. She notes different ways of engagement within family units:

> Families in all societies have three basic goals for their children. The first goal is the survival goal…Second, the economic goal…The final goal is self-actualization…While the basic goals that parents have for their children are similar, culture can provide differences and variations in behavior and beliefs of patterns (Irfan 2008, p. 149)

Irfan (2008) argues that all Muslim parents have their common goals for their children. However, diversities in Muslim families' ways of setting family goals are due to differences in cultural beliefs. Likewise, Muslim families who hold on to orthodox views of Islam, for example, will be different from moderate Muslims in their ways of bringing up their children (Al-Mateen & Afzal 2004; Becher 2008), and this difference occurs because religious values are an important source of parenting in Islam (Becher 2008).

In addition, regarding the diversity in Muslim family practices, Cheryl S. Al-Mateen and Aneeta Afzal argue that:

> In the United States, there has often been confusion regarding what characteristics come from being raised in Islam. Muslims have cultural influences from religion and from their racial or ethnic background and country of origin. Cultural differences may be related to history of Islam, in general, and to the politics and particular history of the racial/ethnic group...an individual or family may be considered devout, fundamental, moderate, or even lapsed in regard to the adherence to Islamic teaching (Al-Mateen & Afzal 2004, p. 184)

Islam is shaped by culture and likewise, Muslim cultures are influenced by Islamic values (Duderija 2008).

For instance, in his study of Lebanese families in Australia, Humphrey (1998) found that Lebanese Muslims usually live in extended families, and they regard their families as a place of cultural production (Humphrey 1998) through observing traditional practices at home; Lebanese Muslim families in Australia, especially the first generation, maintain Lebanese cultural practices while living in Australia.

In addition, studies about Muslim families of South Asian background such as those by Al-Mateen and Afzal (2004), Becher (2008), Irfan (2008), Qadeer (2006), and Stewart, et al. (2000) have found that South Asian Muslim families emphasise children's obedience and respect to parents and the elders in their family (Basit 1997; Irfan 2008). In fact, South Asian Muslim parents teach their children to respect their teachers at school and behave themselves modestly upon interacting with friends. Although Muslims of South Asian background emphasize the extended family, such a family structure is not so common in the British context (Basit 1997). However, these Muslim families usually live adjacent to other relatives (Basit 1997). In respect of ways of educating their children, parents of South Asian Muslims assume that registering physical punishment (within certain limits) is an effective strategy to discipline their children. Such an assumption is derived from their cultural practices rather than religious teachings (Irfan 2008). Irfan (2008) explains in regard to childrearing practices:

> Every society has its own norms for acceptable childrearing practices...in South Asian communities, what might be considered child abuse by

Western standards, may often fulfil a normative function in childrearing
practices (Irfan, 2008, p. 149)

The quote by Irfan (2008) indicates that there are different views of
how childrearing should be performed. She identified the disjunction
between western standards and South Asian family practices, which are
shaped not only by religious doctrines but also by cultural practices.

For example, the South Asian families focus on the *izzet*, the family
honour, which is culturally constructed, and thus not necessarily shared by
other Muslim families of different ethnic backgrounds (Basit 1997; Qadeer
2006). For Muslims of South Asian background, guarding the family *izzet*
is strongly required within the family, and this 'cultural baggage' to
borrow Kaya's term,[5] is also shipped into the Western context (Basit
1997). The *izzet* drives Muslim parents to implement strict regulations for
their children, especially their girls. Such a protective attitude, however, is
often seen by mainstream society as a form of family oppression to their
children (Basit 1997). Values of home such as respecting elders and
teachers, restraining from talking to strangers, and guarding the family
*izzet*, certainly help shape the identity of young Muslims. Such values are
brought by young Muslims to their interaction in schools and wider
communities.

Another study has found that the participants from Turkish Muslim
families exercise a form of family hierarchical authority (Küçükcan 2004).
The family hierarchy is represented through a fixed division of responsibilities
within the family unit. For example, husbands are responsible as family
breadwinners, while wives are mostly confined within the home taking
care of familial issues (Küçükcan 2004), and such a hierarchical line of
authority is also found in the study of Becher (2008), who examines the
family practices of South Asian Muslims. The traditional form of family
structure is featured in earlier immigrant families, but is not necessarily
typical of contemporary Turkish families in the West. However, most
traditional values are still practised in the present Turkish families as well
(Küçükcan 2004).

As a result of different family practices and different ways of
understanding Islam, Muslim families' ways of bringing up children are
varied. Muslim families of Arab backgrounds and South Asian backgrounds,
for example, would use different ways of childrearing from those of the

---

[5] The term has been used by Kaya, I. (2004). Turkish-American immigration
history and identity formations. *Journal of Muslim Minority Affairs, 24*(2), 295 –
308 upon discussing American Muslims of Turkish background Muslim identity
construction

Indonesian Muslim families. However, apart from distinctive cultural values, religious devoted parents indeed play an important role in the shaping of young Muslims' identity (Stokes & Regnerus 2009). Devoted parents would be more likely to pay attention to their children's religious education. For example, Krause and Ellison (2007) and Stokes and Regnerus (2009) found in their studies a correlation between religious parents and the religiosity of their children. They suggest that if the parents are religious, their children will most likely become religious. This also suggests that less religious parents will have children with a lower level of religiosity. This is because less religious parents may regard as their priority issues other than the transferring of religious values to their children. In my research, I will explore to what extent Indonesian Muslim parents invest efforts in shaping their children's Muslim identity. I also identify whether Indonesian Muslim parents in the study provide 'sacred time' in their family.

Culture rather than religion may be the deciding factor in the ways parents educate their children. In a study on Arab family in the USA, Barazangi (1989), for example, found that the doctrinal teaching of Islam within the Arab families in the USA is not a religious teaching, it is a cultural belief among some Arab families in the USA. In playing their role as parents, Arab Muslim parents in Barazangi's (1989) study emphasized perseverance in following the dress code. They see that protecting their children's dress code is one way of exercising their parenting roles. As parents, they perceive that it is their role to make a habit of wearing a headscarf for their female children. Barazangi also suggests that Muslim parents of Arab background in his study impose a stricter dress code on their daughters and relax the dress code for their sons.

However, other studies, such as that by Mishra and Shirazi (2010) have found that in exercising their parenting roles, some Muslim parents do not see the need to apply strict regulations regarding their children's dress code. Some of them as indicated in Mishra and Shirazi (2010) do not impose the dress code to their children because they do not want their children to be seen as different within the mainstream societies of the West. In line with this fact, another study conducted by Bayoumi (2010) found that some Muslim parents of Arab background in the US discourage their children from exposing their Muslim identity through performing *ibadāt* in public for fear of public discontent (Bayoumi 2010). Findings of these reviewed studies add to our understanding that Muslim family practices, especially of families living in the West are shaped by multiple factors. They are shaped by religious teachings as indicated in religious texts. The family practices are also shaped by cultural practices of certain ethnicities and are influenced by the social and political conditions of the societies in which Muslim families reside.

Although diversities within Muslim families in the West are evident, Muslim parents across cultures still engage in continuous and constant efforts to shape their children's Muslim identity through various means (Ansari 2004; Johns & Saeed 2002; Yasmeen 2002). One of the common efforts taken in shaping their children's Muslim identity is through sending them to weekend schools, known as the *madrasah*. In this particular type of informal schooling conducted in many mosques, young Muslims are given the opportunity to learn the *Qur`ān* and other kinds of Islamic knowledge. They are also taught to behave modestly in their society as a representation of their Muslim identities (Johns & Saeed 2002).

Studies by Michael S. Merry found that, in addition to sending their children to Islamic weekend school, most Muslim parents participating in her research indicated their intention to empower their children through high academic achievement (Merry 2005a, 2005b). For this reason, Muslim parents in her studies, make a tremendous effort to send their children to the best schools they can afford (Merry 2005a). A study on Muslim students in Belgium reveals that Muslim parents believe that academic success will enable their children to integrate more easily and improve their lives (Merry 2005b); it is seen as a factor that uplifts Muslim social mobilization (Kaya 2004). In addition to finding a 'good' school, Muslim parents in the West also seek schools accommodative to the preservation of their cultural values. Such an intention indicates that immigrant communities wish to transfer religious and cultural values to their children, as well as maintain these values. In relation to my study, I examine the aspirations of Indonesian Muslim parents regarding their children's education.

In another study on parents' aspirations for their children's education, Zine (2007) found that most Muslim parents in her study in the Canadian context appreciated the academic quality of schooling in Canada. However, Zine (2007) found that Canadian Muslim parents are worried that school environments in Canada challenge their children's ways of being Muslim. As a result, they would rather minimize their children's interaction with the outside world out of fear of cultural and religious contamination (Zine 2007). Lewis (2007) also found a degree of protection exercised by Muslim parents in Britain. He argues that Muslim parents prefer their children to study in an institution closer to home. They are concerned with the possibility that their children will have to live in a mixed-sex dormitory if they study in faraway universities.

A study conducted by Collet (2007) examined resistance among a traditional Muslim group in Toronto on the public school's policy. The research focused on how the Muslim Somali in Canada respond to the policies and practices of Canadian public schools, especially those located in Toronto area. The Muslim parents interviewed suggest that schools are venues of identity construction. They challenge the Canadian government to alter the curriculum contents which are biased to certain ethnicities and religions. In addition, they are concerned with gender-integrated facilities and programs. They are also against the curriculum that covers sexual education. Among their requests is the possibility to withdraw their children from participating in the school programs that involve mixed gender activities, such as some sports activities and swimming lessons (Collet 2007).

As discussed earlier in this section, Muslim family practices in western society are complex and complicated and are shaped by multiple factors as mentioned earlier. As a result, these different ways of bringing up children lead to different responses of young Muslims. For example, as reviewed earlier, Muslim parents make extra efforts to send their children to high-achieving schools. They also request them to attend weekend school in addition to their formal schooling. They expect that their children become knowledgeable about Islam as a way to guard their Muslim identity. At the same time, they expect their children to gain high academic achievement in their formal public schooling as a way to gain a better future in their host land. As reported in some studies, these expectations are seen as a burden by young Muslims (Sarroub 2005, 2007; Sirin & Fine 2008). This means that these young Muslims have to work harder to excel in academic, religious as well as in social domains to meet their parents' expectations.

A clear example of this phenomenon is revealed by Sarroub (2005) in her study of Yemeni-American girls. She found that Muslim girls of Yemeni background worked harder to ensure that they performed well in their school. In addition, they continuously negotiated their lives within the three settings of family, community, and school. As a result of the stringent rules of their parents, which even disallowed them from reading American teen magazines for fear of cultural and religious contamination, these young Muslims found the classroom to be an oasis that gave them more freedom than their home environment (Sarroub 2010). Unlike Basit's (1997) findings, which suggest that young Muslims' conform to their parents' rules, Lewis (2007) has suggested that most young Muslims are frustrated with their parents' 'overprotective' rules.

This section describes multiple factors shaping Muslim family practices in the West. Religious teachings and practices, ethnic cultures, and cultures of host countries shape Muslim family practices. In the following section, I describe the roles of Muslims within the religious spaces in the *ummah* in shaping young Muslims' identity.

## Muslim Community (The Ummah)

I start this section with a discussion on how Islamic teaching governs the lives of Muslims within the *ummah*. The second issue discussed in this section is in regard with how Muslim communities in the West construct and negotiate their ways of being Muslim.

### *The Ummah: An Islamic perspective*

In addition to the Muslim family, Muslim community or the *ummah* is also an important space and environment for nurturing young Muslims' sense of identity (Yasmeen 2008). As Muslim family practices are governed by *shari`a* (Islamic law), practices within Muslim communities are also guided by the *shari`a*. This suggests that Muslim ways of interaction within their community need to be in line with Islamic teaching. Riaz Hassan says that:

> the *ummah* can be viewed as collective identity … individuals developed it by first identifying with values, goals, and purposes of their society, and then by internalizing them. This process, besides constructing individual identity, also constructs the collective identity. Rituals and ritualised behaviours of the society further reinforce it and give the members a sense of similarity, especially against 'Others' whose collective identities are different (Hassan 2006, p. 314)

Hassan (2006) suggests that the *ummah* is a venue to shape collective Muslim identity. In the attempt to construct collective identity, Muslim community establishes religious spaces, such as mosques and Islamic schools.

Religious centres such as mosques (*masjid*) and weekend schools (*madrasah*) are communal religious spaces for the worship of the Muslim *ummah*. These spaces are also social and educational sites where the transmission of religious knowledge from religious teachers and community members to the young generation of Muslims occurs (Woodlock 2010b). In addition, these religious spaces are also used to run cultural and social events aimed at fostering a sense of solidarity and compassion amongst

Muslims. This suggests that in these religious spaces, the process of *tarbiya, ta'dib* and *ta'lim* also takes place. This educational process is the responsibility of all Muslim families as well as Muslims within their immediate community. As suggested earlier in this chapter, Muslim parents, especially those living in the West gain advantage from the existence of these religious spaces. For example, they invite their children to the mosque to join the Islamic congregation held there. Most of them also take advantage of the weekend school, in which young Muslims learn how to recite the *Qur`ān* and learn other branches of Islamic knowledge.

Because the mosque and Islamic school are central religious spaces, Muslim communities, whether living in a majority- or minority Muslim country, use these religious institutions as a means to strengthen their Muslim identity and that of their children (Küçükcan 2004; Yasmeen, 2008). Most research on Muslim community in many parts of the western countries recognizes the important roles of religious institutions such as mosques for Muslims in the West: in Australia (see Dunn 2004; Johns & Saeed 2002; Saeed & Akbarzadeh 2001); in the USA (see Byng 2008; Lotfi, 2001); in Britain (see Anwar 2008; Naylor & Ryan 2002), and in Canada (see Azmi 1997; Dizboni 2008). These religious spaces are undoubtedly important in the attempt to shape and strengthen Muslim identity.

It follows that most mosques and Islamic centres in Australia are used as a venue for educational processes, such as the *Qur`ānic* lessons, and constitute places to transmit Islamic knowledge to younger generations (Johns & Saeed 2002; Yasmeen 2008). On the weekend, mosques are usually used to cater school activities for learning the *Qur`ān* and other Islamic knowledge such as *Fiqh* (Islamic Jurisprudence) and *Ulum al-Hadith* (sciences on the *hadith*).

In addition to the significance of *tarbiya, ta'dib and ta'lim,* there are other important roles that Muslims are encouraged to take within their lives in the *ummah.* For example, Muslims are required by the teaching of Islam to spread the messages of Islam, known as *da'wā.* In the early Islamic history, Prophet Muhammad (PbuH) paid attention to the improvement of the religious knowledge of his companions through the mosque, which enabled him to transfer Islamic knowledge and values to his *sahabāt.* The prophet's companions then travelled to many parts of the world in the attempt to *da'wā* (spread) the religion to other places. In line with the parenting role in Islam, Muslims are encouraged to implement the best way possible to perform this religious duty, *da'wā.* As Islam, itself means peace and submission (Marranci 2008), one of the Muslims' religious duty is to spread peace to their societies.

*Allāh* stipulates that Muslims engage in *da'wā* and spread peace in Sura *Ali-Imrān, ayāt* 104.

> Let there arise out of you a group of people inviting to all that is good (Islam), enjoining Al-Ma`ruf (all that Islam orders) and forbidding Al-Munkar (all that Islam has forbidden). And it is they who are the successful (*Ali-Imrān, ayāt* 104).

*Ibn Kathir* interprets this verse as the encouragement from *Allāh* for a segment of Muslim community to spread the message of Islam, although this duty is an obligation of each and every Muslim. Prophet Muhammad (PbuH), as narrated by Abu Hurayrah as recorded by Muslim, says:

> Whoever among you witnesses an evil, let him change it with his hand. If he is unable, then let him change it with his tongue. If he is unable, then let him change it with his heart, and this is the weakest faith.

This narration is an indication that Muslims while living within the *ummah*, are encouraged to spread the truth and prevent evil from taking place within their environment. To fulfil this duty, Muslim communities have established religious spaces, through which Islamic rules are taught.

The other religious duty that shapes Muslim identity is the adherence to Islamic principles regarding the *muamalāt* (Muslims' interaction with others). Muslims are encouraged to engage in social activities with others regardless of their religious belief. However, in their engagement, Muslims are stipulated to hold onto the Islamic principles. Islam expects that Muslims hold firmly to Islamic principles as prescribed in the *Qur'ān* and the *Hadith*, which then leads them to have a collective Muslim identity, in turn shaping their ways of being Muslim. Muslims' commonalities in faiths and rituals motivate them to give more attention to the needs of the Muslim *Ummah*, especially those of the Muslim minorities in the West. This research also examines how an Indonesian Muslim community centre acts as an educational site within the Indonesian Muslim community in Australia and how its various programs shape the Muslim identity of Indonesian Muslim youth in Australia.

According to Ramadan (2004), there are several main responsibilities of Muslims within their Muslim community, the *ummah*. First, they are encouraged to be involved in charitable acts to help those in need. The *Qur'ān* states that:

> And in their wealth is the right of him who asks, and him who is needy (*Az-Zariyat* 19).

This *ayāt* reminds Muslims to fulfil another basic requirement, which is the giving of the *zakāt*, which is a portion of wealth (2.5%) taken from the rich to be given to the poor. The *zakāt* aims to uplift the poor's financial conditions and to encourage empathy and compassion. Therefore, the commitment to fulfil the *zakāt*, for example, marks the level of one's religious piety (Dean & Khan 1997; Hassan 2008). In the time of the Prophet Muhammad (PbuH), the prophet assigned a number of companions to take the *zakāt* from Muslims living in the Islamic worlds. The obligation and the encouragement to engage in mutual help through spending a portion of one's property represent the characteristics of Muslims and indeed shape one's Muslim identity.

In addition, the other feature of the Muslim community or the *ummah* is the emphasis on the unity of Muslims. Islam stipulates that Muslims consider their fellow Muslims as their families. The prophet encourages Muslims to support their fellow Muslims through alleviating their hardship. This suggests that Muslims are encouraged to pay attention to the social and financial conditions of other Muslims. The Prophet Muhammad (PbuH) suggests that 'Muslims are brothers to other Muslims'. In fact, the prophet also emphasizes that the perfection of Muslims' faith lies in according other Muslims as much love as they accord themselves.

The prophet says in various narrations as recorded in a number of collections of the *Hadith*:

> The believers are but a brotherhood. *Means*, all of them are brothers in Islam, *and in another narration*, the prophet says: Allah helps the servant as long as the servant helps his brother. The prophet also says: A believer to another believer is like a building whose different parts enforce each other. The Prophet then clasped his hands with the fingers interlaced

*Allāh* also says in the *Qur`ān* in *surā Al-Hujurāt*, *ayāt* 10:

> The believers are but a brotherhood. So make reconciliation between your brothers, and have *Taqwa* of *Allāh* that you may receive mercy (*Al-Hujurāt*, *ayāt* 10).

The messages from the religious texts illustrate 'ideal' attributes of the Muslim *ummah*. They indicate that Muslims are encouraged to look after their lives and the lives of their fellow Muslims as well. Muslims are also invited to engage in mutual help and to spread peace within their lived settings. Therefore, there is an urgent need for religious spaces, such as mosques and Islamic schools to allow Muslims to fulfil these religious duties.

The verses of the *Qur`ān* and the messages from the *Hadith* provide encouragement for Muslims to fully engage with their Muslim communities through fulfilling educational, economic and also spiritual needs of another fellow Muslims. In addition, the teaching of Islam stipulates that Muslims establish good relationships with non-Muslims. This means that they are not only encouraged to pay attention to their fellow Muslims but are also invited to spread peace within their life environment, in which Muslims and non-Muslims co-exist.

In the following section, I examine the Muslim communities' complexities and challenges in fulfilling their religious duties living in western contexts.

### *The Ummah: Negotiating religious and cultural values*

Muslim communities exist in many parts of the western world. Their settlement in new societies through family reunion has created ethnic communities within the mainstream community. For example, there are Asian communities in Britain (Abbas 2005; Anwar 2005; Dwyer 1999a, 2000); Lebanese communities in Australia (Humphrey 1998; Tabar, Noble, & Poynting 2003), and Turkish communities in USA (Kaya 2004; Küçükcan 2004).

Although Muslim communities exist in many western societies, they are still perceived by mainstream communities in the western countries as troublesome and threatening to the nations. This kind of racialization is parallel to the gender politics of male and female Muslims (Bayat & Herrera 2010). While the former is seen as a threat for security, the latter, especially regarding the wearing of the veil, is considered to pose a threat to national identity. This suggests that negotiating ways of being Muslim youth in the minority Muslim countries is more problematic than for those living in the majority Muslim countries. The responses to these misfortunes are varied; some youth choose to be radical, some choose to take Islam as their identity marker, some others only hold Islam as their normative norms (Bayat & Herrera 2010). However, this statement cannot be generalized to all non-Muslim western countries, since some countries are more accepting toward Muslims (Esposito 2010). In spite of the complexities in ways of being young Muslims in non-Muslim countries, they enjoy more freedom to express their youthfulness due to lack of social control by their Muslim relatives (Bayat 2010).

As Muslims in the West from certain ethnicities establish concentrated communities, they impose rules and habits, which are not necessarily consistent with Islamic values. In addition, these ethnic communities provide a space for sharing of common religious and cultural values, and the communities also facilitate access to ethnic and religious foods such as the *halal* butcher (Dwyer 2000). In spite of such advantages of being within the ethnic communities, feelings of discomfort also emerge, especially within young Muslims. The literature suggests that Muslim girls of South Asian and Arab background are being watched by their fellow male Muslims within their communities (Dwyer 1999a, 2000; Sarroub 2005).

As suggested earlier in the previous section, the mosque is the central venue of the Muslim *ummah*, especially for those living in the West, who establish mosques, through which they nurture their children's Muslim identity and also improve their level of religiosity. However, Muslim communities' ways of managing these religious institutions are not immune to the ethnic diversities of Muslim communities, and thus they are quite diverse, following different ethnic cultures. This diversity is indicated by the numerous Islamic centres, mosques, Islamic schools, and *Qur'ānic* schools that have emerged in particular ethnic enclaves in western societies such as in the USA, Britain, Canada, and Australia.

These centres are established by certain ethnic communities, and thus cultural practices taking place in these various Muslim communities reflect the particular ethnic cultures (Azmi 1997; Lotfi 2001; Shih 2000). Cultural diversity among the Muslim community centres to a certain degree shapes ways of being Muslim. For instance, Lebanese mosques would be different from the Turkish mosques, and likewise, mosques of the Pakistani community will have some differences from Indonesian mosques in their ways of conducting Islamic teachings and structures of the mosques, the language of instruction as well as benefits given to Muslim communities (Shih 2000).

Woodlock (2010b) advocates the establishment of mosques featuring ethnic identification, seeing this to be urgent in non-Muslim societies like Australia. This is because the ethnic mosque is often used as the mechanism to control certain ethnic minorities (Lotfi 2001; Naylor & Ryan 2002; Woodlock 2010b). Mosques of the Arab community are usually assigned a special *imam* (the Muslim cleric) from overseas whose knowledge about local contexts is limited. In addition to the assigned *imam*, Woodlock (2010a) argues that most mosques, especially those belonging to Arab communities segregate women and men; the mosque committee orders limited access to the mosque for women, and most often the access is available only via the back door. Language diversities are also a common feature of mosques in the western world. For example, the mosque of the Albanian community and of the Turkish community in Victoria, Australia, use their ethnic language and Arabic as a medium of *khutba* (the Friday sermon).This, however, is not a religious teaching; it is more a cultural doctrine for certain ethnic groups.

Due to these diversities within Muslim communities, ways of taking full advantage of mosques also differs. Employing segregation in the mosque and registering strict rules in the utilization of the mosque indeed contribute to different ways of being Muslim. Insights on the diversity in Muslim communities have prompted me to raise questions on Indonesian community practices, and identify how they contribute to the construction of Muslim identity of young Indonesians living in Australia.

While living in the West, Muslim communities invite their children to attend religious gatherings at the mosque and also attend the weekend school. However, young Muslims do not always follow their parents' requests. They do not always concur with their parents' views on certain issues. They tend to enjoy being among their fellow classmates, spending most of their time engaging in social activities (Bayat & Herrea 2010). In their work on being young and Muslims, Bayat and Herrera (2010) note:

> Muslim youth, like their global counterparts, have come of age during a technological and communication revolution. New information communication technologies (ICT), from the mobile phone to the Internet, have changed the landscape of youth learning, culture, sociability, and political engagement (Bayat & Herrera, 2010, p. 10).

Young Muslims' engagement with modern technologies shifts their intention to attend the mosque and their weekend school. They relate to people in their age group and within their safe zones, they also make connections with people beyond their locality. As a result, some of them do not take their parents' ethnic values for granted. Some others, in fact, question cultural practices exercised within their ethnic community (Bayoumi 2010; Kibria 2007; Mondal 2008). This complex factor in young Muslims' identity construction is eloquently narrated by (Herrera & Bayat 2010a):

> In both the global North and South, Muslim youth navigate between asserting their youthfulness and oftentimes their Muslimness. But this maneuvering is mediated by a host of social, economic, and political settings within which these youths operate (Herrera & Bayat 2010a, p. 362)

The narration shows complexities in young Muslims' ways of constructing their identities within their lives in western environments, and thus a large number of studies have found that young Muslims in the western states hold multiple identities; while they maintain their ascribed Muslim identity, they take up other identity markers. Their ways of engagement in the mainstream society seem to be smooth (Bayoumi 2010; Kaya 2004; Mondal 2008; Sirin & Fine 2008).

In addition, young Muslims' engagement in the host countries seems to be different from that of their parents (Kibria 2007; Küçükcan 2004). Some are found to leave their religious values and take different identity markers. Other studies, however, show the contrary phenomenon, where some second generation Muslims attempt to return to the 'new Islam'[6]. Findings of some studies confirm that most second generation Muslims hold somewhat different perceptions of Islam to those of their forefathers; these young people attempt to return to the genuine Islamic principles, which are free from cultural boundaries (Bayoumi 2010; Dizboni 2008; Kibria 2007; Mishra & Shirazi 2010; Nielsen 2000).

For example, in a study conducted in Britain and USA, Kibria (2007) reveals a new phenomenon within Muslim communities in the West. She argues that there has been evidence that most Muslim youth in the west engage in 'revivalist Islam'[7], as the result of the "social and psychological dislocation of migration" (Kibria 2007, p. 245). There are certain factors that lend significance to the emergence of revivalist Islam. Muslim youth living in the West tend to return to pure Islam as a result of their discontentment with their parents' ways of being Muslims (Bayoumi 2010).

In addition, the revival of Islam has also occurred when Muslim identity is contested and confronted (Mondal 2008). For example, after 9/11 people in the global arena started to ask questions about Islam, and such attitudes have encouraged some young Muslims in Mondal's (2008) study to look back into their religious teaching and begin to learn more in-depth about their religion, and through engagement in the learning journey about Islam, those young Muslims living in the global north have recognized the beauty of their own religion. Mondal (2008) then found that for many young Muslims, Islam is highly compatible with their lives

---

[6] The term has been used by Kibria, N. (2007). The 'new Islam' and Bangladeshi youth in Britain and the US. *Ethnic and Racial Studies, 31*(2), 243-266 when discussing Bangladeshi youth's ways of constructing Muslim identity

[7] It refers to "a concern for scripturalism and totalism, a return to basic principles and an emphasis on the significance of Islamic thought for all aspects of life (Kibria, 2007, p. 244).

in western countries. One of Mondal's participants notes in the following narration:

> It was very intensive and it basically opened my eyes up to the fact that Islam was very, very accessible, easily accessible; it was for everybody to understand. It wasn't just for the scholars or the intellectuals, it was for everybody right up from the most lay people to the scholars. And it really brought it home to me that in many ways I was already practicing Islam in terms of the fact that I tried to be honest, and that's big thing in Islam...(Mondal 2008, pp. 32-33)

This shows that some young Muslims in Britain have started to learn more deeply about Islam, and thus they see that Islam is not confined only to the ritual performance in the mosques. It is a way of life applicable in daily life. In fact, Mondal (2008) suggests that most young Muslims in his study found that Islam has enabled them to widen their horizon and go beyond their comfort zone of the family circle and the boundary of their hometown.

However, in her study of Bengali Muslims, Kibria (2007) notes that the first immigrant families perceived that their youth were not able to recognize their origin, and at the same time they were not accepted by the mainstream culture. Therefore, some young Muslims' ways of being Muslim are worrisome for the Muslim parents because they are considered to have drifted away from their religious and cultural values. The parents find that their children are developing different attitudes from theirs. On the one hand, these young Muslims are reluctant to leave their parents' ethnic cultures, on the other, they prefer to be called British in the case of young Turkish Muslims (Küçükcan 2004), and to act like other British people. In the study of Turkish Families, Küçükcan (2004) found that while young Turks still believed in basic Islamic principles, their Islam seemed to have taken on a symbolic attachment only. The study also reveals that the young Turks only possessed low levels of Islamic knowledge although parents had consistently facilitated the transmission of religious values. This group of young Muslims took Islam as a symbolic identity instead of their religious identity (Kaya 2003, 2004).

This information leads to my inquiries on how Indonesian parents see their children's attitudes and to what extent they are worried about their children's sense of Muslim identity. It has also encouraged me to examine to what extent Indonesian Muslim youth in the study conform to their parents' ethnic values, the values of their host society and to Islamic values.

## Multiple-Shifting Ways of Being a Young Muslim

In this chapter, I conceptualized Muslim identity through the discourses of religious texts. The *Qur'ān* and the *Hadith* prescribe certain Muslim characteristics and also attributes of Muslims. The basic tenet of Muslim identity as described in the first main section of this chapter focuses on the observance of the *ibadat* in Islam. The *Qur'ān* and the *Hadith* describe Muslims as those who are required to submit themselves to the will of *Allāh*. In addition, the chapter has examined the ways in which the Muslim family and the *ummah* are constructed as educational and social sites in shaping the identities of young Muslims. I also discussed these issues in relation to Muslims and young Muslims living in the West.

Various studies have found that young Muslims living in non-Muslim countries and in the West such as the USA, the UK, Australia have multiple, shifting identities. Studies on young Muslims found that while they embraced their parents' cultural and ethnic values, they also engaged with other cultures, including those of mainstream youth. Social and political conditions have also complicated Muslim youth' ways of being Muslim.

# CHAPTER THREE

# TOWARDS UNDERSTANDING INDONESIAN, AUSTRALIAN, AND MUSLIM IDENTITY

This chapter provides a background on 12 young Muslims' shared understandings on three issues: first, it discusses their essentialized understanding of Muslim identity. The second issue discussed is in regard to their essentialized understanding of being Australian, and the last issue discussed in this chapter concerns with their essentialized understanding of Indonesian identity. These understandings are regarded as being essentialised because they were rigidly and narrowly confining characteristics of Muslim, Australian and Indonesian identity as expressed by these young Muslims.

## Perceiving Muslim Identity

The participants of this study hold similar understandings on the attributes of Muslim identity. Three major themes of Muslim identity emerged from my fieldwork. First, the 12 young Muslims indicated that Muslims are those who have the following three qualities: the *tawhid* (belief in the oneness of God)*,* the *ibadāt* (the rituals), and the *akhlāq* (conduct). Second, they linked Muslim identity with the action of wearing the *jilbāb* (the Muslim dress code), and they saw it as a specific marker of religiosity. Third, they constructed Muslim identity through the commitment to promote good relationships with fellow humans.

### *Being devoted and faithful Muslim*

All young Indonesian Muslims participating in my study noted that to be called Muslims, one needs to have a strong faith in the oneness of God. The *tawhid* is the most important component of being Muslim. In the Islamic teaching, the *tawhid* is the core requirement for someone to be called a Muslim. It is a declaration of faith, in which all Muslims, either those who were born Muslims or converted to Islam, are obliged to declare the word of *tawhid*. For example, when someone intends to convert to

Islam, he or she is required to utter the declaration of faith, which is the belief in God as the sole deity and that the Prophet Muhammad is God's messenger (refer to Chapter Two for more details). For example, some of them noted:

> A good Muslim is the one who is very strong in religion ... even if you don't pray, you don't do anything [bad], as a Muslim, you don't eat pork ... that is one thing that any Muslim does not do ...(Salma, Year 12)

> I think you have to be a good person and you have to really believe in *Allāh*. I don't think if you broke a couple of rules; if you want to call the rules, I don't think that will make you a bad Muslim. It is just you have to believe in religion I guess and you just have to value it (Suci, Year 10)

These quotes see Muslim identity in terms of the belief in *Allāh* (*tawhid*) as the one God and having strong faith. For these young schoolgirls, the basic tenet of being Muslim is to have a strong faith in their religion, which is the belief in the existence of *Allāh*. Although some Muslims fail to show their religious conviction through ritual performance, having a strong faith which is the belief that there is no deity of worship except *Allāh* is an important marker of Muslim identity. This understanding is generated from Salma's quote: 'even if you don't pray'. The quote indicates that even though Muslims sometimes fail to pray, they are still considered as Muslims as long as they have a strong faith in *Allāh* and Islam. Salma's and Suci's quotes confirmed Ramadan's (2004) conception of Muslim identity suggesting that it is closely related with the *tawhid*. As noted in Chapter Two, Ramadan constantly notes in many of his books that the first and the foremost important component of being Muslim are faith and spirituality (Ramadan 1999, 2004).

In addition, some others in this study linked being Muslim not only with strong faith but also with the actualization of the faith through ritual fulfilment (*ibadāt*). Young Indonesian Muslims suggested more comprehensive ways of understanding Muslim identity. While not ignoring the significance of faith, Darni and Yani suggested that Muslim identity is also related to the commitment to observing the obligatory rituals. This perception is in line with Riaz Hassan's conception of Muslim identity, in which he sees that the performance of religious rituals is an expression of being Muslim (Hassan 2008). Their interview quotes suggest this way of seeing Muslim identity:

> A good Muslim should do all obligatory stuff; being understanding and respectful to others, this is hard, probably if someone asks about Islam and if they know it, they can explain it properly, if not they just can keep quiet

so no bad things would be said about Islam that can be more misunderstood to other non-Muslims (Darni, Year 12)

Praying five times a day but knowing what to do and not to do [because] I know that there are a few Muslims that pray five times a day but they are pretty bad as well, but they know what values are and stuff and just have a good character I guess (Yani, Year 12)

Performing religious obligations is the core component of being Muslim as suggested from the quotes. Young Muslims in my study noted that 'praying five times' is a prerequisite for being Muslim. For example, Hafnizar suggested in the interview that those who do not perform the prayers are not considered real Muslims. In his own words:

I think he is not a type of Muslim [those who do not do *salāt*], he calls himself a Muslim but doesn't do all stuff, it is a kind like a hypocrite (Hafnizar, Year 9)

Hafnizar linked the performance of the religious rituals, such as the *salāt* to the essence of Muslim identity; those who fail to do this are seen as hypocrites or as not 'Muslim' as Fadil (2005, p. 145) puts it.

The other young Muslims argued that the possession of good conduct (*akhlāq*) is the central part of Muslim identity. In addition to emphasizing the observance of the *ibadāt*, the youth in my study emphasized another important dimension of being 'good' Muslim, which is the possession of good conduct (*Akhlāq-al Makhmudāh*), which they saw as the attribute of 'good' Muslims. For Yani having the commitment to show religious piety through ritual performance and having good conduct are the essence of being a Muslim. The absence of these two qualities is thus seen as a deficiency in being Muslim. Hanafi also voices similar perceptions on being Muslim, stating:

A person who is kind, a person that tells their Muslim brothers and sisters if they [the non Muslims] are doing something bad for them, do not angry with people who call you terrorist ... a person who has a good knowledge about Islam, and a person who try hard to memorize the *Qur`ān* and other stuff (Hanafi, Year 11)

Giving advice among Muslims and being patient in the wake of unjust treatment are features of good conduct in Hanafi's perception. In addition to having good conduct, Hanafi adds another dimension of Muslim identity, which is acquiring sufficient knowledge about Islam and having high motivation to learn the *Qur`ān*.

This understanding of *Muslimness* is in line with the discourses of the religious texts, the *Qur`ān* and the *Hadith*, which specify *akhlāq-al makhmudāh* as one of the basic tenets of being Muslim, and in fact the Prophet Muhammad (PbuH) himself was sent to improve the conduct of mankind (refer to Chapter Two for more detail). In addition to the performance of the prayers, Muslims were seen as those who achieve a balance between their engagement with the obligatory rituals (*ibadāt makhdah*) and their social lives. Fatma states:

> Probably someone who does a basic stuff like pray five times a day and read *Qur`ān* and stuff like that and they do all that and live a life too, so it is not just all of that the whole time, it is not just the Muslim stuff all of the time, you have to be balance (Fatma, Year 11)

Fatma saw Muslims as those who have a balanced life, meaning that they do not only perform the obligatory and the voluntary *ibadāt* such as the recitation of the *Qur`ān* but also engage and socialize with surrounding people. For example, Muslims are allowed to do some social activities such as going camping and engaging in sport and music as part of their lives, and she does not see that being involved in such activities will denigrate one's belonging to a Muslim faith. This definition also suggests that Muslims are not those who only limit themselves to the ritualistic sphere, but they also integrate with people in the communities as well.

In addition to such ways of understanding Muslim identity, most young Muslims in this study related Muslim identity to the dress code. The donning of the veil (*jilbab*) was considered as a specific marker of Muslim identity. In the following section, I will describe these young Muslims' voices on another *essentialized* notion of Muslim identity.

## *Wearing the headscarf (Jilbāb)*

Both male and female young Muslims in my study linked Muslim identity to the donning of the veil, seeing this as a form of identity marker. This kind of understanding is found in many studies such as that by Ali (2005), Cole and Ahmadi (2003), and by Zine (2006). The *jilbāb* was indeed perceived by all the participants as a religious marker. Although most of the girls stated that they do not consistently wear the headscarf in their daily routine, all of them saw the headscarf as a Muslim-specific marker, and some considered it as a religious requirement. Ikhwan, for example, states:

> Sometimes it is obvious that they are Muslims, then they are not wearing
> so you don't realize that they are    Muslims; they look just Australian. If
> they wear you can tell that they are Muslims then if they are not wearing it
> right … Yeah I do [appreciate] because they are very brave to wear it
> outside like everywhere because people mostly see them as like Muslim so
> they know what to associate with …(Ikhwan, Year 11).

The sense that the *jilbāb* acts as an identity marker that differentiates
Muslims from non-Muslims was shared by all young Muslims in this
study. That this type of identity marker is also used as an expression of
religiosity is revealed in many other studies (see Mishra & Shirazi 2010).
Even though the 12 young Muslims in this study saw it as a religious
marker, out of the six female students in this study, five of them did not
always wear the veil for multiple reasons, which will be explained in
chapters to come in this book.

In addition to the above aspects of their essentialized understandings of
Muslim identity as discussed earlier, these twelve young Muslims also
indicated that interaction with others was seen as the essence of Muslim
identity. This essentialized understanding of Muslim identity is described
in the following section.

## *Integrating rather than isolating with others*

In my fieldwork, I found that all participants suggested that the basic
tenet of being Muslim entails participation and engagement with
surrounding people. In addition to linking Muslim identity with the dress
code, Ikhwan holds that the ability to engage with the community is also a
central part of Muslim identity; he states that:

> Good Muslims that can mix with non-Muslim people but still keep their
> religion at the same time, not afraid to do his religious stuff in front of
> them [non-Muslim friends] (Ikhwan, Year 11).

Ikhwan perceives that Muslims are not exclusive. They are required to
interact and mix with other people beyond the boundaries of their religious
communities. However, he also maintains that in their interaction with a
wide range of people, Muslims are encouraged to be persistent in holding
to their religious principles and practices.

It has been noted in Chapter Two that Islam encourages its adherents to
integrate with the community surrounding their residences. Prophet
Muhammad (PbuH) himself while living in the new city, Yathrib, which
later became known as Medina, integrated and interacted with the residents

of Medina regardless of their clans and religions (Al-Mubarakfury 2006). In Ramadan's (1999) conception of Muslim identity, he also reiterates the necessity of participation in the environment in which Muslims live. Although participation within a particular community is seen as necessary, participating in non-Muslim communities may be difficult (Qardawi 2008).

This section has revealed three *essentialized* understandings of Muslim identity as reported by Indonesian young Muslims. These *essentializations* of Muslim identity, which are gained through exposure to Islamic teaching at homes, weekend schools and mosques, are closely related to the discourses of religious texts. Belief in *Allāh*, observing religious rituals, and good conduct are important components of being Muslim as prescribed in religious texts. Ramadan (2004) and Zine (2008) also noted that having these three Islamic components was seen as one of the prerequisites of being Muslim. *Tawhid*, for example is a representation of *imān* and it is the first pillar of Islam, the *sahadāh*. Next, *ibadāt* and *akhlāq* are also foundations of Islamic teaching as represented in the pillar of Islam.

In addition, the donning of the headscarf is also believed by mainstream Muslim communities to be a religious requirement and is seen as the characteristic of devout Muslims as suggested by most of the participants in this current study and those by others researchers (Ali 2005; Cole & Ahmadi 2003; Hamdani 2007; Read & Bartkowski 2000). In fact, wearing the *jilbāb* as a religious requirement is stated in at least two verses of the *Qur`ān* in spite of varied interpretations of the *ayāt* (see Chapter Two for detailed explanations of the verses). Finally, the ability to promote relationships with others is seen as another *essentialized* understanding of Muslim identity. Although Ikhwan, was the only participant to explicitly state this notion, all young Muslims in the study indirectly perceived that interaction within the community in which they lived was important.

This section shows that all young Muslims in this study see the essence of being Muslim through an essentialized understanding of Muslim identity. This understanding of Muslim identity reflects their engagement with the teaching of Islam within their home environment and their immediate family. In spite of this essentialized understanding, not all of them adhere to these markers in their daily lives, which I discuss in following chapters

In the following section, I move on to discussing how young Indonesian Muslims in my study understand Australian identity.

# Perceiving Australian Identity

This section identifies how young Indonesian Muslims in my study perceive what it is to be Australians. Whether their responses correspond with widely perceived notions of Australianness is also discussed in this section. Five themes emerge from this study: stereotypes, habits, physical appearance, a length of stay in Australia, and 'a fair go'.

## *Being laidback and arrogant*

Most young Muslims in my study refer to Australian identity through stereotypes such as 'laidback', 'dumb', 'talkative', 'annoying', 'arrogant', 'joke around', and 'show off'; and habits such as drinking beer, liking footy and barbeques. Suci, for example, said:

> …the people are laidback like they are very relaxed and nothing like bother them… I think that what most people would base it on, the stereotypes (Suci, Year 10)

> …I don't know they [Australians], it is just laidback everyone is taking it easy…they work hard when they need to (Yani, Year 12)

These quotes represent the stereotyped characteristics of Australians. The majority of young Muslims in this study use the term 'laidback' to represent Australian identity. The term refers to the state of being relaxed.

In their understanding, Australians are those who do not spend time to work hard. They see Australians as people who are relaxed in their effort to gain financial benefits. This definition emerges from these young Muslims' lived experience with 'Aussie-Aussie' friends either in their schools or the wider Australian community. During their engagement with their classmates at school and other broader contexts, they encountered situations, in which their 'Aussie-Aussie' friends tended to act in ways that corresponded to the stereotypical understanding of Australian identity.

In addition to the terms 'laidback' and relaxed that represent their perceptions of Australian identity, some other participants described Australian traits through 'negative' attributes. My research participants, for example stated that Australians were:

> People who talk too much and … they are annoying, they always joke around, they are dumb, they are dumb like in education stuff, they cannot [do] math, they cannot spell precisely … (Hanafi, Year 11)

The expressions of 'talk too much, annoying, joke around, and dumb' are pejorative terms that emerged during my communication with my research participants. Hanafi, for example, as seen in the quote, viewed Australian identity as such due to his experience while studying in an Australian public school. Therefore, these pejorative terms only referred to some of their peers at school. They did not apply to all Australians in a general sense. Another student, Hafnizar, also commented:

> Ok in my class has five Australians, and they are all like the same personalities, they all like show off cause they think they good at sport, and they are very arrogant, not all of them, and some of them are racist … they arrogant, they think they are the best of everything, they are racist … (Hafnizar, Year 9)

Some of my research participants seemed to generalize Australian identity. For example, in defining Australian identity, these Indonesian young Muslims told me that Australians are the same in their characteristics. They told me that Australians 'are all like the same personalities'. This statement seems to be judgmental. However, it is understandable because it reflects their daily experience when interacting with them, especially at school. One of the participants, for example, reiterated that out of five 'white Australians' in his class, all five thought that they were good at sport and this made them arrogant. Another student, Fatma also said that 'they think they are good'.

There is evidence in some studies, one of which is that of Ata (2009) who found that students of mainstream culture see Muslims negatively. Muslim students at the same time also depict Australian students with negative attributes. Some young Muslims in my study, however, expressed the view that these negative attributes were not because of any experience they had had of discrimination. Their narration about Australian identity is drawn from the attitudes shown by some of their 'Aussie-Aussie' classmates.

In addition to these negative attributes, some of my research participants associated Australian identity with habits practised in the mainstream society. Suci, for example, linked Australians to footy and drinking beer as she said that: "…you have got to like footy, you have got to drink beer and everything like that". While living in Australia, these Muslim youth have observed that people living in Australia usually engage in a certain type of sport, such as 'footy' (Australian-ruled football). These Muslim youth also observed that drinking alcohol is a common activity taking place in Australia. These observed habits shaped these Muslims' ways of perceiving what it is to be Australian. This understanding of Australian identity was also narrated by Hanafi when he stated that Australians:

> always drink beer and they say 'what's up mate', they always end their talks like 'mate', but they are very sporty (Hanafi, Year 11).

In addition to the habit of drinking alcohol that constitutes Australian identity for the youth in this study, my research participants also told me that communication styles also construct Australian identity. For example, they claimed that their Australian peers were always using a particular expression when they spoke. The expression of 'what's up mate' is seen as an expression used by Australians and thus it became a particular attribute of Australian identity. While some young Muslims linked Australian identity with 'drinking beer' and 'sports', other young Muslims related Australians to the habit of engaging in barbeques and attending parties. Darni says:

> Yeah, pretty much all that and they really good in the sport and barbeque … that is the stereotype, and other Australians who are not white, do like sport also and then they like barbequing and they like party too so ya (Darni, Year 12)

This narration suggests that Australian identity is always related to the stereotypes and perceived habits of being sporty and attending barbecues. These attributes seemed to be associated with being 'white', though Darni and others indicated that if someone is not white but they enjoy doing sport and barbeque, he/she can be considered as an Australian.

In this discussion, I have identified participants' views that there are two attributes of Australian identity, including stereotypes such as being 'arrogant and laidback', and habits that are commonly practised in the Australian society, such as playing sports and consuming alcohol. In the following analysis, I provide other attributes expressed by the participants, which are related to physical appearance.

### *Being white and blonde*

Some young Muslims in my study defined the attributes of Australian identity as aspects of physical appearance. Most of them perceived that Australians are white. Because of this belief, they did not see themselves as Australian (I return to this issue in the following three chapters). For them, whiteness and blonde hair were seen as the representation of Australian identity. Earlier studies on Australian identity conducted by

Zevallos (2005) also found that Australian identity is oftentimes referred to as being based on being white and being blonde in addition to other attributes. Some of the young Muslims participating in this study stated:

> Australian is someone with white skin and maybe blonde or brown hair or something like that, with blue eyes or something (Suci, Year 10)

> I think, at the back of my mind I think Australians are like white people…I don't know they just look like Australian stereotype blonde head (Darni, Year 12)

For these young Muslims, Australians must be white. This suggests that non-white people were not considered Australians. In addition, those who do not take on some stereotypes and habits that are linked to the attributes of Australians could not be perceived as Australians.

These narrations from some of my participants indicate that physical appearance determines for them which group someone belongs to. For example, most of these young Muslims did not categorize themselves as Australians because of their different physical appearance. Although most of my participants engaged with activities commonly undertaken by their Aussie-Aussie friends, such as being sporty and attending parties, they did not see themselves as Australians, just because of their different skin colour. In the following three chapters, I will discuss in more detail these young Muslims' ways of positioning themselves within the Australian contexts. This information is consistent with arguments given by Marranci (2008), who suggests the feeling to be someone, shape people's identity.

In the following discussion, I provide the other two attributes of Australian identity as expressed by most of my participants.

## *Length of living in Australia and 'a fair go'*

Some young Muslims in this study suggested that Australians are those who have spent a considerable amount of time in Australia. Yani, for example, stated:

> People who have been here longer than, say, they've been here since they were three but they were born overseas. I'd consider them Australian because they've been raised up in this environment (Yani, Year 12)

This narration identifies Australian identity through the length of stay in Australia. Kabir (2008b) also found in her study that Muslims who had been living in Australia for a long period of time, viewed themselves as

Australians and they had a strong connection to the country. Some of the Indonesian Muslim youth in my study considered that those who had grown up in Australia were Australians. This definition of Australian identity allows people of various backgrounds to be considered Australians as long as they have stayed for a number of years in Australia. As narrated in the quote, Yani believed that those who started living in Australia at an early age, and those who had been exposed to Australian mainstream culture could be considered part of the Australian society. Other young Muslims also noted similar understanding of what contributes to an Australian identity. Imani, for example, stated:

> Anyone who lives there [Australia] and grow up there [Australia]…yeah like raised up or something here, grew up or born, so yeah" (Imani, Year 9).

Although stereotypical definitions of Australian might also emerge in their description of Australians as noted earlier, they preferred to see Australians mainly as those who live in Australia and hold an Australian passport. Salma, though, constructed Australians in a different way. She linked Australian identity with 'fair go' attributes. She suggested that Australians are open-minded people. They welcome people of different backgrounds, even though she also found that she could not ignore some emergent stereotypes about Australians. She said that:

> An Australian I guess ya someone who is accepting and is open to everyone's culture because Australia is a multicultural country, right…like they are always willing to give help like I find that Australians are really nice, I mean they do anything and they are Australian…I guess you just need to have an Australian passport (Salma, Year 12)

Salma's perception of Australian identity seems to contradict most opinions on Australians given by my participants in this study. Salma perceives that Australians are those who possess the quality mentioned in her narration. She views Australians as open-minded and very nice people. This perception emerged through her lived experience, in which she observed that Australians like to help others. Somewhat similarly, Ikhwan also agreed that Australians could not be defined only through physical appearance, such as being white people. For him, there are many white people who are not necessarily Australians. In addition, he also did not conform to the linking of the attribute of heavy drinking to Australian identity. He suggested that there are many people who also drink beer but do not live in Australia.

Multiple understandings of what defines Australians emerged in my study. These young Muslims did not hold a single definition of Australianness. For example, Darni provided three ways of being Australian: physical appearance, habit and also a length of stay in Australia, and such multiplicity in understanding what it is to be an Australian applied to other young Muslims in my study. This indicates that understanding being Australian is indeed complex. Salma at least shows her confusion in explaining what constitutes Australian, as she says that:

> I reckon the Aborigine are [Australian] because they are here first and Australia is their country, but again, is that the British one who make Australia, or it is already called Australia (Salma, Year 12).

This narration suggests that Australian identity is multiple and also complex at the same time. Salma seems to raise questions about who should be called Australians, the aborigine or the Anglo-British people. Such a complexity in deciding who Australians are also emerged in some other studies, one of which is by (Zevallos, 2004, 2005). In her interview with Latin American and Turkish second generation in Australia, Zevallos found that most participants are confused on who and what Australian culture is. In spite of such difficulties, Zevallos' (2004) participants across ethnic groups referred to the terms 'laid-back, beer, and footy'(Zevallos, 2005). Drinking beer and being laidback as essentialized notions of being Australian were also found in the study by Philips and Smith (2000).

Having understood how young Indonesian Muslims in my study define Muslim and Australian identities, I now turn my discussion to analyse how they define Indonesian identity.

## Perceiving Indonesian Identity

During the interview with these 12 young Muslims, they told me about their perceived markers of an Indonesian identity, namely eating Indonesian food, having Indonesian parents, and participating in Indonesian culture and traditions.

### *Preferring Indonesian food*

Some of the young Muslims saw themselves as Indonesian because of the type of food they customarily eat. Suci and Salma said:

> Because I still do a lot of things that are within the Indonesian culture as well. Like I still go back to Indonesia pretty often and my family is

Indonesian, I eat the food if there's a food festival or something and I have Indonesian friends and stuff like that, so I think I'm both (Suci, Year 10).

I was born in Indonesia and I live in the Indonesian family, I will be pretty traditional I guess because we eat rice every day (Salma, Year 12)

The two quotes link Indonesian identity with the type of food they eat and also with their engagement in Indonesian cultural and food festivals.

## *Having Indonesian parents*

Other students in the study defined Indonesian identity through their birth into an Indonesian family. They suggested that those who were born to Indonesian parents are seen as Indonesian. This is in line with their ways of defining themselves. Most of them see themselves as Indonesian because of their family heritage. Imani and Fatma stated:

Well, I am mostly, like I am really, I am like Australian more, but Indonesian blood. Like I don't know, yeah Indonesian blood like, yea I do things the Indonesian way (Imani, Year 9)

Yeah because I was born in Indonesia and I want to keep my Indonesian (Fatma, Year 11)

Imani's words suggest that although she perceived herself to be more Australian because she had been living in Australia for her entire life, her Indonesian heritage seemed to play a greater role in determining her identity marker. In line with Imani, Fatma also argued that the fact that she was born to Indonesian parents made her see herself as Indonesian.

## *Practicing Indonesian culture(s)*

Some other students in the study identified that certain ways of doing things also determined one's identity. For example, one of the participants asserted that his habit of taking off his shoes upon entering his home was a marker of his Indonesian identity. For example, Hanifa said:

I still can speak Indonesian and I act like an Asian person...you know when I go home I take off my shoes... people see me as an Asian...because I am discipline, when I got into their house right it is always messy and they don't try to clean it, they just oh oh stop it, leave it like this, whereas in my family I have to discipline like clean up the house and the stuff (Hanafi, Year 11)

In this quote, Hanafi provides three traits that represent the Indonesian identity. The first trait is the capability to speak the language. He suggested that although he had spent a considerable amount of time in Australia he was still able to speak Indonesian, and this ability to speak the language represented his sense of belonging toward Indonesian identity.

The second trait drawn from the interview quote was being disciplined. Hanafi and some other students in this study linked Indonesian identity with 'discipline'. For example, he indicated that his identity was linked to always meet the demands of a certain daily schedule, such as attending the madrasah and taking his shoes off upon entering his home. The final trait obtained from the quote is being clean and tidy. He compared and contrasted his home environment, especially his clean room with those of his colleagues, which he found to be dirty and untidy.

## Summary

In this chapter, I present markers of the Muslim youth's essentialised understanding of Muslim identity: being devoted and faithful, wearing the headscarf, and integrating with others. Their definitions of being Muslim parallel with notions of Muslim identity as prescribed in discourses of religious texts as noted in Chapter Two. The *Qur'ān* mentions:

> The only saying of the faithful believers, when they are called to *Allāh* and His Messenger to judge between them, is that they say: 'We hear and we obey.' And such are prosperous ones (An-Nur: 51).

> Then do you believe in a part of Scripture and reject the rest? Then what is the recompense of those who do so among you, except disgrace in the life of this world, and on the Day of Resurrection, they shall be consigned to the most grievous torment, and Allah is not unaware of what you do (Al-Baqarah: 85)

Two main attributes of Muslims are revealed in these two verses, total obedience, and full observance. *Ibn Kathir* argues that faithful believers always hear and obey *Allāh*, and through that kind of total submission, one attains success. In addition, as reported by *Ibn Kathir*, *Abu Ad-Darda'* perceives that total obedience to *Allāh* is the essence of being Muslim.

As suggested by these *ayāt*, being a Muslim represents the commitment to obey the commands of *Allāh*. For example, when Muslims are asked to perform the *salāt*, they will obey and act upon fulfilling it. Likewise, if they are prohibited from engaging in certain acts, such as consuming alcohol, they consistently abstain from it. In line with the messages in the first *ayāt*, the second verse indicates that Muslims are represented as those who are perfect in fulfilling their religious duties. They obey all *Allāh*'s commands, insofar as not fulfilling one religious duty and leaving others undone. Referring to the discourses of religious texts, Zine (2008) and Ramadan (2004) see Muslims as those who adhere to the commands of Allah. Therefore, being committed to rituals such as praying and fasting is a strong indication of Muslim identity and all students in this study held this essentialized understanding of Muslim identity.

The chapter also reveals how the 12 young Muslims in this study defined Australian identity. They defined being Australian through various attributes, such as stereotypes, habits, physical appearances and traits – ones however that most of them felt did not apply to them. This finding is not uncommon given that previous studies (Zevallos 2003, 2004, 2005) have discovered similar notions of Australian identity. Finally, this chapter also revealed the 12 young Muslim voices on Indonesian identity.

# CHAPTER FOUR

# IDENTITIES IN-BETWEEN:
# AUSTRALIAN-INDONESIAN MUSLIM

## Introduction

In the previous chapter, I discussed my research participants' (twelve young Muslims') essentialized understandings of Muslim, Australian and Indonesian identity. In this chapter, I discuss the ways in which a group of five young Muslims in my study constructed and negotiated their Muslim identity within their family and religious spaces, such as the *masjid* and the *madrasah*. These five young Muslims took on some markers of the 'good' Muslims and some markers of essentialised understandings of 'Australian' and 'Indonesian'. I illustrate the ways in which they did this in their family and the *ummah* spaces. In this chapter, I also discuss parenting styles and parents' religious and educational aspirations for their children.

## The Five Muslim Youth and Their Parents

In this section, I provide a brief discussion on the 5 Muslim youth and their parents. I also discuss their schooling and social backgrounds. I also discuss their parents' professional backgrounds and their reasons for migrating to Australia.

'I am an Australian-Muslim of Indonesian background' is an expression shared by five young Muslims in this group, Billah, Zaki, Imani, Hera and Suci. All of them were born in Australia to Muslim parents. Billah and Zaki were in Year 11 at the time of the interview. There were also two Muslim girls in this group, Suci and Imani, who were in Year 10 and Year 9. Hera had studied in a private Islamic school in Melbourne before she moved to an Australian public school. At the time of the interview, Hera was in Year 12. These 5 young Muslims follow their parents to the mosque and religious activities occasionally, especially in the month of Ramadan and when other special events were held.

The parents of all these five students are Indonesian Muslims except Zaki's mother who is an Australian of Anglo background and converted to Islam upon marrying his father. They come from families who work in factories, while Hera's parents own a small *halal* café and Billah's father is a professional plumber. Most of the mothers of these young Muslims are housewives, except Zaki's mother who works in the City Council and also Imani's mother who works in a Health Service Centre. The parents of some of them migrated to Australia in the 1970s and some in the 1990s. All of them indicated during the interview that migrating to Australia enabled them to improve their economic status. Billah's father, for example, argued that he is more comfortable living in Australia. He asserted:

> I have tried to live in Indonesia, but I feel more comfortable living here in Australia, in which I could make a good living, and raise my children (Oman, Billah's father).

These parents were involved in the Indonesian Muslim community centre and actively attended the religious sermons there and also those taking place within homes of the Indonesian Muslim community. For example, Ahmad, Zaki's father, attended the Islamic sermons on Friday nights, Saturday nights and Sunday mornings. While in the mosque I found him performing the *salāt* in a congregation; this commitment to prayer is one of the markers of practising Muslims as suggested by Hassan (2008). Zaki's mother, however, rarely attended the mosque. Billah's parents attended the Islamic sermon run on Friday nights. Junaidi, Hera's father, attended the religious sermon taking place on Sunday morning, and when he was in the mosque, he frequently acted as the *muadzin* (the caller for the *salāt*) while her mother only occasionally attended this religious space. Imani and Suci's parents only occasionally visited the Indonesian mosque during regular Islamic teaching. However, they attended the mosque during special events taking place there, especially in the month of *Ramadhan*.

## The 'melting pot' phenomenon: The Australian young Muslims

Young Muslims in this group regarded Islam as one of the important components of their identity as they live in Australia. Some of them asserted:

> Yeah it is [Islam is important], cause it is something I grow up with, it gonna be always a part of me and I will not change like for my friends or anything (Suci, Year 10)

Islam has made me who I am; Islam and my family have brought up this me and guide me to the right way, I believe in, I believe in Allah and stuff (Billah, Year 11)

...I am sure of what I believe in though I may not be praying all 5 prayers a day and read Qur'an every day (which I should be doing, I know it is not something what you mould around something else) I know my heart. I believe in Allah because I would be empty, not knowing what higher power there is. It is just not logical to believe that all this due to a big bang (narrative)-(Hera Year 12)

As they were born into Muslim families, they have been raised to believe in Islam, and thus it has been personalized in them. I label them as quiet observant Muslims referring to the typologies offered by Yasmeen (2008) because they do not fulfil all their religious obligations. The comments also indicate that they have acquired some knowledge of Islam. They have Islam in their heart, or 'Islam of the heart' to borrow Killian's (2007) term. They knew about the 5 pillars of Islam from their parents and the religious classes they attended. They also understood that one of the most central religious rituals among the five pillars is the *salāt*. However, they described themselves as not very religious Muslims due to the fact that they were not always persistent in performing the *ibadat*. For example, Billah confessed: "I don't think I am strong in religion, in the middle or something". Billah indicated that he was not a strong Muslim because he did not always practise the *ibadat* as required by Islam either at home or in other spaces.

Just pray, but sometimes I got told to pray but some other time I just do, and it's fine, I didn't mind...I pray at home sometimes...yeah I should have started it whenever I have time and stuff (Billah, Year 11)

At home I don't really pray 5 times a day, I usually pray 3 times a day or something, depending on how much homework, essays, assignments or whatever I have. Praying isn't always in my head, like to do Maghrib at night or whatever. But it's always good to try and remember you have to do it (Narrative)...I don't really feel uncomfortable like it is pray time, No I don't really have it in my head like when I am at school (Imani, Year 9)

Because there's not really enough time because now I am in Year 10 I have to be in every single lesson to catch up if I have the exam or whatever, and also there is not really place to do it, so it is really hard. Sometimes that is because the people not really the teacher, so sometimes they are a bit hard too (Suci, Year 10)

Right now I don't think so [pray five times], which is bad, I know it is
important but I still don't do it…No no they probably understand but it is
only my choice whether I want to pray at school or not, I don't think I am
comfortable at school (Hera, Year 12)

These comments confirm the young people's earlier expression of what
it is to be Muslim. They had an *essentialized* understanding of Muslim
identity. They understood that Muslims are encouraged in the religious
texts to adhere to the 5 pillars of Islam. In the interviews, they told me that
they understood that performing the *ibadat* is an important marker of
strong Muslims, and those who do not do so are not 'strong' Muslims.

Even though they did not see themselves as strong Muslims, they told
me that they believe in Islam faithfully and that *Allāh* the almighty is the
Supreme Being who regulates the entire universe. They were aware of the
rules that pertain to them as Muslims. For example, they believe that
performing the daily *salāt* and reading the *Qur`ān* are important aspects of
being Muslim. In fact, Ika said that he believed in Islam and regarded it as
important for the afterlife. Imani linked Islam with the afterlife and with
her parents' observance of religious principles; she opined that:

Ya it is (important) for the afterlife and because my parents have gone to
Hajj already, yea I guess it is pretty important (Imani, Year 9)

Islam is important because "I grew up with" was articulated by all
these five young Muslims. They described themselves as Muslims and as
always being Muslims regardless of their lack of religious conviction. This
information reveals that some second generation Muslims take Islam for
granted and regard it as part of their identity that has been ascribed to them
through their family, as argued by many scholars (Dwyer, 1999b; Killian,
2007; McAulife, 2007; Ramadan, 2004).

While they tend to take on their parents' religion, the young Muslims
in my study engaged with the essentialised understandings of a strong
Muslim in different ways, and these were again different from that of their
elders (Bayat & Herrera, 2010; Raby, 2001). They usually engaged in
certain religious and social activities, which were not necessarily as
important for their elders.

The Muslim girls in this group, Hera, Imani and Suci did not wear the
headscarf as they felt that it was a marker of 'backwardness' and that
wearing it would result in their friends' not wanting to interact with them.
They also told me about the discomfort in wearing the headscarf as it is
associated with stereotypes of a traditional Muslim woman. Suci
comments:

I probably would not be confident (wearing the veil), not that I got friends who questions but it would...I mean not everyone is ok with me, so I am not sure what people are gonna say about me, probably because of the stereotype and stuff that probably like, they don't want to hang out with me anymore (Suci, Year 10)

Her lack of confidence in covering her head is justifiable, since discourses of veiling as a sign of backwardness and patriarchal oppression have been part of an on-going debate in the western world (Gendrot, 2007; Read & Bartkowski, 2000), and in the Muslim world as well (Hamdani, 2007). Suci then explained that she respects those who wear the veil and are able to live their lives in Muslim minority countries, one of which is Australia. She asserted:

I don't think I could be as brave and also it'll be a big change, because I haven't worn one before like that, so I don't know if I could (Suci, Year 10)

Likewise, Hera indicated that she did not feel very comfortable about wearing this specific religious marker. She asserted that:

Ya I think it [Islam] is important but sometimes I don't know like wearing *hijab*, I am still not comfortable wearing the *hijab* or anything, maybe when I got older I would (Hera, Year 12)

While Hera felt uncomfortable about wearing the *jilbab*, Imani considered it as a voluntary action in Islam. This kind of perception indeed discouraged her from wearing the veil. She said that:

I am like because you have a decision (about wearing the veil) if you want to wear it and if you don't want to wear it (Imani).

These comments indicate that prejudicial sentiments may emerge toward Muslim women who are veiled. This also suggests that this particular specific marker of being a Muslim woman, the veil, is still not entirely accepted even in such a multicultural country like Australia. The quotes show the level of discomfort about wearing this religious marker in public domains as suggested by Suci and Hera. In addition, as they saw wearing the *jilbab* as not obligatory for Muslims as expressed by Imani, these young Muslim girls chose at that time not to do so.

In the series of interviews with the five young Muslims in this group, they indicated their engagement in various activities in and out of home ranging from academic to social activities, in addition to their religious activities. One of the students, for example, explained that in addition to reviewing her lessons for school, she also took piano lessons.

> I go to school, of course, usually I start about 8.20 am and I get home at about 3.30 pm, and I usually sit and have a snack after school, I do some homework and I go to my computer and like every Tuesday I have a piano lesson, I leave the house about 7.15 am and I get home about 8.30 am every Tuesday, I don't know, nowadays I get a lot of homework, so usually I do that on the weekdays (Suci, Year 10)

The hectic schedule as experienced by young Muslims in this study is a common phenomenon among Muslim families, since their parents set a high expectation regarding academic achievement for their children. Most of them attempt to secure their children's future through encouraging them to engage in many academic and non-academic activities daily (McGown 1999; Sarroub 2005).

Most of these 5 Muslim youth were involved in sports and other non-academic activities as seen in their interview narratives below

> Yeah I do basketball, badminton… I practice badminton every Friday after school, basket I usually play during play time or lunch … I am like a leader that we go camping someday, somewhere in a tent and hiking and stuff like that (Imani, Year 9)

> I do soccer and then running, sprinting a hundred metres and two hundred metres … It is like we have a partner and we have to do dance and stuff, and we started dance class, which is really fun (Billah, Year 11)

Suci was in her school band. Hera was the only one in this group who did not show much interest in any sport. She insisted:

> No sport no sport I am not very sporty, I am not doing much because Year 12 is too busy you cannot do anything but I have a part time job (Hera, Year 12).

Hera's reluctance to be involved in sports and other such extra-curricular programs was because of her heavy schedules at school that requires much of her attention.

For these young Muslims, being Muslim did not mean merely the performance of the *ibadāt*, or merely the engagement with activities run in the mosque. Their comments indicate that engaging in activities common among most teenagers in Australia while holding firmly to their religious values was also seen as one way of being Muslim. Some of them stated:

Like sometimes I go to party and they drink alcohol, eat pork or something of course I gonna say no, and my friends like they won't force me to do anything and understanding, so it is important to me...I just go to my friends' house tonight and watch the movie (Suci, Year 10)

Ya, I go but only go to the one I want to go, I go with my friends and if there is no, my friends, I don't need to go, or if the school function, I go... No, I won't drink...No I don't want to drink and they don't force me to because they know I won't, they force my other friends who are not Muslim but she also says no (Hera, Year 12)

These comments above indicate that Islam to some extent also shaped their social behaviour. On the one hand, they participated in social activities and interactions with teenagers from a range of cultural backgrounds, yet they also held on to their Islamic principles. While they attended most of the parties with their friends, they negotiated their ways of being Muslim through abstaining from participating in activities which were in conflict with their religious values, such as drinking alcohol. This way of being young Muslims where there is a sense of balancing between being Muslim and also being part of the youth culture is also seen in other studies (see Masquelier 2010; McAulife 2007).

Imani enjoyed attending parties as seen in her interview quote below:

I like, well I like going out, sometimes parties and stuff like that ... Yeah a little bit [laugh], I don't know what you have though ... I don't know maybe I just want to try it [alcoholic drink], it is not like, it is like drugs, but I don't actually do drugs, but I don't actually do drugs ... like drinking is just one sip and that's all (Imani, Year 9)

Imani sees herself as a young Muslim and does not strictly adhere to some Islamic practices such as not drinking alcohol. In saying she was only having one sip of drink and did not do drugs, she seemed to indicate that she felt moderate in her behaviour compared to others.

In addition to attending their friends' parties, most of the young Muslims in this group engaged in many activities with their friends during the weekends:

Well if it's the weekend sometimes I'll go to my friend's house or to the movies or maybe a party. If it's like weekdays probably my homework and I just stay home and I just watch TV or go on the computer if I've got no homework or something...Not every weekend and not every night. Usually, it's just one night I go with my friends and then the other two I stay at home or go with the family (Suci, Year 9)

We usually go to Southland, hang out in the shopping mall, walk around looking for some places to lunch, talk about the news or talk about going out (Zaki, Year 11)

As young Muslims in Australia, they participated actively in numerous activities and interacted with youth from various religious and ethnic backgrounds. Some of them asserted:

I hang out with a small group, I usually hang out mostly with a few people, I don't hang out with the big group. I usually mix with others because everyone knows everyone by Year 12 (Hera, Year 12).

My group is just like a mixture of non-Aussie and Aussies, and they are a cool group. I just hang out with them and stuff, yeah it is really most of the friends in school know that I am a Muslim, and they have no problem with that, it is fine yeah (Billah, Year 11).

I also found that these five young Muslims connected with the global youth culture by accessing YouTube, blogging, Facebook, and using other social media. Some of them said:

Sitting in front of computer, chat on MSN, Facebook and stuff like that, check email regularly, download music, stay at home most of the time (Imani, Year 9)

Normally I just do homework because VCE or sit at the computer, eating and praying (Billah, Year 11)

Ya, ya, I do that (watching movie on my computer), like check up the internet or whatever, like usual thing, internet, tv, homework, radio in the morning to wake me up…Movies and driving, which are good but I don't really do much with my parents, we go shopping sometimes. I have my driving lesson with my dad, ya just like before, I drove here, I try to get my license by my birthday but I don't think I will get one (Hera, Year 12)

In some ways, these 5 young Indonesian Muslims reflect some of the findings that Kabir (2008) found in relation to young Australian Muslims. She found that young Muslims in her study are constantly shifting their identities. They

were western when it came to music, sports and reading; they were ethnic when it came to cultural celebrations, they were Muslims when they felt other Muslims were unfairly treated (Kabir, 2008a, p. 1).

In measuring Muslims' religiosity in seven countries, Hassan (2008) includes the frequency of recitation of the *Qur`ān* as one of the dimensions in his study. He argues that it is important to understand how often Muslims read the *Qur`ān* as the basis of understanding their religious conviction. These five young Muslims' comments suggest that recitation of the *Qur`ān* is not their daily habit although they consider recitation of the *Qur`ān* as an important marker of their religious commitment.

To summarise, I see these five young Muslims as being to some extent similar to Yasmeen's category of "quiet observant Muslims" for two main reasons. Firstly, these young Muslims seemed to take Islam for granted because it had been ascribed to them since birth, and second they do not take on all the 5 pillars of Islam all the time, only observing this practice occasionally.

Examining one's level of religiosity through looking at the commitment to fulfilling Islamic obligations and religious duties has been carried out by Riaz Hassan. In a series of his studies, he measured a person's level of religiosity through examining their commitment to performing the *ibadāt* (Hassan 2002, 2007, 2008; Hassan, Corkindale, & Sutherland 2008), and thus came to the conclusion that those who do not fulfil the rituals frequently fall into the category of quiet observant rather than practising Muslims.

This finding is similar to other studies on Muslim youth both in the majority and the minority Muslim countries (Herrera & Bayat 2010b). Dwyer (1999a) also found that most Muslim girls in her study did not express their piety through the fulfilment of the religious duties. They identified themselves as Muslims through their solidarity with their global *ummah*. This finding is also in line with a study conducted by Kabir (2008a) suggesting the young Muslims in her study claimed to be Muslim in solidarity with the globalized Muslim community. Their solidarity was actualized through their feeling of discomfort at what was happening to their Muslim fellows in some Muslim countries such as Iraq and Afghanistan (Dwyer 1999a). Some Muslim girls in Dwyer's research suggested that their feeling of being Muslim was very much connected to their parents' ethnic backgrounds.

A study in Nigeria found that for Muslim youth in that country, being Muslim is not necessarily about engaging in pious activities such as performing the *salāt* and the *sawm* (Masquelier 2010). They consider Islam as an important source that plays a significant role in their lives, and their Muslim identity is shaped by the sense of belonging to the global Muslim *ummah* (Masquelier 2010, p. 225). A study on Iranian young Muslims in the western contexts of Britain, Australia and Canada also discovered that the majority of Iranian Muslim youth take Islam from their parents and are not necessarily fulfilling their religious duties (McAulife 2007). Because they have been brought up to believe in Islam, these Muslim youth in McAulife's study take some parts of Islam, which they feel comfortable with, but leave aside Islamic rituals. For them "Islam remains a cogent part of their Iranian identity as a set of core (national) values that inform everyday cultural and secular interactions" (McAulife 2007, p. 44).

In the next section, I draw on the interview narratives of these five young Muslims and their parents to understand their ways of being young Muslims in their families.

## *Taking on Muslim identity at home*

Most of the parents of this group of participants are from middle-class families. They migrated to Australia for economic reasons and for a better future for their children. Even though Muslim parents in this group believe that living in Australia provides them with better income compared to Indonesia, they are also concerned with their children's Muslim identity. Ahmad, for instance, raised this issue:

> I have a grave concern with my son's religiosity, but I believe that environment shapes one's identity. If he is in the Muslim environment, he will be exposed to Islamic values, I also teach him Islam through story-telling, especially the story of the Prophet Muhammad, and I also encourage him to read Islamic books. Lastly, I make a *do'a* [pray] to Allah to guide my son (Ahmad, Zaki's father)

They are aware that Islam requires them to shape their children's Muslim identity and guide them along the right path in accordance with Islamic teachings. As argued in Chapter Two, the *Qur`ān* and the *Hadith* have set certain principles regarding parents' obligations toward their children. As required by Islam, parents are invited to be the *murabbi*, *muaddib*, and the *muallim* to their children (see Section2.2.1) that enable them to perfect their children's soul, body and mind.

Constructing and maintaining children's religiosity is a concern of all Muslim parents living in the West (Becher 2008; Collet 2007; McGown 1999). Although they live far away from the original home country, Indonesia, Muslim parents living in a minority Muslim country attempt to bring their cultural and religious values with them (Basit 1995, 1997). They transfer these values to their children through the process of instruction taking place at home. This issue was also the concern of all parents in this group. Tiarman, Suci's father, for example, spoke regarding this issue:

> The most effective ways of teaching children are to start from home, and then I sent them to Sunday school. However, after they graduated from primary school, they were reluctant at coming to the school [*madrasah*]. I also showing them that they are Muslims, in which Muslims are obliged to fast and to pray, and we should be committed to show non-Muslims about the Islamic values (Tiarman, Suci's father).

The parents in this group, as shown in the comment, realized that effective education starts from home. They took responsibility in shaping their children's attitudes and identities. Students in this group also saw parenting roles as significant in the formation of their Muslim identity. These roles began with reminding them about Islam. One of them, for example, asserted:

> It's important that my parents remind me every day how lucky I am like if we see on TV, they remind me about Allah and anything…Ya, my parents are the most because they come here like 25 more years ago, and there wouldn't be as many Muslims here … then so life is even harder back then and now I got pretty and yea I realize that… (Suci, Year 10)

> I think it is my family, like how they brought me up; it is a big part and I realize yeah this is [Islam] the right way (Billah, Year 11)

Although Muslim parents were aware of their parenting roles in shaping their children's Muslim identity, all of them agreed that coercions in teaching their children about Islam would, in fact, reduce their possibility to successfully shape their children's Muslim identity. The following quotes indicate how Muslim parents in this group approached their children when teaching them Islam through dialogue. Oman commented:

> I don't force my children, I teach them Islam through dialogue, I have a chat with them about the Islamic principles; about what they should do and should not do as Muslims-(Oman, Billah's father)

Oman asserted that his children understand Islam much better if he approaches them through dialogue. He insisted that he uses reasoning in teaching his children about Islam. For example, he stated that when he teaches his children about some restrictions in Islam, such as alcoholic drink, male-female relationships and other kinds of religious issues, he always gives them logical examples that help his children understand better. For instance, he said he tells his children not to drink alcohol and explains them the negative effects of alcohol.

Likewise, other Muslim parents shared this understanding. In fact, they were aware that Australian law sees child corporal punishment as illegal and impermissible in the Australian society. Aiman noted the need for patience and reasoned dialogue:

> I teach about Islam regularly and slowly, I don't force him, I have to be more patient in instilling Islam to him. Praise be to *Allāh* with His help, hopefully, I am able to teach him Islam and to maintain his Muslim identity (Ahmad, Zaki's parents)

All parents in this group believed that dialogue is the most acceptable way of teaching Islam to their children. In fact, Islam requires Muslim parents to understand their children's 'psychological mechanism' (Ekram & Beshir 2009, p. 17) during their engagement in parenting roles. They further discuss:

> In order to know how to motivate children to function in a useful and cooperative way, we must have some understanding of the psychological mechanism involved…. A child has two major motives that drive his or her actions-the need to belong and the need to gain attention (Ekram & Beshir 2009, p. 17)

In the *Qur`ān, surā An-Nahl ayāt* 125, *Allāh* also reminds Muslims to be gentle and wise in their ways of preaching Islam to someone, and this also applies to Muslim parents as they play their parenting roles. *Allāh* says: "invite the way of your Lord with wisdom and kind advice (*An-Nahl ayāt* 125)". Gentleness and brevity in teaching have been practised by the Prophet Muhammad (PbuH), and thus Muslim parents are invited to follow His footsteps because this kind of teaching does not only yield positive results but also allows them to build good relationships with their children.

In this endeavour, though, Muslim parents in this group faced challenges because their children were born in Australia, a non-Muslim country, in which there might be fewer religious opportunities and activities to nurture their children's Muslim identity compared to Indonesia, a Muslim country. Given these complex realities, these Muslim parents in this group were aware of some of the challenges facing them given the interplay between Islam, popular youth culture, and the broader Australian context. For this reason, parents in this group did not adopt a strict parenting style. Instead, they tried to make their children aware of their religious and cultural identities through visiting Indonesia and getting them to engage with religious practices through dialogue. Rizki, for example, asserted:

> I told them that they only born here in Australia, while we originated from the village [the countryside]. My oldest son has visited Indonesia frequently, and Ika has visited Indonesia 3 times (Rizki, Imani's father)

> The key procedure in instilling Islam to him is to remind him of his background that he is a Muslim, 'Muslim is your religion', and he is proud to be a Muslim and did not hide his Muslim identity, and thus gains respect from his friends. He also takes care of the dietary issue – the *halal* food (Ahmad, Zaki's father)

These parents believed that the home environment is an important source of identity formation, and thus constantly reminding the children about their religious background is significant in shaping the Muslim identity of his children.

Oman expressed his concern:

> At home, I have to keep reminding my children about Islam, I cannot stop doing that…youngsters in the age of 15-16-17 are having a critical change in their personality…it is a common thing in Australia that almost every weekend, teenagers go to party (Oman, Billah's father)

Issues of lifestyle were of concern for these Muslim parents. However, they allowed their children to interact with a wide range of people and allowed them to attend parties, which are commonly attended by many Australian youngsters. Ostra, for example, commented:

> I allow my children to attend parties, I have never prohibited them from attending parties, in the end, they quitted themselves…I gave them two requirements if they decided to attend parties: First, they have to restrain themselves from drinking alcohol, and second, I should take and pick them up to and from parties myself (Oman, Billah's father).

Although parents in this group seemed to be more flexible in terms of home regulations, all of them held the similar aspiration that they wanted their children to grow up to be righteous Muslims. For example, Ahmad and Oman stated:

> I wish my child can be a righteous Muslim … I don't care what culture he wants to take, either being an Indonesian or an Australian as long as he is a righteous Muslim, that suffices to me … I wish his partner would be a

Muslim girl, I don't know, but I have to make a *do'a* to Allah. (Ahmad, Zaki's father)

Besides making maximum effort, we also make constant prayers to Allah … we pray that Allah will make my children righteous Muslims. I was not concerned with their worldly career, they can be anything as long as they are righteous Muslims was fine with me. In my opinion, there is no difference between one occupation and others (Oman, Billah's father)

The study also reveals that young Muslims in this group were aware that their parents have played their parenting roles to teach them about Islam. Their parents are also remindful about their religion. Some of them described their awareness as follows:

Yeah, there are a lot of people that influence me to do better things. Like my brother will always remind me if I forget to pray he'll tell me to pray, he just always reminds me. And my parents always remind me to be thankful for everything I have and if you've got no one to turn to you've got Allah, so it's like it reminds you that there's always something there for you, but yeah I think it's a blessing (Suci, Year 10)

Imani said:

My parents…my parents always remind me to that … not really (do not pray together at home) but during *Ramadhan* we pray *Magrib* together … they ask me whether I want to come … like pray and stuff like that, like I don't know, telling me not to do, like fun stuff and like that (Imani, Year 9)

Hera also stated that her parents have been significant in shaping her Muslim identity. She noted that "mom and dad told us to pray and we have to learn the *Qur`ān*". The request to fulfil religious obligations is an indication of parents' concern with their Muslim identity. She also suggested that her parents' expectation of her ability to recite the *Qur`ān* and that sending her to an Islamic private school were part of their efforts to guide her in being a Muslim.

Although these Muslim parents wanted their children to be righteous Muslims, they realized that it is difficult for them to expect their children to enact all markers of 'good' Muslims. This is because raising their children as Muslims in a minority Muslim country like Australia can be challenging as has been noted earlier. Juhana, for instance raised this issue:

At least Hanifa is aware that she is a Muslim. I also expect that she understands some Islamic rules and regulations that she is not allowed to break, and I notice that she is aware of these Islamic rules (Junaidi, Hera's father)

Although these parents were concerned with their children's Muslim identity, they sent their children to public schools rather than the Islamic schools here in Australia. They had multiple reasons for their decision to send their children to public schools. Some of them regarded public schools as providing a space that helps their children integrate well into the Australian mainstream society. Others thought that Australian public schools could provide their children with good opportunities for academic excellence. Oman, for instance, asserted:

> We are not against Islamic schools. We just felt more convenient sending children to public schools. In fact, I don't see a big difference between Islamic and non-Islamic school, to me all of them are the same. Why this specific public school? Because academically, it is a prestigious school in the area (Oman, Billah's father)

Academic rank or school quality seemed to be among the reasons Muslim parents in this group sent their children to public school. Indonesian-Muslim parents in this group also felt that being in a public school provided their children the opportunity to develop a 'balanced life':

> I don't intend to send my children to Islamic schools since I don't agree with segregated religious schools ... I told my children that we live here in Australia, we have to have a balanced life and understand how other people's ways of life (Tiarman, Suci's father).

> I want to give a chance to my children to interact. I told them 'you are Muslims' so just go and interact with people around you be they Muslims or not. I believe that schooling is one of the best places to develop such interactions. There are only two consequences of this interaction, first, either my children will give a good example to their friends and influence their friends or they get influenced, and fortunately, so far my children are able to influence their friends, or at least are able to guard their *Muslimness* (Oman, Billah's father).

Some of the parents in this group believed that public schools have helped their children to integrate into mainstream Australian society more easily. They, in fact, suggested that their children have not shown any sign of discomfort being at their school. Some of them reiterated that public schools accommodate religious differences. Tiarman, for example, noted:

> The school here is good, if there is a class on Christmas, the school usually send us a notice letter first, then we decide to send our children to join the lesson or not, and we explain to the children the reason we don't let them join the program (Tiarman, Suci's father)

Regarding the public school, the youth shared common views to that of their parents, they elaborate:

> I don't know but I think it is a common thing now that there are a lot of different religions and the school, they understand, and sometimes, they just ask questions like fasting (Suci, Year 10)

> Being an individual in a public Australian high school is good because everyone is different, they have their own religions, backgrounds, beliefs and whatever. Myself, being an Australian/Indo-Muslim, educating at a public high school, full of Christians, Catholics, and many other religions out there, is pretty interesting. You learn about other religions (Imani, Year 9)

Unlike the other parents, Junaidi, Hera's father did not have as strong faith in the public schools as did the other parents, as this is evident in his decision to send his children to an Islamic private school. For Junaidi, Islamic school would help his children recognize Islam, and help them to hold onto their faith. However, Hera decided in favour of public school she was no longer interested in an Islamic school. Therefore, in Year 9, she moved to a public school. In her new school, Hera professed feeling more freedom, since socialization and interaction with students of different sex were possible. Junaidi realized that moving Hera to a public school was a difficult choice. In such a difficult situation, he then argued that the best thing he could do was to give balanced exposure to both secular systems at school and the Islamic environment at home and at the mosque.

The other parent, Ahmad intended to send his son to an Islamic school. However, he chose the public school for his son's health issue. In fact, he wondered whether a public school would distance his son from Islam. However, he believed that the home environment would play greater role in shaping his children's Muslim identity. Aiman explained:

> Actually, I want Zaki to attend the Islamic school, I discuss with his mother and we decide to send him to public school because we don't think there is a facility for a student with autism in the Islamic school.... Regarding my son religiosity, it depends so much on how I guide him and how I create a Muslim environment for him. No matter what type of school he enrols in as long as his religious identity is well guarded, it will be fine (Ahmad, Zaki's father)

All Indonesian-Muslim parents in this group had some concern with their children's religiosity. They were aware of their parenting roles and what was expected from them by Islam. They indicated that they wanted their children to be righteous Muslims and that education for this goal starts from home. They believed in dialogue with their children and therefore that their children should have choices in taking on different identity markers, be these Muslim, Australian or Indonesian. They sent their children to public schools as they also wanted their children to have a 'balanced life' and interact with young people from different backgrounds and also be part of the broader Australian society. The parents of the 5 young Indonesian-Muslims were clearly practising Muslims. Hera, one of the young Indonesian-Muslims in this group captured the fact that the parents in this group are also moderate Muslims:

> ...you got the orthodox and you got the moderate, I think we fall into the moderate, if we draw the line between fundamentalism and moderate, we're close to moderate (Hera, Year 12)

In the following section, I examine these five young Muslims' ways of being Muslim in the religious spaces of the *ummah*.

## *Partly participation within the ummah: Masjid and Madrasah*

For Muslims, the mosque or *masjid* is considered as one of the most important venues, in which various religious activities are performed (Johns & Saeed 2002; Marranci 2003). Since it is an important religious space, Muslim communities are encouraged to establish this type of religious space. The *masjid* is used to run the weekend *madrasah* (Islamic weekend schools) as a means to teach Muslim children about the *Qur'ān* and about Islam in general, to present Islamic sermons, and to conduct other types of Islamic activities.

The Indonesian Muslim community centre, which is established in a particular part of Victoria, is the central venue for most Indonesian Muslims. Most Indonesian Muslims in the community visit the space once in a while, and some visit it more regularly. The parents of these five Muslims told me that these two religious spaces are very important to them. The activities in the *masjid* and *madrasah* have provided the parents with the opportunity to introduce aspects of Islam to their Australian-born children. Ostra, for example, stated:

> There was an Islamic study group where Muslims held religious programs. My wife is very committed at inviting the children to come along with us.

Participating in the study group give a positive impact on our children's religious identity as well as ours (Oman, Billah's father)

Tiarman also voiced similar feelings:

Alhamdulillah, I have a large number of Indonesian Muslim friends living in Melbourne. We then established Islamic learning circle and my wife was very active at teaching children about Islam. When they reached the age of five, I took them to the madrasah but there were not many Muslims back then (Tiarman, Suci's father)

The parents interviewed perceived that, as a minority community, Muslims need to pay great attention in their attempt to establish a religious centre. However, they realized the difficulties they faced in requesting their children to attend the *masjid* and the *madrasah*. They commented:

Before we owned our personal religious centre, I sent them to somewhere else. We also conduct door to door learning circle, but now it is difficult to invite them to the Islamic program. They tend to say 'not again' (Rizki, Imani's father)

I take him to the mosque and the *madrasah*, but then he does not necessarily do what I want him to do. If he is in a mood, he will definitely attend the religious space (Ahmad, Zaki's father)

Giving exposure to Islamic teaching has become one of these parents' priorities. They saw the *masjid* and *madrasah* as two places that enable their children to grasp some knowledge on Islam. Nevertheless, as these comments have noted, these young Muslims did not necessarily abide by their parents' requests. Although their children showed a sense of reluctance in attending the religious spaces, the parents did not pressure them in this regard. Tomi, for example, commented:

We are not actively involved in the Indonesian community centre but we frequently visit the place. I take them to the centre to familiarize them with the Indonesian and Islamic cultures, such as when there is a marriage celebration, I invite them to attend the centre. In the month of *Ramadhan*, I encourage them more to attend the centre, but they tend to say 'not again' ... I want them to come to the mosque and at least listen to the *adzan* [the call for prayer] to remind them about Islam (Tiarman, Suci's father)

This comment suggests that the parents were not very strict in enforcing the Islamic regulations on their children. One of the main reasons they take their children to the religious spaces was to introduce them to Islam and the Indonesian culture.

As a result of their parents' request to attend the *masjid* and the *madrasah*, the five young Muslims in this group have visited the Indonesian religious centre along with their parents or siblings at least once. Two of them attend the space frequently, and the other three young Muslims showed no commitment to attending these religious spaces on a regular basis.

These five young Muslims attended the Indonesian Muslim mosque occasionally, especially in the month of *Ramadan* and during the special events held there. For example, the Indonesian mosque invites Muslim scholars from Indonesia to give a talk about Islam on a regular basis. The Indonesian Muslim communities living nearby and also in different suburbs in Victoria are invited to attend the program. Therefore, along with other Indonesian Muslims, they attend the mosque to listen to a talk given by Indonesian Muslim scholars. In the program, the scholars oftentimes speak the Indonesian language, which is not understood by many young Muslims growing up in Australia.

The language was one of the biggest barriers for the five young Indonesian Muslims in participating actively in the mosque's programs. They explained that there is no point in coming to the talk since they have no capabilities in communicating in the Indonesian language. Some of them point out that:

> I don't really visit it because I don't understand so, it is not really useful if I go but not really understand it, sometimes like my parents would go and they take me but not always (Suci, Year 10)

> I always go to *Masjid* every night in the month of *Ramadhan* to pray. And when there is a speaker I try to listen, depending on what language they are talking (Narrative)-(Imani, Year 9)

Research shows that language has become one of the sources of intergeneration conflicts (Marranci 2003) within the Muslim community in the West. As young Muslims are born and/or grow up in the English-speaking countries, they soon adopt the dominant language, which is English, and most of the time, they leave their heritage language. In fact, oftentimes, Muslim parents themselves communicate with their children in English to facilitate their children's accessibility to education in English-medium schools. The young Muslims in this group were speaking fluent English, while they did not have the capability to communicate in Indonesian very well.

In addition, the distance can be an inhibiting factor for some of these Muslims to attend the mosque. Hera, for example, suggests that her far distance from the Indonesian mosque discouraged her from visiting the space. In addition to distance, school homework and other academic issues distracted her from coming to the mosque regularly. She asserted:

> I usually not really wanna come because I have homework, usually during the week I am always busy and I won't have time for myself, but if something is very important, I probably go (Hera, Year 12)

The obvious reason for their lack of enthusiasm to visit the mosque is the language barrier and also their hectic schedules.

Most of the young Muslims in this group expressed their lack of enthusiasm for attending the *madrasah* or the Islamic weekend school. They said they find it boring and that it was very difficult to get up earlier in the morning. Some of them expressed their concern due to their parents' enforcement of attendance at this particular space. One of the students put these points as follows:

> My parents force me to go to weekend school but I don't go any more …my mom taught how to read *Qur'ān*…I used to go to Islamic weekend school…I just cannot get up on every Sunday morning…probably yea I will attend the weekend school again…Yeah, I don't like…like it is all about religion you know, like it is boring, one boring subject. So like normal school you have different other subjects (Imani, Year 9)

Multiple factors inhibit some young Muslims in this group from attending the *madrasah*. One of the major issues is the fact that they have to get up early morning to attend the school since it starts around 10 am. The type of the lessons being taught, which are all about religious issues, is also a factor that discourages most of young Muslims from attending the space. Studies have shown that dealing with religious issues is not a concern of youngsters (Saktanber 2007). They pay more attention to the lessons that best suit their social lives, such as music or sport.

Attending the *madrasah* is also difficult for some other Muslims. Suci, for example, explained that it was difficult for her to get along well with her Muslim friends at this Islamic school:

> I met a lot of new friends, at the time to me it just like the school day so I didn't like it, it just like one free day in the week so I don't like the sense of it, but yea I like it because I met a lot of friends and stuff … think that a lot of the kids there went to Islamic schools and I went to a public one, so we kind of had, we were kind of different in interest and stuff, I don't

know why it just ended up that way. So it was harder for me to make friends in the Islamic school than it was for me in the public school (Suci, Year 10)

Suci provided some contradictory statements in this comment. On the one hand, she was happy attending the *madrasah* because of the possibility to make new friends. However, on the other, she found it hard to make friends with her fellow Muslim students in that particular learning space. This fact is interesting to note because Suci seems to have had interests that conflicted with those of with her fellow Muslim students who actually shared a common belief, and at the same time, she was able to engage well with her non-Muslim friends at school.

In addition, Hera who used to attend an Islamic private school stated that she did not need to attend the *madrasah*, since she had gained basic Islamic knowledge from the school she used to attend.

Hera states:

No, I went to [the name of the Islamic school], so I got all my religious education from there and then whatever else I left out I usually ask my friends at [the name of Islamic School] anyway, so it is alright (Hera, Year 12)

Unlike the other three young Muslims in the group, two of them enjoyed going to the *madrasah* for a number of reasons. They said:

It is a kind of both, sometimes my parents ask me to go and sometimes I can go, I can have fun and something, Friday, most of them are kids, but Sunday is fine. On Fridays there are rarely my age kids…in the Sunday school, learn like learning Qur'an and Iqro' and then the teachers give us the talk or something and discuss Islam and different topics (Billah, Year 11).

I go every other Sunday but sometimes, I go every Sunday…Ya, I kind of enjoy it (being at the mosque) … pretty much learning iqra' (Zaki, Year 11).

The expressions indicate that although some of the Muslim youths in this study claimed to attend the mosque, their presence at the mosque was not always the result of genuine interest. Their parents seemed to exercise their authority in asking them to attend this particular learning space. However, two of them realized that attending the *madrasah* would give them some benefits since they could learn various kinds of knowledge there.

This section identifies two major issues faced by young Muslims in this group. In regard to participation in the mosque, these young Muslims were discouraged by the language barriers, though they were invited by their parents to attend the mosque and listen to the sermons given there.

## *Being young Australian and Indonesian-Muslim*

Ways of being Muslim are multiple and shifting depending on the settings and situations where Muslims live (Duderija 2008; Hassan et al., 2008; Sadat 2008). The five young Muslims in this group, Billah, Zaki, Imani, Hera and Suci were aware of their sense of belonging to the Muslim *ummah*. All of them claimed to be Muslims and regarded it as their main identity marker. They saw themselves as Muslims at home, in the religious centre and they also carried their Muslim identity with them as they live in the broader Australian society. However, their Muslim identity was related only to their adherence to Islam. They do not link being Muslim so much with the obligation to strictly adhere to the 5 pillars and fulfil religious duties.

When they were at home and the Muslim community centre, they tended to engage in performing some of their religious rituals. However, they did not see it as their priority. They fulfilled the religious duties at home because of their parents' teaching about their roots and background. Therefore, they tended to behave in Islamic ways at home and in the mosque out of respect for their parents and elders. They respected their parents and attempted to comply with their regulations as expected in the Indonesian and Islamic values (Tuncer 2000), but at the same time, they engaged in popular youth cultural activities such as partying, socialising, sports activities, digital technologies, and other youth activities. They do not attend the *madrasah* and other kinds of religious learning circles frequently. Given the intersection of these many identity markers, they perceived themselves as moving among multiple identities. One of them asserted:

> I think I am Australian with Indonesian heritage, so I've always got an Indonesian culture in me and then; but I may be an Australian citizen and I might live a lot of my life in the Australian culture, but I've also got the Indonesian culture that I've always got with me as well... I don't really know because the Australian culture that I guess I have some part in and then I'm not really sure... (Suci, Year 10).

The parents of these five young Muslims told me that it sufficed for them to find that their children could understand the basic knowledge of

Islam and believe in Islam as their religion. They did not expect their children to follow all the Islamic rituals and regulations as they are Muslims living in a non-Muslim country, Australia. At home, young Muslims may take up the markers of 'good' Muslims such as fulfilling some of their religious duties and respecting their parents, while in the other settings they may take up some markers and leave the others. The series of interviews and personal narratives have shown that parents play a central role in shaping their children's ways of being Muslim.

## Summary

The five Indonesian-Muslim youth in this group suggest that being a Muslim is a matter of understanding the basic principles of Islam and believing in Islam as their religion, and one does not have to strictly adhere to Islamic rituals and regulations. They take on some of the markers of being a 'Muslim', some markers of being 'Australian' and some markers of being 'Indonesian'. They are balancing being Muslim, Australian and Indonesian. One of them stated:

> So like you'd have to fit some things so that they fit around being a Muslim, so there's no drinking, but you can still go to the footy and watch it and there's still things you can do. You can still if you want, you can go clubbing or whatever, but you've just got to know what you can't and can do (Suci, Year 10).

Even though the study reveals that young Muslims in this group prefer to see themselves as Australians, they believe that their Aussie-Aussie friends do not see them as Australian because of reasons they voice in the quotes. In their own words:

> Probably if people saw me they wouldn't think of me as an Australian, probably because I look different and I have different skin, and that's probably what they would base on (Suci, Year 10)

> I have like a mixture… I am Australian, I don't know…yeah [she thinks that she is an Australian]…because I have been mostly, nearly the entire of my whole life, so yeah, my whole life …Yeah I guess so [Australian – thinks that she is an Australian] (Imani, Year 9)

The comments indicate the reason they believed others do not see them as Australians is the fact that they are not white.

In the next chapter, I look at a group of six Indonesian Muslim youths' ways of being Muslim in Australia.

# CHAPTER FIVE

# HYPHENATED-IDENTITIES:
# INDONESIAN-MUSLIMS IN AUSTRALIA

## Introduction

This chapter reports how a group of six young Muslims constructed their ways of being Muslim within their family and Muslim community environment. This group of Muslim youth was negotiating a balance between being Muslim, Australian and Indonesian; they use hyphenated-identities when describing themselves. I also discuss the ways in which their family dynamics and their engagement with activities in the Indonesian Muslim community centre shaped their identity strategies. While there are some similarities in the identities of this group of six Indonesian-Muslim youth and those of the group of five Muslim youth discussed in the previous chapter, there are also major differences between these 2 groups of Muslim youth. The two groups were similar in their interactions within the broader Australian society and in their youth activities. However, there are differences in the ways in which they engaged with Muslim identity and religious understandings and practices.

## The Six Muslim Youth and Their Parents

In this section, I provide a brief discussion on the 6 young Muslims and their parents. I also discuss their schooling and social background. Their parents' professional background and their reasons for migration are briefly discussed.

The six Muslim youth in this group see themselves as Indonesian-Muslims who live in Australia. Unlike those in the previous group, almost all students in this group were born in Indonesia and moved to Australia as young children. Only one young Muslim in this group was born in Australia. While five were born to Indonesian Muslim parents, Yani was born to a mixed family background. His mother is an Indonesian, while the father is an Anglo-Australian who converted to Islam upon marrying his mother. There are two female Muslims in this group, Salma (Year 12) and Fatma (Year 11). The other four students in this group are Yani (Year 12), Hanafi (Year 11), Ikhwan (Year 11), and Hafnizar (Year 9).

The parents of the young Muslims in this group are professionals with a university degree or postgraduate qualifications, unlike the parents of the group of youth in my previous chapter who did not possess any university qualifications. Sandra and Ikhwan's parents obtained their doctorates from Australian universities, Fatma's mother also has a doctorate from an Australian university, while Hanafi and Hafnizar's mother is a Ph.D candidate, and Yani's father is an engineer. The Muslim parents of four young Muslims in this group migrated to Australia for their own postgraduate education initially. Salma and Ikhwan's parents first travelled to Australia to pursue their masters' and doctoral degrees, and later on decided to settle permanently in Australia for the future of their children's education. Hanafi and Hafnizar's mother also arrived in Australia for her masters' degree, while Fatma's father settled in Australia because of his job transfer. He was transferred by his employer in Indonesia to work in Australia for a number of years. While in Australia, her mother also pursued a doctoral degree. Yani's mother came to Australia through her marriage to an Australian citizen.

Initially, no parents in this group had planned to settle in Australia permanently except Yani's mother who had settled in Australia joining her husband. Most of them, in fact, planned to return home, to Indonesia, upon completing their studies and also upon completing their job contract, as in Fatma's case. However, these parents observed that over the period of their stay in Australia, their children seemed to enjoy studying in Australian schools. Their children soon adapted to the Australian life and spoke fluent English. One of the parents in this group asserted:

> My children grew up in Australia, while we pursue our doctorate degree, and they feel comfortable living in Australia and they do not want to return to Indonesia anymore (Deni, Salma and Ikhwan's father)

This quote suggests that most Muslim parents in this group decided to apply for permanent status in Australia for the sake of their children's education. They told me that the schooling environment in Australia is much better compared to schools in Indonesia. They also suggested that their children experienced culture shock upon returning back to live in Indonesia. Deni told me that upon his completion of his doctoral degree, he invited his family to settle down in Indonesia. However, his children faced difficulties adjusting to the school life in Indonesia. Because of this reason, they applied for permanent resident status in Australia.

In addition, apart from this reason, their decision to stay permanently in Australia was also due to the fact that there are many Muslim community centres in Australia. They told me that the availability of these various Muslim community centres provided them the religious and community support in educating their children to be Muslims. For example, all of the Indonesian-Muslim parents in this group told me that they see the Muslim community centres here in Australia as an oasis. This was one of the reasons behind their motivation to settle permanently in Australia.

The parents of these 6 Muslim youth placed much emphasis on religious education for their children. They valued the activities held in the Islamic community and saw these activities as valuable in developing their children's religious identity. Deni, Salma and Ikhwan's father for example said:

> I try to be active in the Indonesian Muslim community, especially those originated from West Sumatra. In fact, I am the founder of *minang saiyo* Muslim organization. We run weekly meetings, in which Muslim communities and their children get together. Initially, my children were not interested in coming but then they also have fun-(Deni, Salma and Ikhwan's father)

Taking part in activities in the Islamic environment was considered an important strategy to build their children's awareness about their Muslim identity. Given the importance of such community, Deni and other Muslim parents founded an ethnic based Islamic circle, known as *Minang Saiyo*. There are many small study groups in Melbourne belonging to Indonesian Muslims, one of which is *Minang Saiyo*, which focuses on religious teaching. These study groups are established based on certain ethnicities within Indonesia. The *Minang Saiyo*, for example, is a study group whose members are from West Sumatra. There are no differences in the ways the groups are run. Most of the groups focus on fortnightly sessions of religious teachings. Although some Muslim youth in this group were not always keen on attending the programs of the *Minang Saiyo* and other Islamic learning circles, these young Muslims at least gained some benefits from interactions with other Indonesian Muslim youth of a similar age.

Most Muslims parents in this group perceived Islamic communities as important cultural and educational sites where their own and their children's Muslimness and Indonesianness could be shaped and nurtured. Because such Islamic environments are not easily found in Australia, the parents took advantage of the existing Indonesian Muslims' religious centre through various means of participation. First, they took part in the Indonesian Muslim mosque. For example, Hazny, Eko and Deni were very active at attending religious programs in the Indonesian mosque. They also held a strategic position in the Indonesian Muslim community. Fatma's father was the mosque treasurer, while Hanafi and Hafnizar's father was the treasurer of the Indonesian Muslim Community of Victoria (IMCV). While most of the Muslim parents in this group were active in the mosque, Yani's parents did not make visit the Indonesian Muslim community centre frequently. However, they visited the mosque located adjacent to their home.

In the following section, I discuss the six participants' multiple ways of being Muslim in Australia.

## *Integrating ('the salad bowl') in the wider Australian Society*

I identified five young Muslims in the previous chapter who had something in common in their ways of being Muslim within multiple contexts. Some of their attributes and characteristics are found to be different from those examined in this chapter.

Like their fellow Muslims described in the previous chapter, the six youth described in this chapter took aspects of being Indonesian and Muslim as their main identity markers and also saw Australian aspects as a part of their identity. Their Australian part derived from their place of residence. They also saw Islam as important to them because they had been taught about Islam and to believe in it since childhood. Their commitment to fulfilling their religious duties is the representation of their perception of Islam as their religion. Most of them said:

Ya, … that's my religion, in which I grow up to, I got to believe it and I guess it is important … we were raised to study, live and believe in Islam, and we still do, and my mom tries to help us believe in religion (Fatma, Year 11)

Yeah, a little bit [the way he is brought up] … Since I was little I was brought up how to pray, to look after people and to treat them right and stuff and I have been used to it and now it is just what I do … Yeah like if I don't pray and if I miss the prayer, it's just like I have to double the prayer, the next prayer time to combine it and I also fast (Yani, Year 12)

Yes, it is important to me but I don't know, yes yes yes important … why … because I grow up believing in so yea … I am still going to Saturday school, so they teach me more in depth about the whole religion and stuff,

like what happen if you do something bad, is just doesn't keep you in line.
Like you try to be a good Muslim (Ikhwan, Year 11)

These young Muslims' narrations indicate the important roles of
parents in providing their children with Islamic knowledge. Their voices
provide insights that parents are encouraged to play their parenting role as
*murabbi, muaddib* and *muallim* from the early years of their children.
Educating children about Islam from an early age is important in providing
a basic understanding of Islam, which later on becomes the basis of their
Muslim identity formation.

In his study, Mondal (2008) reveals that education about Islam is
important as a way to infuse Islamic values in young Muslims. This is
because education enables someone to revive their Islamic awareness. By
so doing, Muslim children will recognize Islam and take it as their main
identity marker. Yani's expression 'since I was little I was brought up how
to pray', indicates that Islam has been ascribed to him by his parents since
childhood, and through such efforts, has Yani recognized Islam and is
aware that it is his religion. He was not only aware of his religious
affiliation but also took efforts to fulfil his religious duties. As explained
in Chapter Two, Islam requires Muslim parents to teach Islam to their
children since childhood.

Although the six young Muslims recognized Islam through their
heritage, they had also gained a good level of understanding about Islam.
In fact, for them, Islam had become their 'chosen identity' (Peek, 2005), in
which they intentionally chose Islam as their main identity markers and
they firmly believed in Islam (Peek, 2005). Hanafi and Salma, for
example, explained:

> Ya, I think religion is important ... Islam is important in my life, without
> Islam I think I will be lost, like when there is a free time I don't know what
> to do, if I am a Muslim, right, in the free time, I just could read Qur'an, I
> will do *tasbih* [a special kind of recitation to remember Allah, (sic)] or
> something like research the Islamic history, if I am not a Muslim I don't
> know what to do (Hanafi, Year 11)

> Yes, it is and I like to think that I am very religious person just because the
> way I was brought up and I go to Saturday school as well outside of
> normal school (Salma, Year 12)

These two comments represent their inner voices, by which they
identify themselves as Muslims because they feel so. Marranci (2008)
states that the 'feeling to be' is important in one's ways of being Muslim.
When Hanafi commented that 'without Islam, I think I will be lost', he

indicates that Islam has indeed been personalized in him, and then he actualizes it through practising instead of keeping it in his heart. The quote also indicates that Salma believed herself as a religious person. This feeling to be a religious person has shaped her Muslim identity as indicated by Marranci (2008) who utters that identity is a personal feeling to be something. In addition, Sandra's comment illustrates that the action of attending the *madrasah*/the Saturday school represents one's level of religiosity.

The six young Muslims in this group see themselves as 'practising Muslims' referring to Yasmeen (2008) or referring to Mondal's (2008) term, 'principled Muslims'. I identify them as practising – or principled – Muslims because they observe basic Islamic rituals such as the *salāt* and the *sawm* across the settings.

Although studies about Islam and Muslims reveal multiple ways of being Muslim (Bayat & Herrera 2010; Masquelier 2010; Mondal 2008), the essence of religiosity is in the commitment to fulfil religious duties (Hassan 2002, 2007, 2008; Hassan, et al. 2008). The six young Muslims in this group were found to be practising Muslims as seen through the eyes of these scholars. The six young Muslims in this group observed the five-times-daily *salāt* and also the *sawm* during the month of *Ramadhan*. In addition to their level of practising the *ibadāt*, they were knowledgeable of Islamic regulations, such as regarding some basic religious rituals. Their knowledge on Islam, which was obtained from their family and in the *madrasah* enabled them to understand some basic Islamic rules. For example, they understood how to make up their prayers when they missed them. They were aware that failure to fulfil their religious obligations is sinful, and thus felt sorry for their incapability to fulfil their religious ritual duties. This indicates that their belief in the importance of performing the *salāt* is a sign of religiosity. Some of them stated:

> I regretted it and like I think what I should do to make up and I just think back what have I done so I miss the prayer, I feel sorry (Ikhwan, Year 11)

> Very bad very bad I cannot not pray even if I was in the situation like once in the tram or something and it is nearly *magrib*, and there is no room, you know, to pray on the tram, I cannot not pray, I will never do it on purpose maybe when the time is so close, I thought it is still *ashar* but it already *magrib*, I feel so bad (Salma, Year 12)

Practising Muslims are conscious about their *ibadāt* (Hassan, 2007). They always make efforts to fulfil their religious duties. As practising Muslims, these six young Muslims fulfilled their religious duties.

Fulfilling religious rituals, such as the *salāt* is one of the most challenging rituals to perform in minority Muslim countries such as Australia. Unlike the *salāt*, the *sawm* can be performed much more easily and is less challenging. However, the majority of Muslim youth in this group claimed to pray across the settings: home, mosque and beyond the boundaries of these two spaces. Some of them asserted:

> No no difficulties praying at school, I just ask for a room, I just ask one of the teachers to open up one of the rooms, sometimes my friends join me...No, they don't, they watch, I mean some other people watch (Hafnizar, Year 9)

> Well I close the door so they cannot see, and if they see me praying, I will be totally ok, and I will explain the reason I am praying... I have to ask my coordinator whether I can stop studying and just pray. Most of the time he allows me because I only have 20 minutes of my lesson left, you know before lunch time and usually, he lets me go (Hanafi, Year 11)

> Yes, it is not actually a room, it's like another room but no one uses that a lot and you got the key from the office and then...because *dzuhur* time is at 12 o'clock now, so we do that during lunch time, we just get all the boys that want to pray, but some of them don't do it, so we just get the boy like go to the toilet, make *wudhu'* and pray (Ikhwan, Year 11)

These comments show their level of religious piety. They did not only pray while they were at home, but all of them except Fatma performed the *salāt* while they were in other contexts. For example, if they were at school Hafnizar and Hanafi who go to the same school, requested a space for them to pray at the school. Ikhwan also stated that he was able to fulfil his religious duties beyond his Muslim environment, such as at his school. In contrast, young Muslims in the previous group showed less enthusiasm to fulfil their religious duties.

Although two young Muslims in this group did not pray beyond their specific religious spaces, they managed to make up their prayers (for example between the *dzuhur* and the *ashar*)[1] when they arrived home. Fatma, for example, states:

> Not at school, I just don't feel comfortable praying at school ... because it's just weird with the non-Muslim friends, I pray and they wait and they're watching and it's really awkward ... I don't know, because I'm used

---

[1] Islam gives the flexibility to its adherents to join their *salat* such as *dhuhur* with *ashar* and *magrib* with *isha* when they find difficulties performing the *salat* on time

to it, because I don't pray at school, I just pray when I get home ... Not
really, because I know I'm going to pray at home (Fatma, Year 11)

Fatma felt awkward to pray in public spaces within the Australian
wider society. Her sense of being uncomfortable to perform prayers other
than within the limits of her private and family spaces prevented her from
praying elsewhere. Certainly, performing religious rituals in public is not
as common in Australia as it is in Indonesia.

Even though this discussion shows a different degree of performance
of religious duties among these six young Muslims from that of students in
the previous group, they seemed to share an understanding with their
fellow young Muslims in the previous group regarding the veil. They were
not comfortable with wearing the veil despite their belief that it is a
religious requirement.

Like other young Muslims in previous group, they regarded the veil as
a religious marker that differentiated them from their non-Muslim peers.
However, the two young female Muslims in this group were not very
consistent in their engagement with covering their heads, wearing the veil
on certain occasions but leaving it off on others. For example, they wore
the headscarf when attending the *madrasah* and the mosque but did not do
so when they were in different settings. In spite of being faithful to Islam,
they were not ready to wear the *jilbab* due to lack of confidence. For
instance, Salma noted that:

Just because I started school without it [the veil], if I start right away I am
ready with it. I am just not confident enough to start it now (Salma, Year
12)

It appears that Salma did not feel comfortable to wear the *jilbab*, since
it would make her look different in terms of physical appearance. This fact
also applied to Fatma. However, they regarded Muslim women who cover
their head in such a secular society as more confident and braver than they
were. Salma, for example, spoke to me further in regard to the veil:

When I do wear my veil, you feel a bit less comfortable in some areas of
Australia, just because all the things that have been happening in media
you feel a bit more like someone's looking at you (Salma, Year 12)

The negative discourses of the media coverage about Islam, especially
the controversial issue surrounding the veil, are seen as a driving force for
Sandra's reluctance to wear it. This also indicates that ways of being

Muslim are closely linked with social contexts as suggested in Chapter Two.

Muslim identity is multiple and fluid (Kabir 2010; Mishra & Shirazi 2010; Nielsen 2000; Werbner 2004). Take Salma as an example. She saw herself as a very religious person due to the fact that she prays five times, fasts in the month of *Ramadhan*, and goes to *madrasah*. This suggests that her ways of being Muslim were realized through practising the religious rituals. However, her Muslim identity was also multiple; she was a practising Muslim when it came to the observance of certain rituals. She stated:

> It is not like a set thing straight away, when I was young yes I said yes when I am going to university, now I gonna see how it looks and I am not gonna force, I mean probably going to Saturday school first, and then wear it and then no going back you know, I wanted to wear and I want to stay, I don't want to have doubt and take it off like my friends, I want to be confident and happy when I am wearing it not just because I want to please my principal or anything like my *madrasah* teacher (Salma, Year 12)

Salma indicated that wearing the veil was one of the biggest challenges in her ways of being Muslim, while she did not encounter as much challenge in performing the *ibadāt* such as the *salāt*.

Fatma also stated that wearing the *jilbab* is not a choice in the present times since she was worried that being in the veil would trigger different treatment from their colleagues and Australian society, but she felt that veiled Muslim girls must be braver than her in terms of wearing their Muslim identity.

> I don't know, I'm just not comfortable yet...yes, I think so [people will probably treat her differently]...yea I think so [those who wear the veil are braver than her] (Fatma, year 11)

Although she did not seem to consistently cover her head, she perceived it as an important marker for Muslim identity.

The other four Muslim schoolboys in this group were also in agreement with Fatma and Salma, stating that those who put on the veil must be braver and more confident than those who do not. They also claimed that it would be easy to judge someone a Muslim or not through the type of attire they wear. For this reason, they argued that the *jilbab* is a Muslim specific marker. Ikhwan for example said:

> Sometimes it is obvious that they are Muslims, then they are not wearing so you don't realize that they are Muslims; they look just Australian. If

they wear you can tell that they are Muslim then if they are not wearing it right ...Yea I do [appreciate] because they are very brave to wear it outside like everywhere because people mostly see them as Muslim so they know what to associate with....(Ikhwan, Year 11)

Ikhwan indicated that the veil differentiates Muslim from non-Muslim girls. Since wearing the *jilbab* in such a secular society is difficult, Ikhwan highly appreciated those who assert Muslim identity through wearing that specific religious marker.

As these six young Muslims believe that they could be both Australians and Muslims at the same time, they felt comfortable interacting with their classmates during the school hours and during their spare time as well. Watching movies and doing sport are some activities performed by these young Muslims together with their friends; Muslims and non-Muslims. Some students in this group, in fact, joined their school sport team such as the cricket and the soccer teams. Yani said:

Yeah, I do school sport and stuff, like cricket and stuff and then we have rock climbing and go camping and stuff ...No, I just hang out with friends, watch movies and play games and something (Yani, Year 12)

Other Muslim youths, Ikhwan and Hafnizar played soccer at school, while Sandra in addition to participating in sport, was very good at music. Hanafi and Fatma were not very concerned with sport. However, they engaged in other kinds of student organizations.

All young Muslims in this group believed that engaging in the global 'youth cultures' (Bayat & Herrera 2010) did not denigrate their sense of belonging to their Muslim identity. In fact, this kind of engagement enabled them to be part of the broader Australian society. My interaction with these six young Muslims brings to mind Ramadan's (2004) argument that Muslim minorities should be confident of being part of the broader society without the feeling of marginalization and hold firm to their Muslim identity at the same time. This phenomenon is also revealed in the work of Abid (2006), Lathion (2008), Mondal (2008), Raedt (2004) and Sirin and Fine (2008), which suggest that young Muslims in their studies engaged with other cultures of their host countries but still took on their Muslim identity.

My study also reveals that in their engagement in the host society, the six young Muslims in this group were aware of their religious duties and understood their religion's expectations. Ikhwan, for instance, told me that:

If I hang out with … if I make a plan to go out with my friends I usually do it after the actual prayer time, I pray at home and meet them, and then I only do in between, I don't hang out like the whole day or the whole night, if I do and I am at their house, I will ask them if I can pray … I hang out with Australians but keep religion for yourself, like they know you are the Muslim because you do the stuff and after that you just go to play with them (Ikhwan, Year 11)

The quote indicates that interacting with friends across religions will not put one's religious identity at risk. As explained by Ikhwan, he interacted with and has non-Muslims as his friends, yet is also a Muslim youth who follows some of the religious practices

Sandra and Fatma also visited their friends' houses and sometimes they also attended their friends' birthday parties. In fact, Fatma stated that sometimes her friends slept over at her house, and some other times, she went to her friends' houses. However, she made sure that she did not consume non *halal* food. She suggests that her friends are aware of the religious restrictions that Fatma has to fulfil. Likewise, Salma admitted that in Year 12, she had been to her friends' birthday parties and also school parties more often. She says:

Because I am in Year 12 I have got a lot of parties at the moment, like I got five parties last week, I go to the parties sometimes not everyone of course and I find that you are not pressured into anything, it is your own choices, they don't go out and say, here drinking-drinking like that. It is more like your own debate you had inside your own body, like thinking oh oh I want to try this, no one force me, they all know that I don't drink so they don't offer me, there maybe occasionally drunk person saying common let drink, you know you are a Muslim. I have a couple of friends who at their own choice don't drink, they just good people they don't want to drink and so here I am not pressure to anything (Salma, Year 12)

Salma suggested that her friends did not force her or did not even encourage her to do something conflicting with the Islamic regulations. Salma felt she did not encounter any kind of peer-pressure during her interactions. The study by Zine (2001), however, found that young Muslims in her study encountered a certain degree of peer pressures.

Although all of them tended to interact with a wide range of friends, two young Muslims, Haniafi and Hafnizar, did not enjoy as much freedom as some other friends in this group did. They were restricted by some rules of their parents. Hanafi and Hafnizar did not visit their friends' houses or attend school parties, and in fact they were not allowed to go out at night.

The study also suggests that the young Muslims in this group saw Australia as a democratic country, in which the rights of its citizens or permanent residents are respected. They also agreed that Australia had a clean environment and a good quality of education. However, they also realized that Australia was not their parents' home country, and thus they were mindful of taking extra cautions while living as Muslims in Australia.

## Being 'Religious' Young Muslims within Domestic Life

All Muslim parents in this group were concerned with the influences of certain types of cultural practices in mainstream Australian society on their children. They told me that the habit of consuming alcohol and sexual intimacy before marriage are some of the issues that may challenge their children's identity. In addition, they were aware that facilities that cater to Muslims' needs are not as easily found in Australia as in Indonesia. This lack of religious facilities that exert a positive influence on their children added to their concerns as they played their parenting roles in Australia.

Although Muslim parents in this group showed their deep concern about their children's Muslim identity, they shared a common perception with those in the previous group that coercion in raising their children should be discouraged. They told me that they avoided forcing their children to engage in certain religious activities. For example, in regard to their children's social lives, they seemed to be flexible. Although it is a fact that some parents restricted their children's activities beyond their home boundaries at night time, the majority of parents allowed their children to get out at night and participate in various activities.

In addition, they told me that they promote dialogue with their children. Some of them asserted that they regard their children as their friends with whom they could share jokes. In spite of such interactions, the parents noted that whenever their children showed disrespect toward them, they immediately reminded them about the Islamic values to which they should commit. Salma and Ikhwan's father, for example, noted:

> They sometimes act like Australians, if they have gone too far in their behaviour, I would tell them that we have our own values. I realized it was difficult to control them indeed, I just make a *do'a* [to Allah] (Deni, Salma and Ikhwan's father)

This narration suggests that Deni and some other parents tried to build good relationships with their children. However, if their children showed disrespectful attitudes Deni and other parents reminded them to behave well. In addition, they told me that one of their responsibilities as parents was to shape their children's attitudes, so that they know about being modest upon interacting with others.

In terms of the type of attire, some of the parents do not seem to set strict rules. These parents only emphasized modesty regarding the types of clothes to wear. This suggests that they did not set a strict rule regarding the types of clothes their children choose to wear as long as it showed modesty. However, regarding their attendance of *madrasah* and the performance of religious rituals, these Muslim parents seemed to be more serious. They consistently encouraged their children to attend the *madrasah* and other kinds of Islamic learning circles and asked them to fulfil their religious duties.

Fatma's parents, for instance, invited her to attend the Sunday morning learning circle. Although she was not very enthusiastic about attending the mosque for that purpose, her parents seemed to be consistent in their request. Hazny asserted:

> I used to attend the *pengajian* run on Friday nights, I also joined the one on Sunday morning, and then I preferred to come to the Sunday one. I also used to invite my children to come along with me but it was difficult to invite Fatma because she tends to compare [with other friends who did not come to the mosque]-(Hazny, Fatma'a mother)

Although parents seemed to be consistent in their request for their children's attendance to the religious space, the children did not always abide by their request. If they indeed attended the religious settings, some of them did not seem to enjoy being in that space (I will return to this issue later in the next section).

As these Muslim parents believed that effective education starts from home, they took various teaching roles at home. Some stated that accompanying children to learn about Islam or 'being there' to borrow Becher's (2008, p. 101) term, for their children was an effective way of teaching. Hazny, for example stated:

> I usually give a special care for Fatma. She is different from her sisters. She grows up here in Australia and lives in the Australian environment, in which she interacts with mostly non-Muslim friends. Sometimes, I read Islamic books for her because I believe that the attempt in shaping children's Muslim identity should start from home. I have to negotiate my ways of teaching her about Islam (Hazny, Fatma's mother)

As we see from the comments, the parents in this group realized that the discourse of 'being there' is important to shape Muslim identity of their children. Hazny believed that the home environment was the first educational site for every child, and thus she spent times reading Islamic books with her children.

Other parents act as a role model for their children, as Deni and Eko reveal:

> We have to be the role model for them. I invite them to pray in congregation, but I realize when they are grown up, it is difficult to ask them to pray together. However, we always remind them about the *salāt* and the *zakat*.... Unfortunately, I do not have sufficient Islamic knowledge, so I just teach them about wisdom (Deni, Salma and Ikhwan's father)

> Parents should be the role models for them. If we are going out, when it is the time for prayer, we immediately perform the *salāt*, and they join with us too. They have got used to doing the *salāt* in public (Eko, Hanafi and Hafnizar's father)

For these Muslim parents, one of the important parenting roles to exercise is modelling. They suggested that when asking their children to perform the *salāt*, they invite them to do it together in congregation. They showed that they also performed the Islamic rituals. This strategy allowed their children to imitate their practice. The strategy used by these Muslim parents is in line with Ekram and Beshir's (2009) suggestions. However, they are also aware that when their children grow up, they find it more challenging to invite them to pray in congregation. The parents told me that when their children reached the secondary level, they did not always follow the parents' requests. Their reasons varied. Some indicated that they were fully occupied with school work and thus did not have time to attend the mosque to listen to sermons about Islam.

During my interview with these six young Muslims, I uncovered their perceptions of their parents' ways of exercising their parenting role. Young Muslims in this group explained that their parents, especially their mothers, played a significant role in reminding them about Islam. They told me that their mothers were always 'getting into their ear'. The mother according to them always reminded them about the *salāt*, their ways of interaction with friends, and about their interactions and attitudes in public spaces. Fatma said:

> Ya I study sometimes, ya my mom teaches me Qur'an and makes me read Qur'an...Like we were raised to study, live and believe in Muslim, and we still do, and my mom tries to help us believe in religion (Fatma, Year 11)

In the following extract, Yani also stated that his mother was persistent in reminding him about many issues. He asserts:

> All the time, she always reminds me … No, I'm just used to it now. She just reminds me all the time. 'Do this, do that, don't do this, don't do that.' Every time I go to my friend's house 'Don't do anything bad' so yeah (Yani, Year 12)

These comments show the significant role of parents in the construction of their children's identity. The comment also suggests that parenting roles at the domestic level were taken mainly by mothers. This indicates that mothers played a more significant teaching role at home. In other studies, the mothers were found to be more active in persuading their children to follow the religion, especially in migrant communities (Becher 2008; Irfan 2008; Yasmeen 2002). However, there are also studies suggesting otherwise. Some Muslim parents are in fact worried about the safety of their children if they look too religious (see Bayoumi 2010; Mishra & Shirazi 2010). For example, some of them have discouraged their children from expressing their Muslim identity so openly that it might trigger prejudice and stereotypical attitudes to emerge.

As shown in the comments, the parents of these six Muslims in this group played significant roles in shaping their children's Muslim identity. However, parents' demands were not always followed with their children's total obedience. They argued that being a devoted Muslim does not necessarily mean that they should not enjoy life. As youngsters, they indeed required some freedom in their lives. Hafnizar and Hanafi, for example, complained about their parents' ways of imposing strict regulations on them.

> Oh, I just talk to them, and I am not allowed to go out much … I don't really mind with the regulation and the rule but I do like go out once and a while and stuff…I think so because I never thought of that …Yea I guess so but it is for our good yea … (we need to have) some freedom … yes like once a month (not every week) …Ya I did with my parents like last Thursday because I gonna watch with my friends but my parents didn't let me and then they say just watch with us the movie (Hafnizar, Year 9)

Hafnizar realized that parental restrictions were for his own good, and serve to protect his Muslim identity. Nevertheless, he could not resist expressing his expectation to have some fun and freedom with his schoolmates, as he argued that youngsters like him should be allowed to have some freedom, although not much. He added that the restriction not to go out at night, for example, could be seen as a form of denial of his freedom as a Muslim youth.

In addition, he was sometimes not interested in listening to his parents' teaching about Islam at home. He stated:

> They will give me like a long lecture about Muslims like being a good Muslim and being away from bad stuff like girls and all that you know … yeah (I get bored) they say a lot … no, I just listen … yea everything is alright, I don't mind with that but I don't really like it because we are not allowed to play on the computer, I am not allowed to watch TV much, I am not allowed to get out much…we got banned yesterday because we are playing too much…no I just read the book, ya but I want to play and watch tv and stuff…because it is holiday we should be allowed to play (Hafnizar, Year 9)

The inability to express their youthfulness by engaging in young people's lifestyles (e.g., playing games on the computer, watching TV, and going out at night) was seen as a challenge to being Muslim at home. The fact that Hafnizar complained, however, does not suggest that he was not happy with his parents. Actually, he understood such rules and regulations. However, as a young Muslim, he was not able to resist the sense of freedom enjoyed by his non-Muslim friends.

Besides the strict home regulations, parents' constant requests for praying were also felt as a burden by some Muslims such as Yani. He argued:

> Since I was little if I didn't pray she yelled at me, then I just get used to it, say like if I hang out with friends I know what time I have to go home and pray, and sometimes they know I am Muslim so I pray at their house, say like on Saturday, before cricket I go to my friends' houses and pray (Yani, Year 12)

The mother has given Yani strong roots for his Islamic identity; he just became used to praying and following the essentialized notion of being a 'good' Muslim. When he was asked if he found difficulties negotiating his Muslim identity during interaction with his friends, he answered:

> I don't really mind really because I still get to hang out with them, but sometimes it limits you to what you do and stuff and mom will be like 'Go home this time, you have prayer'. And you're like 'Yeah' and you know you have to cut maybe going to your friend's house short just to pray … It's probably mom really. I just keep learning because of mom because she keeps getting in my ear about it and stuff. So probably mum, yeah (Yani, Year 12)

The comment indicates that some of the parents in this group emphasized the need to perform the *salāt*. The persistent request to do the *ibadāt* had shaped and strengthened their level of religious piety. Because of this important role of the mother in the formation of one's Muslim identity, Islam provides a special position for mothers and requests Muslims to respect and take care of their mothers.

While Hanafi and Hafnizar showed their level of comfort in meeting their parents' requests to attend the *madrasah* and the *masjid*, four other young Muslims in this group showed more complex attitudes toward abiding by their parents' desire that they attend the *madrasah*. I return to the issue of weekend school in the following section. Salma and Ikhwan said:

> They take us every Saturday to *madrasah*, everything still dawn you know, sometimes me and Ikhwan no not really want to go but for them, you have to go, you have to go and that they always force us and yea they pay for our camp (Salma, Year 12)

> …This year and the year before we have been learning the same things or more mature stuff which is kind of boring I don't know why because it gets the common sense, not to do that, not to do this, that is alright but because our teacher just reads from a book (Ikhwan, Year 11)

Participating in the *madrasah* was highly encouraged at home as parents, especially the mothers, were considered to be determined in their request for them to attend this particular Islamic learning space. However, they started to be increasingly unwilling to attend. The reasons for their reluctance to attend the *madrasah* varied; one concerned the period of learning, which takes place early on the morning in the weekend. Yani also expressed similar concerns, he said:

> I don't learn much from Sunday school really, I don't know, it's just the same stuff every year, I tell mom that but she doesn't listen…Just they teach the same stuff every year every year, just like I have been in the top class like 3 or 4 years now, and it just the same stuff the same stuff, different teachers but the same stuff (Yani)

This comment indicates some complexities regarding some young Muslims' presence in the mosque. They stressed that they had been attending the school since childhood, and thus no new knowledge could be gained from that particular educational venue. However, Muslim parents in this group seemed to be strict in regard to their children attending the *madrasah* unlike the Muslim parents in the previous group. As the parents perceived that the Islamic environment, such as the *madrasah* and the *masjid,* are important venues in shaping one's Muslim identity, they were very serious in asking their children to participate because exposure to certain values will shape one's ways of being.

Although the section explains that to some extent, they were not happy with their parents' regulations, these young Muslims felt blessed being born into a Muslim family. Like other young Muslims in the previous group, their parents were their inspirations and sources of their Muslim identity. They were thankful of the parental supports gained. For example, their parents' persistence in sending them to the *madrasah* indicated their parents' level of seriousness about shaping their Muslim identity. One of them, Fatma, stated that she was glad of being born into her Muslim family because she was continuously introduced and reminded about Islam. However, what made her even happier was the fact that her parents are not very restrictive. She declared:

> Yeah, I feel blessed, because it's not strict at all, it's really laid back, but we're still strong as Muslims, but we're not strict like don't do this, don't do that...My mum always reminds me to *salāt* and she tells me to read the Koran and stuff like that. She helps me (Fatma, Year 11)

Fatma felt that the parents' relaxed regulations increased her comfort in being Muslim at home. Her parents did not set strict regulations toward her in terms of her social life, but they were serious in regard to the performance of the *ibadāt*. She adds:

> Yeah, we have an interesting family, there's always something going on and it's entertaining...Good, I don't know, it's good, they treat us the same now, because we're older, there's no real difference to how they treat with my other sisters. But bad, I'm the baby of the house and they always tease me (Fatma, year 11)

For many Muslims in this group, their family was the primary site that shaped their Muslim identity. Sandra, for example commented that she was in fact very glad at having been born into a Muslim family. Otherwise, it would have been difficult for her to get exposed to Islam. Through birth into a Muslim family, she recognized Islam and embraced it following her parents. She said:

> Well I am actually really glad because I know probably if I wasn't born into a Muslim family, it would be very hard to convert to Islam if I was not exposed to this faith and then I learnt in my Saturday school in *madrasah*, yea it is a blessing we have it easier because like we are told to believe and

yea when you are young you just take the religion of your parents, but now I am older I have chosen this and I know that it is right to me maybe when I was younger yea I get it from my parents, yea I am glad because I just have it easier if there in front of me already (Salma, year 12)

For Sandra and also other students in this group, their parents were a source of Muslim identity. Therefore, being part of the Muslim family is a blessing for them, since through this they have been able to recognize, believe and take Islam as their religion. In spite of taking Islam through heritage, upon learning more about the religion they became more comfortable with Islam.

As explained elsewhere, in terms of the type of clothes their children should wear, these Muslim parents were not very strict. They seemed to let their children to the choose types of clothes they intend to wear as long as it represents modesty. Salma stated:

My parents are not forceful at all in the headscarf thing, like I ask my parents there was a stage after a *madrasah* time, every day I found in the *madrasah* is always a religious thing and values and that very very religious like I do everything and then you know slowly fades away. Yea they are not forceful at all in that choice like they say you don't have to and I ask them what if I started wearing it and they said yeah it is your own choice, we will be happy and they not forceful (Salma, year 12)

Since the obligation of the *jilbab* is subject to multiple interpretations in the discourse of the religious texts, some parents were more relaxed in terms of asking their children to be committed to wearing it.

Like the parents in the previous group, Muslim parents in this group chose to send their children to public schools. Although the schools did not necessarily cater to religious needs, Muslim parents sent their children to public school for various reasons. Some believed that public schools would prepare their children to integrate with the broader Australian community. For example, Deni asserted:

I send my children to Australian public school to make them become the Australian plus ... my children should be involved in the Australian society and they should be able to connect themselves with the Australian society ... become political figures, decision-makers, but are still the strong Muslims, and one way to realize such expectations is through sending them to Australian public schools, in which they interact with students from multi religions and ethnicities, and in turn such interactions enable them to integrate with the wider mainstream culture (Deni, Salma and Ikhwan's father)

The other parents also pointed out that public school would enable their children to be well prepared in facing their life in Australia. For example, through enrolment in the public school, their children would understand cultural practices taking place in the Australian society. Eko, for example, elucidated:

> I have a little discussion with my wife, and then we decided to send them to public school and at the same time guard their Muslim identity. Lives in Australia are difficult, therefore, I trained my children to be confident in expressing their identity, and we also expect them to create their own praying spaces in their public school (Eko, Hanafi and Hafnizar's father)

The quote indicates that parents felt that interacting with people beyond their safe zone of the Muslim community would allow young Muslims to be confident and expressive regarding their identity. For instance, they were confident about performing their religious duties in public because they had got used to doing it beyond their own home boundaries.

The parents also saw public schools as important venues for preparing their children to gain university entrance. Therefore, they sent their children to public schools. Dodi, for example, said:

> We see that my children's public school was ranked high and we wished that he could also enrol in a good university, we also know that their schoolmates are good students (Deni, Salma and Ikhwan's father)

Although they sent their children to public schools, they saw the possibility to shape their children's Muslim identity in other venues. They stated that there are many Muslim communities and mosques in Australia. These religious spaces are important venues for Muslim parents to raise their children in accordance with Islamic principles. Fatma's mother for example, asserted:

> We live in an environment that is conducive to the protection of my children's Muslim identity. For that reason, I was not very worried about my children's identity, since in Australia we also find environment that supports [their Muslim identity)-(Hazny, Fatma's mother)

Salma and Ikhwan's father also stated that in Australia, some Muslims are in fact more religiously devoted than those in Indonesia. Therefore, he reiterated that his children would be exposed to a Muslim environment that enables them to protect their Muslim identity.

I am a bit worried of my children's religiosity. Nevertheless, after I do
informal survey, I found that here in Australia, there are more Muslims
who are more devoted that those in Indonesia (Deni, Salma and Ikhwan's
father)

However, the Muslim parents I interviewed told me that Australia is
not a Muslim country and facilities that cater Muslims' needs are rare. In
addition, ways of life in Australia are also different from those in
Indonesia. The wider communities do not have much knowledge about
Islam and Muslims. These conflicting realities experienced when living in
Australia required these Muslim parents in this study to take extra care
regarding their children's Muslim identity and their ways of being in
Australia.

In the following section, I examine their ways of being Muslim within
the religious spaces of the *ummah*.

### *Active involvement within Religious Spaces of the ummah: the Masjid and Madrasah*

Like the parents in the previous group, the parents in this group
believed that the *masjid* and the *madrasah* were important venues for
identity construction. However, the parents in this group took firmer action
in requesting their children to attend the weekend school. For example,
when their children showed some reluctance to attend the religious space,
they persuaded them to attend the weekend school and convinced them
that the religious space would benefit them. Hazny, for instance, stated:

It is not her first time attending the *madrasah*. Initially, I have to make so
much effort in inviting her to the weekend school, and she does not show
as much complaint in coming to the *madrasah*, but I still need to persuade
her to attend the religious space (Hazny, Fatma's mother)

Indeed, what distinguishes these parents from the group of Muslim
parents discussed earlier is their consistency and persistence in requesting
their children to attend the *madrasah*. Some of them asserted:

I sent my children to the *madrasah* since they were 10 and
12 years old. They have got used to their *madrasah* now
(Deni, Salma and Ikhwan's father)

I asked them to attend the Indonesian mosque since they were in Grade
one, but since there are no permanent *Qur'ānic* teachers in the Indonesian
mosque, I then send them to the *madrasah* in the other Islamic centre (Eko,
Hanafi and Hafnizar's father)

The comment shows that these parents had sent their children to the *Qur'ānic* School since they were in primary school. The parents seemed to have succeeded in keeping their children in the *madrasah* for a number of years. This indicates that the Muslim parents in this group had been more persistent in their attempts to take their children to religious spaces, in which they could learn Islam and also the *Qur'ān*.

In addition, almost every Sunday morning, Eko and Hazny come to the Indonesian mosque and listened to the Islamic teaching delivered there. They also invited their children to come along with them. As I observed in the mosque, Eko and Hazny sit with their children and ask them to stay focused on the program. These parents engaged with the discourse of 'being there' in nurturing their children's Muslim identity. As they invited their children to the mosque, sat with them and requested them to stay focussed on the programs at the mosque these parents showed their seriousness in shaping their children's Muslim identity.

As their parents required them to attend the religious spaces, all Muslim youth in this group attended the *madrasah*, which in turn accorded them a fair knowledge of Islam. They were knowledgeable in certain aspects of Islamic jurisprudence and also capable of reading the *Qur'ān* fluently; most of them, in fact, had memorized some short *surā*.

For Muslims living in Australia, the mosque and the *madrasah* are two invaluable entities within the heart of the Muslim community in the West (Johns & Saeed 2002), this need is not an exception for Muslim communities in other non-Muslim countries.

During my interaction with these six young Muslims in the interviews, I witnessed two forms of responses and attitudes in regard to the two Muslim spaces. All students in this group regarded the *madrasah* as the venue to gain Islamic knowledge. They realized that through attending the Islamic weekend school, they gained much knowledge about Islam. The *madrasah* at least enabled them to obtain basic knowledge about Islam if not all branches of Islamic knowledge. Fatma, for example, mentioned:

> I learn Al-Qur'an and the basic knowledge of Islam, you learn like students living in Australia and how they deal with the community and the stuff like that…Yeah, but I'm thinking of going to Indonesian mosque with my friend…Yeah, I learnt a lot yeah…Just thing I didn't know; they teach us about living in Australia, in this environment, being a Muslim in this environment and stuff like that and how to deal with things in the Muslim way and stuff like that (Fatma, Year 11)

Another young Muslim, Hafnizar, also expressed a similar opinion, saying that:

Yeah, I like Sunday school because they teach me more about the religion ...I learn to read Al-Qur'an really better now, fluently, not much mistake and faster, and also I learn a bit Arabic and I memorize the meaning of surah, and Islamic study like the history of Islam and stuff (Hafnizar, Year 9)

Some other students, such as Yani saw the space as helpful in giving him an understanding of ways of interacting with people. He says that he learnt "what you need to do and how you go about treating people, just fundamental stuff".

These comments indicate that the *madrasah* was believed to be a learning venue where participants could obtain various branches of Islamic knowledge. They learned about the *salāt*, the *sawm* and also learned some Islamic principles on their ways of interaction with other people living in Australia. Although some of them had lost interest in attending the weekend school, they did not ignore the fact that the *madrasah* helped them to be knowledgeable in Islam. Besides being seen as a learning space, the weekend school popularly known as the *madrasah* was perceived by these six young Muslims as their venue to connect with their Muslim fellows physically and emotionally.

Muslims in the West are struggling to gain a social space that enables them to interact with other Muslims, and the mosque is a central social, educational and religious space for these Muslim communities (return to Chapter Two for more details). As important venues in Islam, the mosque fulfils multiple functions, one of which is its use as the learning space (Johns & Saeed 2002). This learning space enables Muslim youth to interact with their Muslim counterparts.

Six Muslim youth in this group narrated during the fieldwork that being in the *madrasah* allowed them to find a space and to interact with their Muslim friends, who have many similarities. Some of them indicated that Muslim friends gave them a feeling of unity, solidarity, and peace. Therefore, their interaction with Muslim fellows is the source of peace for them. They express their feeling to each other since their fellow Muslims are better able to understand them than their non-Muslim schoolmates. Salma, for example, says:

I find ya [give positive impact] because I have been going to that school for a long time, since I was in grade 1, I found that when I don't go I start to doubt myself because I am in such in environment at school, I need some other environment where I could talk with people who are actually Muslims themselves and share the same belief as me and who are going to the same situation at school so I find that like a kind of a break from the other... Yeah I really-really enjoy actually my Muslim friends (Salma, Year 12)

The comment indicates that the *madrasah* has provided a major impact on Sandra's ways of being Muslim. The young Muslims in this group found the *madrasah* to be a space that gave them a different feeling, a feeling of peace, which is not necessarily gained in other wider spaces.

In addition to seeing the mosque and the *Qur'ānic* class as learning venues, spaces for interaction, and a peaceful environment, the participants felt secure and that their religious needs were accommodated. Hanafi, for instance, stated:

I feel different because in the Islamic school (Sunday school) nobody call me a terrorist, they always talk to me and because the teachers are a bit nice, we can talk freely and we can interact, in public school you know some people call me terrorist and in the classroom, the teacher is kind of strict, we cannot communicate, we cannot ask question and help each other out, whereas, in the Islamic school, you can do that, you can do both (Hanafi, Year 11

This indicates that the most important spaces for most Muslims, the *masjid* and the *madrasah* help Muslims to feel secure. He added:

On Sunday I don't go to Sunday school in the Indonesian mosque but I go to different mosque ... Yes I enjoy, I can interact and let see...if there is *ustad* from Indonesia visit the mosque I could just listen to them and see what they are talking about, and I could sometimes learn from them you know, learn Islamic values and I could speak Arabic, like you know ustad yahya he taught me how to say in Arabic (Hanafi, Year 11)

The possibility to interact with fellow Muslims and learn about Islam in the mosque and the *madrasah*, created a strong bond and attachment to these spaces. Although some of the youth developed a sense of discontent with attending the *madrasah,* they still believed that the two spaces are venues that can allow them to develop more peaceful feelings.

In the preceding discussion, I have explained that young Muslims regarded the *madrasah* and the *masjid* as places of knowledge production, a peaceful environment and the space for interaction among Muslims. However, to some extent, they encountered some complexities regarding their participation in the weekend school, though not necessarily in the mosque. Some of them, such as Yani, Salma and Ikhwan, criticized the instructional methods implemented in their *madrasah*. They argued that in spite of their regular presence at the schools, their interest in the school is reduced to a certain degree. Issues of ineffective instructional methods, long teaching hours, and the inappropriateness of the curriculum contents are three major reasons for their lack of interest in the weekend school. Ikhwan says:

> I don't like to go because lots of stuff he teaches is in the book, so he just like teaching us reading it to us so I see that I can read at home by myself and it is fine, but my mom wants me to go because my teachers and *ustad* know all the stuff that he is really good and stuff like that, she wants me to learn from him but to be honest, I could learn the stuff by myself at home 6 *shubuh* time until 1 o'clock by myself by reading the actual book by myself. I don't see any point for me to go but my mom wants me to go ... I am fine because friends are there, we just talk and stuff like that, but it just drag on a little bit, you know what I am saying (Ikhwan, Year 11)

Ikhwan's main concern with his *Qur`ānic* school were its 'ineffective' teaching approaches. Therefore, he did not see any point of attending the weekend school any longer. This claim was also confirmed by another two, Salma and Yani, who found that the *madrasah* did not implement innovative teaching methods and curriculum. Yani asserts:

> yea, yeah, maybe the teachers...I don't know maybe how they teach. They are not real teachers... they weren't really certified teachers. They were just like helping out and sometimes they don't know how to act around children so they'd be very harsh on some people (Yani, Year 12)

Salma voices a similar view, as she says:

> we don't really learn new *ayat* or surah we just listen to his lecture, we learnt a bit of *tajwid* but because me and Ikhwan have been going since we already know it all and he is like a mix class of people ranging from the uni students and stuff we don't know a lot of them know about all of this thing because they are not practicing Muslim before so even if they are older than us like already in the uni and in fact some of them do not know how to pray so that my teacher goes to like all basic and I guess I get just a little bit boring me and *Ikhwan* since we know it already just repeating again and again (Salma, Year 12).

The complexities of attending of the *madrasah* as described by Yani, Ikhwan and Salma who attended the centre regularly need further scrutiny. Their lack of enthusiasm toward attending the *madrasah* does not suggest that they lacked religious conviction. They were practicing Muslims and in fact saw Islam as their chosen 'identity'. However, the mismatch among the curriculum content, the teaching approaches, the learning period and their expectation as Muslim youth reduced their enthusiasm in their participation in these important religious spaces.

This section has revealed multiple perceptions about the *masjid* and the *madrasah*. The six young Muslims in the group realized the significance of attending these two religious spaces in the process of identity maintenance. They gained much knowledge about Islam in the two spaces, perceiving that the spaces allowed them to gain peaceful feelings and interactions with other fellow Muslims. However, some resistance regarding their participations in the mosque and the *madrasah* emerged. The section also reveals their ways of being Muslim while in the mosque and in the weekend school. They tended to engage with the essentialized notion of Muslim identity, in which they observed religious rituals and in fact, they wore modest clothes and also put on the veil.

In the following discussion, I examine their multiple shifting identities.

## *The hyphenated identity: Indonesian young Muslims in Australian*

The six young Indonesian Muslims in this group seemed to observe the rituals, such as the five-times-daily prayers across the settings. Most of them in the group prayed at home, within the religious spaces and beyond the two sites, while the group of young Muslims in the previous chapter did not perceive being Muslim merely through fulfilling religious duties.

In terms of their perceptions toward living as Muslims in Australia, they seemed to have a common understanding. These six Indonesian young Muslims told me that they held the firm belief that they could be both Muslims and Australians at the same time. This finding is in line with many other studies on Muslim identity (Basit 2009; Kabir 2010; Mondal 2008; Sirin & Fine 2008). Although they believed that they could be both Muslims and Australians, they asserted that they needed to negotiate certain values. For example, while they felt they were free to do what other 'white Australians' do, they had to be cautious in preventing themselves from being engaged with activities such as drinking alcohol, eating pork and many other religious related issues, which are in conflict with Islamic principles. Yani said:

Well, you can do what Australians do really, except drink and stuff. But yeah, you can still be a Muslim, you can still have fun and stuff, but you've just got to know your values about being a Muslim, so that's fine (Yani, Year 12)

For Yani, while participating in the mainstream society, Muslims are encouraged to hold firm to their religious values. However, they also need to negotiate certain issues. For example, they can have fun and engage in many social activities with their non-Muslim friends but they are not encouraged to engage in activities that are in conflict with Islamic teachings, such as drinking alcohol.

In a similar tone, Fatma explained that to be both Australians and Muslims, they are invited to balance their lives. For example, as Muslims, they are allowed to enjoy their lives while in Australia such as going camping or even attending their school parties, as long as they ensure that they do not commit any actions that may violate the rules of Islam. Fatma, for instance, stated that:

> You just have to, like I said before again, balance everything. As long as you don't do all the *haram* things, but still have fun without doing *haram* things. And yeah as long as you have fun and you enjoy life and do Muslim stuff too and being around Muslim people and Australian people. So you can have both. (Fatma, Year 11)

In this comment, Fatma asserted that taking Islam as her identity marker did not necessarily force her to leave her life and participation in Australian society. She continued to interact well with her non-Muslim friends and lived surrounded by people from mainstream Australia.

When I asked what made them believe that they would be able to live as Muslims in Australia, All Muslim youth in this group argued that if their parents were able to live in Australia peacefully, they could too. Ikhwan, for example, explained:

> I see my parents did and I am pretty sure that I can too because they are Muslims too, they did actually get PR here, they studied here, so that means I can live here without being discriminating as much … and there are other multicultural people that can live here probably like one biggest community that they can live here like well off if they can do, I can do too, why not us (Ikhwan, Year 11)

This comment shows that the diverse cultural Australian society has enabled many minorities to consider Australia as their home. He noticed that people of various religious and cultural backgrounds had settled in Australia well, and this fact made him believe that he could live in Australia peacefully practising his religion.

This positive impression about Australian society derived from these young Muslims' experiences living in Australia. They suggested that they did not encounter any major discriminatory attitudes from students of mainstream culture. However, they also understood that Australia is not their forefathers' country. Therefore, they perceived that mainstream Australians also hold different religious values. As a result, they tend to be cautious in conducting their lives in Australia. Salma, for example, stated that her parents sometimes choose not allow her to go out at night, since they do not totally trust the safety of the Australian society. On this point Fatma stated:

> Because if you live in a Muslim environment, like home you feel more comfortable and sometimes you have to choose the right people, choose the right friends and probably, I don't know … Yeah if you live with a bunch of family and friends who are Muslims and I think I can get through living here if you choose the right friends. As long as you don't let anyone in the way to push you around, you have to stand up … Bad, represent us as terrorists (Fatma, Year 11)

Because of not living in their parents' country of origin Fatma argued that bad things may emerge that could perhaps harm them. Therefore, they suggested that choosing the right friends, living within the Muslim community, and standing up to maintain their values are important strategies to live as Muslims in Australia.

However, some other participants proffered views on more personal issues regarding living as Muslims in Australia. Yani and Hafnizar discussed how Australia is a free country, in which relationships with the opposite sex are very much welcomed. However, Islamic principles do not allow them to enjoy such free activities. In the following comment, Yani and Hafnizar stated that:

> I have a few friends who like to go to party and dance but as a Muslim, I am not allowed to go and have fun like them, which sucks but I understand why (narrative)-(Yani, Year 11)

> The thing though that impacts me most of being a Muslim youth in Australia is that there is a limit in a relationship one can make with a girl. These days, people are used to seeing lots of girls and we have multi-sex classes, we often interact with them. Often once one knows another well, they become good friends. Islam teaches us that it is the limit and we are restricted to only having girls as friends. Boys these days hang around with them and some may have girlfriends. This impacts me most because my peers have girl-friends. I do have friends who are girls which are close to me and yes, I go out with them and other people as friends but I do not have a girlfriend. I am happy to keep it like this as Islam teaches us that *satan* can play with our minds while we are interacting with girls (narrative)-(Hafnizar, Year 9)

While Yani and Hafnizar were quite aware of their religious values, as youngsters, they could not resist the temptation to enjoy their lives as young people. Yani stated that while his friends go to parties and dances, he cannot do so because of the religious restriction, which he dislikes but understands. Likewise, Hafnizar elaborated that in his school, his friends interact with students from the opposite sex and they also have girl and boyfriends. Because of his commitment to observing the Islamic principles, he did not engage in a special relationship with any girls. The fact that they have to comply with religious principles, meant that they had to negotiate their ways of being Muslim in Australia, which they sometimes found it to be difficult.

The information in this sub-section reflects the intersection between ways of being Muslim, being young and being Australian. The Muslim youth in the group were certainly taking Islam as their main marker of identity, which they reflect through fulfilling religious duties. At the same time, they expected to be able to take up the marker of youthfulness and Australian identity, yet remain Muslims. For example, Hafnizar argued that he wanted to remain Muslim but at the same time wished to express his youthfulness and enjoy the freedom enjoyed by his 'Australian' friends.

The chapter has introduced the second group of Muslim youth, which consists of six practising young Muslims. Unlike those in the previous chapter, they claimed they had acquired basic Islamic knowledge. Their parents were educated. Some of them held a doctorate degree from Australian universities, while some other parents were highly professional in their jobs.

Like their fellow Muslims in the previous group, they saw their family as an important site in which their Muslim identity is shaped. They realized that their parents had exercised their teaching and parenting roles at home, and that this had enabled them to acquire Islamic knowledge and be practising Muslims. The parents in this group were not only concerned with their children's *Muslimness* but they also took immediate and firm action in shaping their identity. For example, they strongly encouraged their children to abide by their regulations, especially in regard to attending the *madrasah* and performing the *ibadāt*. The family 'sacred time' and parents 'being there' were also significant in strengthening their levels of religious conviction.

For Muslims in this group, Muslim identity is their main identification marker and Indonesian comes second with Australian in the third place. As we can see in this chapter, Islam is taken across the settings. They are Muslims and Indonesians at home, within which, they are observant

Muslims. They perform the *salāt*, some of them, in fact, perform them in a congregation; some of them also recite the *Qur'ān*. They are also revealed to be obedient children; they respect their elders, conforming to their regulations, and they also help their parents. Upon entering their home, they take off their shoes, and they eat Indonesian food following the rules for ensuring it is *halal*. They also attend the *madrasah*, from where they gain a higher degree of Islamic knowledge. Although they do not visit the Indonesian mosque frequently, they make their way to the mosque when they have time and when Islamic sermons are taking place.

However, in their interaction with parents, they also take the marker of being youth. Some of them wish to have some more freedom and engage in youthful lifestyles such as using global technologies (Bayat & Herrera, 2010), playing games on the computer, getting around with Facebook and other new networking sites. In some instances, they also feel unhappy with their parents' strict regulations. Some do not enjoy the fact that they have to keep attending the *madrasah*. However, in the end, they remain Muslim as they negotiate their expectations and their parents' strict regulations, since they understand that respecting parents is a religious obligation, and thus they try to understand their parents' requests and regulations. The information suggests that at home and in religious spaces they take the markers of Muslim identity and Indonesian identity.

Beyond their two comfort zones, however, the six young Muslims are keen to take their Australian identity as their main identity marker but still keep the other two, the Indonesian and the Muslim. They are very involved with school activities; some of them do sport, and one of them plays music. Since they also take Muslim identity with them while in the broader Australian context, they tend to remind themselves about their religious duties: performing the *salāt*; consuming *halal* food; restraining themselves from engaging in relationships with the opposite sex.

Although they engage in activities commonly taking place in the mainstream culture, when they were asked whether they are perceived as Australians, all of them say that they neither see themselves as Australian nor are perceived by others as such. In their own words:

> when someone asks me where are you from I say Indonesia because I am an Indonesian, I don't see myself as an Australian because I mean I live in Australia but I don't have an Australian passport, I may have an Australian accent or something but I may not be an Australian. Australian is like a weird word I mean. Is the aborigine or the white people Australian? (Salma, Year 12)

Define myself? I don't know I don't usually define. I was born in Australia, but I would rather define myself as an Indonesian but I get an Australian passport, it will be easy to travel around with Australian passport, but I still categorize myself as an Indonesian, I am proud of where I am from but I will be an Australian citizen ... I prefer to be Indonesian I guess ... I just don't want to be like one of another people, like another Australian, I just want people to think that I am Indonesian not Australian, just like that (Ikhwan, Year 11)

If they see me based on look, they just see me as a foreign person...because of my look they obviously know that I am not [Australian] (Salma, Year 12)

As can be seen, on the one hand, young Muslims in this group do not define themselves as Australians. They prefer to be Indonesians but they choose to live in Australia. On the other, they believe that people do not see them Australians because of their differences in skin colour.

This section has described Muslim youth's ways of being Muslim at home and their interaction with their parents there. The section provides insights about the multiple feelings of these Muslim youth regarding their parents' home regulations. On the one hand, they feel comfortable and grateful being born into Muslim families, in which they recognize Islam. On the other hand, some of them feel disappointed with their parents' multiple requirements in terms of religious issues, restrictions at home and their requests to attend the *madrasah*.

## Summary

This section describes the six students in this group as practising Muslims. Their being Muslim has occurred through the efforts of their Muslim parents. However, they pointedly identify themselves as practising Muslims and take Islam as their main marker and their 'chosen' identity. Their ways of practising Islam do not reflect preference toward a certain group of Muslims as suggested by Yasmeen (2005a, 2008) – the orthodox and the moderate. They instead adopt the orthodox and the moderate at the same time; they see that the core component of being Muslim is in religious commitment. They believe that taking an essentialized notion of Muslim identity is the only fixed way of being Muslim. They show their consistency in fulfilling religious duties such as the *salāt* and the *sawm*. However, at the same time, they do not ignore the fact that they can engage in the global youth cultures such as participating in sport, listening to music, playing computer games, and attending birthday parties. They perceive that involvement in those activities is not contradictory to Islamic teaching. The section shows their positive perceptions about the *jilbāb,* although they have yet to be confident in taking it on. However, they firmly believe that they are still 'good' Muslims.

In the next section, I look at a one young Muslim whom I see as being a strong Muslim but also hold to Australian and Indonesian identities.

# CHAPTER SIX

# BEING A STRONG INDONESIAN-AUSTRALIAN MUSLIM

## Introduction

In the previous two chapters, I discussed two groups of young Muslims, who showed some similarities and differences in their ways of being Muslims at home and in the religious spaces. While they took Islam as their identity marker, not all of them expressed their ways of being Muslim through observing religious rituals.

In this chapter, I discuss the identity practices of Darni, a young Muslim girl who showed rather different ways of being Muslim especially in regard to her dress code, even though there were also many similarities with the other young Muslims in the group.

This chapter begins with the introduction of Darni and her parents. As in the previous chapter, in introducing this particular Muslim girl, I also include information on her educational background and on her engagement with various social activities. This kind of information is important to allow readers to understand her much better. In discussing her parents, I also provide information on their social background and their reasons for sending her to the Australian public school.

### *A Muslim Youth and Her Parents*

In this section, a brief discussion on a young Muslim girl and her parents is provided. I also discuss her social activities and her parents' professional background.

Darni was born in 1992 to Muslim parents in Indonesia and moved to Sydney, Australia when she was 3 ½ years old. She started her school years in an Australian private girls' school in Sydney and had many Muslim friends. In May 2005, Darni and her parents moved to Melbourne and enrolled in an Australian public school. She found that the students in her school are originated from different backgrounds such as Greek and Asian.

Darni was 17 at the time of the interview, and she was in Year 12 of a public school. She wears the veil consistently in multiple sites. After getting her VCE, Darni planned to go to a public university in Melbourne, where she will focus on studying Primary Teaching or Nursing. She is the first child in the family, and she has three siblings. She lives with her parents along with her siblings. She comes from a middle-class family; her father works in a Bakery factory, while her mother is a housewife.

Her parents are both from West Sumatra, one of the most populous Muslim provinces in Indonesia. They came to Australia in 1996. Although her parents have been living in Australia since then, they did not obtain permanent status until 2008. Compared to the other families participating in this study, Darni's parents had not yet fully settled down in Australia. They lived in rented accommodation. The father worked in a low paid job factory and the mother was occupied as a housewife and only occasionally took on casual employment. In spite of this condition, they spent time with their children nurturing and shaping their Muslim identity. The parents 'being there' and the 'sacred time' took place within their home environment. This suggests that their hectic working loads did not inhibit them from paying full attention to their children's well-being.

The parents are practising Muslims. They frequently attend the Indonesian Muslim centre and also other mosques in Victoria. Eri, Darni's father, is a regular participant in Sunday Morning Islamic teaching. He took advantage of various Islamic and cultural programs run in the mosque. His regular attendance to the mosque, especially that taking place on Sunday mornings represents his thirst for Islamic knowledge. In 2009, Darni's parents have made a spiritual journey, which is the pilgrimage to Mecca.

Her father told me when I interviewed him that he had not acquired in-depth knowledge on Islam. However, the parents were very concerned with their children's identity and their ways of being Muslim. Eri, for example noted:

> I am indeed worried about my children's Muslim identity. I have seen in Sydney many Indonesian Muslim parents fail to show Islam to their children. In fact, there are many young Muslims of Indonesian background leave home because of their resistance to the Islamic rules (Eri, Darni's father)

As the quote suggests, Eri observes many cases of Indonesian Muslim parents who fail to teach their children about Islam. Upon observing such failure, he told me that he made a commitment to work to the best of his ability to take extra efforts to nurture and guide his children to hold firm to Muslim identity. For that reason, he consistently played his parenting role, such as 'being there' for his children and provided a 'sacred time'.

In the following discussion, I examined Darni's ways of being Muslim in Australia.

## *Being persistent in religious markers*

Although Darni told me that she received Islam through the teaching of her family, she had gained a strong root in Islam. She was not only a religious young Muslim but also a 'good' daughter at home. Her religious piety was multidimensional: "at the behavioural, ethical and cognitive level" (Hassan 2007, p. 437). This suggests that religious piety is not only shown through religious worship but covers all spheres of life including the commitment to ethics and conduct in addition to worship. For example, she did not show any kind of disagreement with her parents' ways of teaching her Islam. Her religiosity covered all these spheres, which made her different from the other Muslim youth in the study.

> She claimed she was a strong Muslim. She said: I think my Islam is pretty strong more than other people because my parents always encourage me to go to Sunday school, read *Qur'ān*, pray

This comment is in line with her ways of being Muslim. She showed her religious conviction in all spheres of life as suggested by Hassan (2007). First, she had gained a strong faith in Islam. In the series of interviews and through reading her personal written narrative, I discerned that Islam was very important for her. She stated that:

> Islam is important to me, it's a part of my individuality, a part of my life and ya…Yes I do [pray], and also in the Indonesian mosque

This narration suggests that Islam had been personalized for her, and it had become a part of her main identity. She also suggested that Islam was not only an important part in her life but was also proud of being a Muslim in Australia. She said that 'I feel proud and I feel confident and do not really care what people think'. This expression indicates that she was very certain about her belief in Islam. The belief in Islam and in the oneness of *Allāh* is a core prerequisite of being Muslim as discussed in Chapter Two.

The second characteristic that counts her as a strong Muslim is in her fulfilment of the religious duties, such as performing the *salāt*, the *sawm*.

For example, at home, she prayed five times daily just like other students discussed in Chapter Five. However, she did not only perform the prayers but also engaged in other kinds of good deeds ordained by Islam, such as recitation of the *Qur'ān* and the seeking of Islamic knowledge. She said:

> At home I practice my religion, I pray five daily prayers; I read the holy book *Al- Qur'ān* and ask for Allah's forgiveness [*istighfar*]. Even eating together with my family is good (narrative)...Sometimes we pray together after the prayer my dad give a small lecture after what he learns at the *masjid*, also he tells us as well to read Qur'an, have Islamic books as well

This quote shows her commitment to several kinds of rituals at home. Praying at home with family was a common activity for her. Her perseverance in reciting the *Qur'ān* at home makes her different from other Muslim youth in the study. It appears from the above extract that Darni engaged in an activity highly recommended by Islam, which is the habit of asking *Allāh*'s forgiveness, known as *istiqhfār* in the Islamic literature.

Like the other students discussed earlier, she was also very committed to fasting in the month of *Ramadhan*. In fact, she spent her nights in that particular month with many voluntary rituals (*ibadāt An-Nawāfil*), such as the special form of night prayer during the month of *Ramadhan* (*salāt taraweh*). During that particular occasion, I frequently saw her attending the Indonesian mosque and praying in congregation, and she also listened to the Islamic sermon given afterward. She told me that the *sawm* for her had been a common type of *ibadāt* since her young age. However, she stated that sometimes during the school day, she feels fatigue and the food just looks so good. She says that:

> Maybe when I am a little tired, hungry maybe it is a bit intimidating but most of the time it is fine. I just have to control myself. It is hard people eating but I feel relief that I can eat at the end of the day...I like fasting, fasting is good but just some days the food look really good, yea you just have to control yourself

Although performing the fasting is not as challenging a religious practice as praying, it becomes complex and more challenging during the academic year. The fasting reduced Darni's concentration on her lessons and her distraction was exacerbated by her friends' eating around her.

Despite her commitment to observing religious duties, she did not ignore the fact that she lives in Australia where she interacts with people from different religions and ethnicities. This awareness required her to negotiate her ways of being Muslim to fit in the broader society. Therefore, she balanced her life between the requirement to fulfil the religious obligations and the necessity to reach out beyond her comfort zone of her family and religious spaces. Darni told me that during her interaction with the wider community, she neither isolates herself nor is being alienated by her friends.

The third important characteristic of her ways of being Muslim lies in her dress code. Although all Muslims in this study, male and female, perceived the veil as a specific marker of being Muslim, and some, in fact, see it as the religious requirement, Darni is the only Muslim schoolgirl in this study who had taken on the veil. She wore the veil across the settings: home, Muslim communities, and the broader society. She is the only young Muslim in this study who wore the *jilbab* persistently, and it had become her daily attire. This contrasted with the other four young female Muslims, who wore it occasionally upon attending the *masjid* or their *madrasah*. She stated that it was an important religious marker for her. This assertion derived from her belief that this specific attire is a religious requirement. She wrote in her personal narrative that:

> Wearing the *hijab* is the first major step I took in being closer to God. I have been wearing the *hijab* since I was in year 7. At first wearing the *hijab* was difficult. It was hot to wear in summer and annoying to put on whenever I went out. I didn't like it. But as time went on and my Islamic knowledge increased I thanked my parents and Allah for seeing how good it is to wear the *hijab*. I actually prefer wearing the *hijab* out now. Instead of styling my hair, I can style my *hijab*. But I know now that not wearing the *hijab* makes me very uncomfortable (narrative)

Believing that donning the headscarf would please *Allāh* led her to be persistent in this religious act. Studies have also uncovered that it is seen as the symbol of religious piety or a sign of a 'good' Muslim (Ali 2005; Cole & Ahmadi 2003; Mishra & Shirazi 2010; Read & Bartkowski 2000; Zine 2006). Likewise, she argued that through donning it, she had made an attempt to be closer to *Allāh*. Her narration also suggests that this particular form of attire is not a difficult religious requirement to perform as long as one has got used to it. She commented on the motivating factor to wear this religious attire persistently:

> Maybe my parents started to ask me to wear it when I was young, I am used to it, I got another level of courage as being a Muslim. When I initially wear it I felt uncomfortable … [now] I feel like ordinary people.

This comment indicates a significant role of parents in the formation of their children's Muslim identity. She told me that her parents were persistent in asking her to wear the Muslim 'specific clothes' since childhood. This encouragement was an important factor that enabled her to be assertive in her Muslim identity through this particular form of attire. Her father also told me during the interview that one of his responsibilities was to invite his children to cover their head from early on in their children's life. Therefore, he suggested that Darni should be committed to wear the religious attire prior to her entrance to a secondary school.[1]

In addition, Darni believed that those who are unveiled perhaps do not practise Islam as strongly as other people who do wear it. In her opinion, Muslims are required to show a good example to the Australian community through wearing Muslim-specific clothes, since it enables them to stand up for their identity. She says:

> They say that it is a girl's choice to wear headscarf or not but I think they do look pretty without headscarf but it is so much better if they did wear a headscarf and acted more Muslim, acted more to the rule of Islam ... They (non-veiled) probably don't practice Islam as religiously hard as some others do and that is a kind of bad example especially in Australia. People think oh you are a Muslim, you have to wear the headscarf, you just attract people here in Australia practising Islam.

These statements 'if they did wear headscarf and acted more Muslim ... they (non-veiled Muslims) probably do not practise Islam...' explains that Darni regard donning the *jilbab* as a strong religious requirement, since for her, those who do not cover their heads are not acting Islamic and do not practise Islam perfectly. This narration also suggests that Muslims do not shy away from judging the religiosity of their fellow Muslims (Hassan 2007).

Like other young Muslims in this study, she saw the veil as a special marker for Muslims. This means that, for her, whether someone is a Muslim can be judged through looking at her headscarf. She indicated that she feels a strong bond with those who wear this specific religious dress. In addition to considering it as the religious marker, she believed that it is

---

[1] I interviewed Darni's father in April and he gave me ideas on his hard work to invite Darni and her other siblings to wear the jilbab. In spite of multiple understandings of the jilbab, Darni's father, Mr. Eri regards the jilbab as a religious requirement. His ways of educating Darni and other children reminds me of the guidelines given by Ekram and Beshir (2009).

a religious requirement and therefore, she attempted to act upon it and wear it to show her obedience toward the teaching of Islam.

The other most important characteristic in her ways of being Muslim is concerned with her perception of her home environment. Like the other young Muslims in the two previous chapters, she enjoyed being Muslim at home. She also asserted that her parents had played a significant role in shaping her Muslim identity. They were consistent in asking her to do worship at home and to pay attention to her conduct. She remarked:

> I think it all of them [shape my religious identity] but my parents insist me to pray all the time and read Al-*Qur'ān* and also my West Sumatran background [has shaped my identity] ... My parents both of them from West Sumatra, they got married and have me. They both very religious in how I see them, they always tell us, the kids, to pray to read *Qur'ān*, and just to remember God.

It appears from these quotes that her parents and her ethnic background were the major sources that shaped her ways of being Muslim. Her parents' persistence and perseverance in teaching her Islam encouraged her to be obedient to the religious teachings such as those requiring her to perform the *salāt* and read the *Qur'ān*. In addition, she assumed that her origin in West Sumatra, one of the most populous Muslim provinces in Indonesia, had influenced her ways of being Muslim.

In addition, she asserted that her parents' passion for encouraging her to visit the Indonesian mosque and other mosques regularly and also to attend the *madrasah* was an important factor shaping her Muslim identity – she became a devoted Muslim and was obedient to all her parents' requests. As a result, she did not feel any displeasure toward her parents' requests. She said:

> I am thankful being born and growing up in the Muslim family cause if I wasn't I would have a hard time finding the religion, which is true. Like I have a friend that reverted to Islam she found Islam when she was an exchange student in Indonesia and she is a Muslim now. Being a Muslim in a Muslim family is a really good, it is a blessing.

She was not only thankful to her parents but also abided by all her parents' regulations. This sub section indicates that parental supports received at home were of great benefit in strengthening her Islam. What made her different from other students in the study was her positive attitude toward her parents' regulation and toward attending the *madrasah*.

However, as described in the previous two chapters, some Muslims in the study were not happy with their parents' requests and their home regulations; in contrast, she did not suggest any discontent with her parents' ways of bringing her up. This section examines Darni's ways of being Muslim in Australia. Her commitment at observing religious rituals made her believe that she is a 'strong Muslim'. According to Darni, being committed to the rituals is one of the characteristics of a 'good' Muslim. In fact, she claimed that her Islam is stronger than that of anyone else. Her definitions of a 'good' Muslim were in line with essentialized understandings of 'good' Muslims as prescribed in the religious texts (see Chapter Two). Mondal (2008) argues that the exposure to Islamic ways of life since childhood is one of the motivating factors that produce a 'strong' Muslim. Darni's strong faith in Islam and her confidence in asserting her Muslim identity through the special type of Muslim scarf are seen as a marker of a strong Muslim. The section also describes Darni as a 'good' daughter. She followed all her parents' request. She did not show any resistance to the idea of attending the *masjid* and the *madrasah* regularly. She also saw herself as an obedient young Muslim due to the fact that she wears the *jilbab*.

Like other young Muslims in the study, Darni interacted with her non-Muslim friends within the Australian settings. Although she covered her hair, she did not see herself as different from her friends from school or those in wider societies. She participated in many activities with her friends. She also made friends with those from various ethnic or religious backgrounds:

> I have a group of friends; they are all from different nationalities. I only have one Aussie friend; they all like; India, Sri Lanka, South Africa as well and the Philippines.

Although her friends come from various backgrounds, she did not find any conflicts during her interactions. They understood each other and attempted to respect their friend's religious beliefs. She said that:

> In school hour, yea sometimes we just talk and sometimes play joke, on the weekend ya go to the movies or to the city just walking around and looking and going to interesting places ... I just interact with them in good manner, I talk to them, we all share group, I don't know pretty normal relationship like friends ... I think I have a fair understanding on the limit for interacting so I don't hug them like other people, I just talk to them like they good friends

This comment indicates that although she interacted with her friends, she was aware of how she should behave among her friends. In her opinion, interaction with all people is not prohibited as long as one knows the limitations as mandated by the religion. She suggested that she has never hugged her male schoolmates in spite of her close interaction with them.

In the next section, I discuss her ways of being Muslim within her family.

### *Being a devoted Young Muslim in the Family*

The previous section discusses Eri's aspirations for his children, especially for Darni. This section explores his parenting roles in greater depth. Although he claimed his lack of parenting and teaching theories, he had managed to shape his children's ways of being Muslim. Eri stated:

> I learn how other parents exercise their parenting roles. I found that most parents do not teach Islam to their children as early as possible and they tend to be forceful in their teaching ... I do not have a certain theory in educating my children, I only ask help from *Allah*, the second thing that I do is that I don't only ask them to practise the religion, we also practise our religion. I have never forced her to do things; I just encourage her to practise Islam. If she wanted to put on the *jilbab*, she should do it immediately by the time she enters a secondary school (Eri, Darni's father)

The quote suggests he had various ways of exercising his parenting roles at home. First, he asked *Allāh's* helps to give him the strength to teach his children about Islam. He said:

> I always pray to Allah to help me guide my children and turn them to be righteous Muslims. Since they were small we talk about sinful activities. We ask them to pray and we model it at home too. For Darni , she puts on veil. I really thank Allah for that. I have never forced her to wear the *jilbab*. I only encourage her to put on veil from early on before she enrols in high school (Eri, Darni's father)

The second theme to emerge from the comment is being the role model for his children. For example, Eri indicated that at home, his wife and he acted as the role model. He told me that as he practises religious rituals at home, he shows his children that fulfilling religious rituals is one of the significant components of being Muslim. Eri, for example reiterated that when he encouraged her to perform the *Salāt*, he himself and his wife exemplified this with their commitment to the *Salāt*; when he invited Darni to wear the veil, her mother showed that she also wears the veil.

Third, he is consistent and persistent about being there for his children. However, he did not force his children to abide by the religious principles.

He was very consistent at reminding his children about Islam and performing the *Salāt* at home. He insisted that guarding children's *ibadāt* is parents' obligation in Islam. He asserted:

> I perform the *salāt* in *Jamaah* [in congregation] but not always. Every morning I wake them up to do the Morning Prayer otherwise [I will be blamed]-(Eri, Darni's father)

The preceding comment shows Eri's efforts at instilling Islam in his children. He was active and proactive in reminding his children about the religious rituals. In fact, he was committed at waking his children up for the Morning Prayer. Besides encouraging his children to perform the religious rituals, he also sometimes gave a short speech about Islam after the sunset prayer. In addition, he was committed to allocating 'sacred time', when he requests his children to engage in the recitation of the *Qur'ān* nightly.

Eri admitted that he is very thankful because he was able to encourage her to wear the veil. He stated that *Allāh* helps him in his process of raising his children. He said that 'it is difficult to invite Muslim girls to wear the veil', and thus his ability to invite her to wear the veil was indeed bounty from *Allāh*.

In addition to constant reminders about Islam, inviting children to visit the Indonesian mosque and other mosques in Melbourne are other ways of teaching children about Islam. On many occasions, I found Darni visiting the mosque together with her parents and the two siblings. Eri believed that mosques allow his children to be aware of their religion. When he was absent attending the mosque, Eri encouraged Darni to come to the mosque by train. He asserted:

> She attends the mosque regularly. If I happened to work, my wife asks her to attend by train. We usually perform the *salāt* in congregation (Eri, Darni's father)

In addition, upon visiting Indonesia in 2008, he invited his children to visit mosques in Indonesia and also in Malaysia. He commented:

> I wish to send my children to Islamic boarding school in Indonesia when we visited Indonesia last year, I took them to mosques in Malaysia and in Indonesia to show them that Islam was big and glorious and to prevent them from thinking that Muslim community was as big as the Indonesian mosque in Indonesia.

Eri told me that he wanted to show his children that Islam is a great religion, and thus make them proud to be Muslims. In addition, while in Indonesia he invited Darni and her siblings to visit a funeral ceremony conducted in the Islamic way.

This section explains how Darni's father emphasized the Islamic way of life. He insisted that his children live in accordance with the Islamic law; they have to pray, read *Qur'ān* and also wear the veil. On the weekend, Darni was required to attend the Islamic weekend school on Sunday and also to attend the Friday's learning circle. In fact, her parents discouraged her from pursuing high social status by becoming a career woman. In spite of these so-called 'strict rules', Darni was happy being in her home; she did not show any complaint or discontent toward her father's ways of raising her within the home environment. She stated:

> I am thankful being born and grown up in the Muslim family cause if I wasn't I would have a hard time finding the religion, which is true. Like I have a friend that reverted to Islam she found Islam when she was an exchange student in Indonesia and she is a Muslim now. Being a Muslim in a Muslim family is a really good, it is a blessing

This preceding comment indicates that she did not feel any discomfort living within her home environment, which is unlike other students in this study. In fact, she was thankful to have received Islam from her parents rather than having to face a difficult time finding and understanding Islam.

As we have learnt earlier, Darni's father, Eri is a religious person who pays much attention to his children's environment. He suggested that an 'Islamic environment' could enable his children to be proud being Muslim. Therefore, he planned to send his children to Islamic boarding school in Indonesia and in Australia. Nevertheless, Darni goes to an Australian public school, which embraces a secular system of education, in which little provision on religion is given. Because of his concern with the religious school, it was interesting to investigate his rationale for sending Darni and her siblings to a public school. During the interview, I found that Eri had come to Australia more than a decade ago. However, he did not receive his permanent visa until 2008, allow him to make a life in Australia. His previous status had in a way restricted him from making choices in his children's schools. Eri explained:

> In the past, I did not have many choices regarding the school, since I did not have a permanent status yet. I just found out the opportunity where I could send my children to school, which did not ask for many admission requirements

The preceding comment illustrates Eri's complex situation. He was faced with a difficult choice regarding Darni's education.

This finding suggests that her father did not have any choice regarding her education. The public school was actually not his main choice; he in fact preferred to send Darni to an Islamic school. The fact that he had to send her to a public school forced him to compensate for the gap in her religious education through various sources. Therefore, as discussed earlier, finding an Islamic environment, which would allow her and his other children to be exposed to Islamic values was his priority. Eri then commented that the home environment and the mosque/the Islamic weekend schools were used as venues to shape and maintain his children's Muslim identity.

In addition, like the majority of Muslim parents in this study, Edi's aspirations for his children are founded on the development of his children's spirituality. For example, he argued that the ability of his children to not only understand about Islam but also observe its teaching was his biggest wish. He said:

> I just expect her to be righteous Muslim. I do not want her to be a career woman because being a career woman will [make her] unintentionally ignore the family's well-being

Eri's aspirations for Darni were very straightforward and simple. He suggested that she should be a righteous young Muslim girl. He did not agree with his child's decision to take a path leading to being a career woman, who spends the majority of her time outside of the house. He perceives that women who are very occupied with their jobs will not have time to spend with the family. Because of that belief, he hoped she would not grow up to be a career woman.

## *Seeing religious spaces as the comfort zone*

The previous two sections noted Eri's parenting styles and roles in introducing Islam to his children. Eri believed that exposures to religious spaces are an important means to introduce Islam to his children. His consistency in asking her to attend the *madrasah* has been successful. Darni for example was active in attending the religious space every Sunday in the Indonesian mosque. In that particular space, she learnt the *Qur`ān* and also other Islamic knowledge. In addition to attending this informal type of schooling, she attended the mosque regularly during some of the weekdays. She said that:

> Sunday for *madrasah*, Sunday school and I used to go on Friday night but
> not really nowadays because uhmm sometimes my dad works late and
> sometimes I have my Indonesian homework to do for Saturday class…Yes
> I do, I read Al-*Qurʾān* with ibu Disti

She indicated that spending some of her time on Sundays for her *madrasah* had become her routine. She seemed to enjoy being in this specific Islamic schooling, which is conducted in the Indonesian mosque. The following two sub-sections discuss Darni's feelings about being in the spaces on Sundays and how these contexts shaped her ways of being Muslim.

For Darni, the *masjid* and *madrasah* allowed her to socialize with other Indonesian Muslim youth. She said that:

> I am glad that I have an Indonesian centre to learn my Islamic values and
> to worship God. I am glad that I have friends that understand my values,
> religions and of course, I try to do the same too … It is great to have an
> Indonesian-Muslim community centre near where I live. I can socialize
> and share experiences with other Indonesian Muslim youth (Narrative)

The fact that these two Muslim spaces enabled her to gain much Islamic knowledge encouraged her to attend the spaces regularly. Her participation in these two religious sites also enabled her to gain access to other Indonesian young Muslims. In line with some students in the previous chapter, she said that she was more comfortable interacting with Indonesian Muslim students since they share many things in common. Her Muslim friends in this type of informal religious school were most likely to understand her better because they have many things in common. In addition, the close distance of Indonesian Islamic centre to her house was another important factor that increases her motivation to visit the centre. She stated:

> I got to meet a lot of Indonesian Muslims as well which I wouldn't have
> met if they are not at my school or anything, we can discuss Islamic stuff
> as well and everyone is pretty friendly, so ya

This comment indicates that the interplay between ethnic identity and Muslim identity is evident (Esposito, 2010). Although Islam is the main identity marker for Muslims, their ethnicities also bind Muslims together as I have described in Chapter Two. Darni and some other young Muslims in the study are more comfortable associating with fellow Indonesian Muslim friends than with those from different ethnicities.

In addition to being able to interact with other young Indonesian Muslims in the mosque and the *madrasah*, the two spaces gave her a much more peaceful feeling. The following comment suggests what she felt being in these two spaces:

> Ya of course (I got a different feeling), at the Indonesian mosque you feel more obedient to *Allāh*. To be honest it is a bit more close to *Allāh*, yeah just learning stuff that you wouldn't learn and have done in the mall, for example. The mall has too many distractions

It appears from her illustration that *madrasah* and the *masjid* have shaped her greater obedience to Islam. She also discussed how the two religious spaces enabled her to obtain a peaceful feeling. This kind of feeling is derived from the possibility that these spaces provide an environment and conditions, which allowed her to practice and exercise her religious beliefs without external intimidations. She stated:

> It is more peaceful at Sunday school and the mosque as well because at school people are not Muslim or Indonesian so they don't understand I guess. In the Indonesian mosque we can express our opinion on the Islamic stuff and we feel comfortable with each other and at Sunday school I am with the people my age, I can discuss stuff that is suitable for my age

Darni compared her life at public school and the *madrasah* and the mosque. In the former setting, she suggested that people perhaps did not understand her religious values, which then could lead to their misunderstanding about who she is, while in the latter two settings, young Indonesian Muslims acquired much better understandings about Islam and Muslims, which allowed her to share many ideas and opinions that they could not do otherwise.

In addition, she perceived her informal Islamic school environment and the mosque as the two most important sources of her Islamic knowledge. Her understanding about Islam had increased as a result of attending these two spaces, the *masjid* and the *madrasah*. Darni explained that while in the weekend school, she learnt many Islamic issues such as the relationships with the opposite sex. She asserted:

> (I do) a lot of things, probably the issue about boy and girl in Islam, the other week we are discussing it, my teacher got a reference from the *Qur'ān* saying about what should we do what should not to do about the relationship and ya I wouldn't have got that if I didn't go to *madrasah*

The comment tells us that she did not only learn how to recite the *Qur`ān* in the *madrasah* but learnt about approaches to social issues that were recommended by Islam. Through her attendance in the informal Islamic school, she transformed herself into a knowledgeable young Muslim, and the *madrasah* is where she obtained much of her Islamic knowledge.

> I think from Sunday school, pretty much where I got much knowledge from as long as my parents and family and Islamic behaviour, I just try to share what we learn at madrasah and try to explain to my non-Muslim friends, just help them to understand me better, my religion better.

Darni's narration explained that the weekend school was one of the venues that allowed her to grasp a greater understanding of Islam, and with such depth of understanding, she attempted to help her schoolmates know what Islam is and who Muslims are.

This section discusses how religious spaces have shaped Darni's ways of being Muslim. The environment and people surrounding her are seen to be factors that shaped her ways of being Muslim. She became more obedient: she prayed in congregation, behaved herself during interactions in the mosque, and also sought Islamic knowledge through the Islamic learning circles held in the mosque (see Becher, 2008).

## A strong young Indonesian Muslim in Australia

Darni shared many aspects of her interaction in the Australian society with many other young Muslims in the study. Even though she is a veiled young Muslim, it did not inhibit her from interacting with the wider community. She was active at her school and also in the broader Australian community. She told me that living in Australia is enjoyable for several reasons, one of which is for its clean environment. She also suggested that her heart has been attached to life in Australia. She has developed a strong attachment and a sense of belonging toward Australian through her life journey in Australia. Although she was born in Indonesia to Muslim parents, she saw that Australia has a part in her identity because she has been living in Australia for a long period of time. However, she still maintained her *Indonesiannes*, since she still engaged in Indonesian traditional dances, ate Indonesian food and had Indonesian ancestry. She said:

> Oh that is the hardest part [of interview question] my background is Indonesian but I grow up in Australia, can I say that I am Indonesian-

Australian…ya cause my parents are Indonesians I grow up here, grow up with the veil is here (Darni, Year 12)

The quote suggests that she has taken multiple identity markers. She saw herself as Indonesian-Muslim because of her birth into Muslim family. However, she believed herself to have an Australian part because of her life period in Australia.

However, Darni did not ignore the complexities and challenges of living Islam in Australia. One of the difficulties of living in Australia for a Muslim is to find a space to pray; she understood that Australia is not a country where the majority of its population are Muslims, and thus finding a space to pray was not easy. For example, she suggested that while travelling around in Australia, she has found it difficult to perform her prayers.

> Maybe trying to pray somewhere, maybe like going out with the school, it's quite difficult and like in work. I used to work like I couldn't pray like *Jama'ah*, it's quite difficult...hmm hmm (have a hard time answering it), what I least like about Australia probably not enough *masjid* or other Muslim that I get to know. It is mostly Christian countries so everything over here is celebrating Christmas and the media, they don't explain Islam more and they always put down on Islam in the media

The comments emphasize that mosques are not easily found in Australia. This lack of the religious space discouraged her from performing the *salāt* effectively. This suggests that social and political conditions of the host countries play a significant role in shaping Muslim identity (Duderija 2008; Kusat 2001).

In addition, fasting in the month of *Ramadhan* in Australia is difficult, especially for youngsters like Darni who interact with non-Muslims friends. Although she stated earlier that she had been fasting since childhood, she still found it very challenging. Besides fasting, covering her head was also difficult in the Australian community; it needed courage and persistence. Darni indicated that those who wear the Muslim attire in the broader Australian community are in the spotlight. For example, she sometimes experienced an uneasy feeling when travelling around and people looked at her with suspicion. She wrote in the narrative:

> Being an Indonesian-Muslim teenager in Australia is challenging, especially that I am a girl and I wear the *hijab* when I step outside my house and why I fast during the fasting month. But most of the time it is fine (narrative)

> The hardest thing about being an Indonesian-Muslim in Australia and being a girl wearing the *hijab* is that some people just stare at you, especially on train. It is quite uncomfortable because being a good Muslim I kept my mouth shut and start not start an argument. But it just annoys me that people stare at you like you are a piece in a museum (narrative)

Difficulties in covering their heads because of the emergence of suspicions are experienced by many Muslim girls in many western countries. As a public discourse, the *Jilbab* is seen one of the most controversial issues. However, Darni seems to be consistent at wearing the veil.

In addition, Darni stated that the veil inhibited her from finding a job. For example, when she applies for a job in a particular food industry, such as the restaurant, she has to negotiate about her dress style; the manager was not comfortable with her wearing the typical religious attire while working; and for that reason, she negotiated her ways of covering her hair. In spite of this difficult situation, she commented that some Australians are indeed respectful on her commitment to put on the veil.

## Summary

The chapter discusses a young Muslim girl seen as a 'strong' Muslim girl. She was born to a Muslim family, and thus she became a Muslim firstly because of her Muslim family; Islam has been imposed on and ascribed to her since birth. In addition, her exposure to Islamic values through parental teaching and through the *madrasah,* made Islam her 'chosen identity' because it has been personalized in her. In fact, her written personal narrative indicated that she had come to a stage where she saw herself as a 'strong' Muslim.

Like some other young Muslims in the study, especially those in Chapter Five, Darni was a religious young Muslim. She performed the *salāt* at home, in her Muslim community, but did not do so beyond these two spaces. However, I treat Darni as a special case in this study. This is because she has confronted her biggest challenge as a Muslim girl living in the Australian secular society through covering her head. The other Muslim girls in this study were not confident with expressing their Muslim identity through wearing Muslim attire. They only covered their heads when attending the mosque or their *Qur`ānic* class. Unlike other girls, Darni confronted her fear and was consistent with observing the Muslim dress at home, upon coming to the mosque and her *Qur`ānic* lesson, and also when attending her school. In addition, she did not show any complaint about her routine coming to the mosque and the *madrasah* and about her parents' home regulations.

Darni holds the attributes of both orthodox and moderate Muslims at the same time. She perceives that the essence of Muslim identity lies in religious commitment. However, she also sees that Islam is a beautiful religion that does not restrict its adherents to interact with all mankind regardless of their religious affiliation (see Mondal 2008). The study found that being in multiple settings did not change Darni's identity as a religious Muslim girl. However, in the broader Australian society, she is discouraged from performing the *salāt*. The reasons are varied as discussed earlier, one being the unavailability of the space to pray. Darni is consistent in reciting the *Qur'ān* at home and also in the mosque when she happens to be in the mosque. In addition to her commitment with observing her religious duty, she also balances her life through interacting with the people living around her and participating in her school activities. Referring to the essentialized understanding of 'good' Muslims as described in the religious texts, she is the 'strong' and 'perfect' Muslim.

# CHAPTER SEVEN

# NEGOTIATING MUSLIM IDENTITY
# IN MULTIPLE SETTINGS

This study examines ways of being Muslim in multiple settings: at home, within religious spaces and also beyond the boundaries of these two spaces. In my attempt to examine the 12 young Muslims of Indonesian background in this study, I sought to understand their voices through interviews, personal narratives and also through observation. In the previous three chapters, I have revealed their multiple ways of describing themselves and their ways of being Muslim within these settings and in broader Australian contexts. This study found that these interrelated settings are proven to have played a significant role in shaping the Muslim identity of the 12 young Muslims in this study.

The study has identified that their ways of being Muslim seem to be different. Some of them take on the markers of 'good' Muslims, such as fulfilling their religious duties and holding firm to Islam as their main identity markers, while other young Muslims do not necessarily take on all these 'good' markers of Muslim identity. However, all of the 12 young Muslims in this study subscribed to multiple identity markers. For example, they take Islam as an identity marker and at the same time, they take Australian, Indonesian identities and also enjoy youth lifestyles, such as attending parties, watching movies and playing around with their friends.

In the next several sections and sub-sections, I summarize the young Muslims' shared understandings on certain identity markers. The chapter also summarizes three groups of young Muslims who have similarities and differences in their ways of being Muslim. In addition, it discusses these Muslims' ways of being Muslim at home and in the religious spaces of the *ummah*. The last section of this chapters deals with the 12 young Muslim's multiple-shifting ways of being Muslim.

# Perceiving Multiple Identities

This section summarizes the 12 young Muslims' essentialized understandings of three identity markers. First, information about their understanding of Muslim identity will be given, followed by information on Australian identity. In the final discussion, this chapter reviews essentialized understandings of Indonesian identity as described by those 12 young Muslims.

## *Muslim identity*

Although the study reveals different ways of being Muslim, the 12 young Muslims in this study define Muslims through essentialized understanding of Muslim identity (refer to Chapter Three). They believe that Muslims should be faithful, which is having a strong *imān*. The 12 young Muslims claim themselves to have a strong faith in their religion. They all see that Islam has shaped their ways of being. In addition, they believe in the oneness of *Allāh* and that Muhammad (PbuH) is His final messenger, which is known as the *tawhid* in the Islamic teaching. These young Muslims' expression in regard to the essence of being Muslim is in line with the findings of research conducted by Hassan (2008). In Hassan's study on the exploration of ways of being Muslim of those living in seven countries, one of which is Indonesia, he found that over 80% of participants in six countries believe in the existence of *Allāh, while* in Kazakhstan only 31% of the participants believe in the existence of *Allāh*. This suggests that Muslims are those who make a declaration of the existence of *Allāh* and they do not doubt about it. As noted earlier, believing in the oneness of God is one of the basic components of being Muslim.

In addition, the young participants identify Muslims not only as those who believe in *Allāh* but also as those who observe religious rituals, which are obeying all *Allāh*'s commands. As noted in previous chapters, all of them understand that believing in *Allāh* and fulfilling religious duties are the essence of being Muslim. However, the study reveals that not all of them take on all of the religious practices. As discussed in the previous three chapters, some of them do not pray five times, while some pray at home and fail to do so in the broader Australian society. For that reason, they are categorized into different groups: those who balance their being Muslim, the practicing Muslims and the strong Muslim. As noted earlier, those in the first group are not perfect in fulfilling their religious duties. The second group shows a higher degree of conviction. In spite of their religious conviction, they do not show it through their physical appearance, such as growing the beard and wearing religious outfits. A student in the third group practices and expresses it through her physical appearance. In spite of their different commitment to praying, they show similar attitudes toward fasting. Most young Muslims admit that they are more committed to fasting than to praying. The reason is that fasting is only conducted once in a year, while Muslims are obliged to perform prayers daily, and such daily rituals reduce their motivation for prayers.

These different ways of being Muslim are not unusual in the Islamic world where some Muslims are practising, while others are non-practicing. As found by Hassan (2008) in his study of Muslims in seven countries, Indonesians, Malaysians, and Egyptians show a higher level of religious observance compared to Pakistanis, Iranians and Turkish, who do not show the same level of religious observance, while Kazaks do not show a similar commitment to observing the rituals.

Even though some young Muslims in this study are not fully committed to fulfilling the religious rituals, they are still Muslims and they claim themselves as such. In fact, the term 'Muslim' is used to identify those who believe in the oneness of God and that Muhammad (PbuH) is the last messenger of God, irrespective of their practising or non-practising of Islamic teaching (Meer 2007). A person may refer to himself/herself as a Muslim just because they belong to Muslim families. This fact is in line with the notion of 'ascribed' Muslim identity, a categorization given by Peek (2005) as discussed in Chapter Two

In addition, the young Muslims in the study link Muslim identity to a sense of moral responsibility. They see that Muslims are those who spread peace and promote good relationships with others irrespective of their level of practicing Islam (Aly 2007). Some of the Muslim youth in this study do see themselves as taking on some of these moral principles and practices. Finally, some of these young Muslims also suggest that covering the *aurat*[1] through wearing the veil is seen as an indication of being an 'observing' Muslim.

Hassan also discovers in his study that 96% of his Indonesian participants regard that wearing the veil is an important marker of being Muslim women. In fact the majority of participants in Egypt (98%), Malaysia (94%), Pakistan (92%), and Iran (76%) see wearing the veil as an obligation for Muslim women, while only 38 per cent of participants in Kazakhstan and 56 per cent in Turkey see wearing the veil as an obligation.

---

[1] Refers to parts of a body which should be fully covered; for women the whole body is considered *aurat* except the face and the palm.

This information suggests that wearing the veil is still seen as one of the religious duties by the majority of Muslim communities, at least in five Muslim majority countries as noted earlier.

The twelve young Muslims in my study have an essentialized understanding of Muslim identity. These youth have a strong faith in *Allāh* although they are different in their religious conviction. These ways of perceiving Muslims are obtained through exposure to Islamic teaching at home and some of them from their *madrasah*. Muslim parents in this study indicate that they take on some of their roles as Muslim parents, *tarbiyah, ta'dib* and *ta'lim* roles. As seen in Chapter Two, Islam requires Muslim parents to teach their children about the Islamic faith, the *tawhid*, and the Muslim parents in this study take on their parenting obligations. In the last three chapters, we have learnt that some of them are concerned with fulfilling their parenting roles. At home, they manage to provide a special time for their children, referred to as the 'sacred time' in Becher (2008). In addition, some of these parents spent a time to interact with their children as a way to monitor their children's attitudes.

In the next section, I summarize how these young Muslims' understand of Australian identity.

## *Australian identity*

The 12 young Muslims in this study define essentialized understanding of Australian identity through various attributes. They link Australian identity with stereotypical traits such as 'laidback' and 'arrogant'. This conception of Australian identity is expressed by the majority of young Muslims participating in this study. The term 'laidback' refers to the fact that these young Muslims see Australians to be more relaxed in their ways of engaging with jobs. One of the participants suggests that Australians only work when they need money. The term 'laidback' referring to Australian identity is not uncommon. In her interviews with Australians of Latin American and Turkish background, Zuleyka Zevallos found that 'laidback' is the term used by her participants to refer to Australian identity (Zevallos 2004, 2005).

In addition, when most of these young Muslims label Australian identity with 'arrogant', the term only refers to their classmates. They do not generalize that all Australians are 'arrogant'. At school, they found that some of their Aussie-Aussie friends acted pretentiously in terms of academic achievement and sports skill. They suggest that some of their friends see themselves as better able to achieve a higher academic standard, which is in fact not necessarily true. Likewise, in relation to sport, most of these young Muslims see that Aussie-Aussie friends are usually boastful, as if they can do better than other non Aussie-Aussie students. There is no evidence found in the study that the participants refer 'arrogant' to others beyond this particular context.

Australian identity is also viewed by most of young Muslims in the study through physical appearance. They say that Australians should be white and blonde. For this reason, these young Muslims do not see themselves as Australians despite the fact they have a big part of Australian identity as their identity marker. Zevallos (2003) also identified that her participants failed to see themselves as Australians because "... Australian identity continues to be regarded as synonymous with an Anglo-Celtic appearance" (p. 81). While some of my participants and those of Zevallos view themselves as not Australian through physical appearance, the study by Kabir (2007) identifies the term un-Australian as "not being born in Australia, not having Australian values and not enjoying popular culture" (p. 70).

Finally, young Muslims in the study define Australian identity through people's life-span in Australia. For some of them, all people who have been living long enough in the country are Australians, regardless of their ethnic backgrounds. As discussed in Chapter Four, my participants who were born in Australia – and some of them understand that their parents have been living in the country in the past 25-30 years – view themselves as more Australians than Indonesians. In addition, most of my participants label Australian identity through the term 'fair go'.

## *Indonesian identity*

It has been noted earlier in Chapter Three that three attributes of Indonesian identity were expressed by the participants. All the participants link the type of food one consumes with identity. Because of consuming the Indonesian food at home, these young Muslims categorize themselves as Indonesians. As discussed in the previous three chapters, all young Muslims assert that being Indonesian is an important marker of their identity. For example, some students in Chapter Four are aware that Indonesian is the significant part of their identity although they prefer to be seen as Australians. The other students also consume Indonesian food, but unlike those in Chapter Three, they prefer to be seen as Indonesians.

The second attribute voiced by these 12 young Muslims on Indonesian identity is through heritage. They see themselves as Indonesian because of the fact that they were born into Indonesian Muslim families. The third way of seeing Indonesian identity is through habitual activities. Some students make a comparison between the Indonesian daily practices and the Australian practices. They see Indonesian identity markers as being disciplined and clean.

This way of understanding identity is in line with how Kabir (2010) perceives identity construction. She notes that identities are created through multiple angles. Kabir states that identity is constructed through the place of birth, the family in which one grows up, and the religion they were born into. These 12 young Muslims construct their identity through these multiple angles. They see themselves as Indonesians and Muslims because of the fact that they were born into Indonesian Muslim families. At the same the same time, they take 'Australian' as the identity marker through the place they were born in and in which they grow up. As a result of this multiplicity of factors that shape these young Muslims' identity, they take multiple identity markers, and thus young Muslims who were born in Australia and grow up in the country see themselves as having multiple-shifting identities.

In the next section, I summarize three groups of young Muslims who have multiple ways of being Muslim.

## Ways of Being Young Indonesian Muslims

This section briefly recapitulates the three groups of young Muslims who are different in their ways of being Muslim.

### *Balancing being young Muslims, Australian and Indonesian*

In Chapter Four, I described five young Muslims, and I see them as balancing their ways of being Muslim. Yasmeen (2008) refers to these types of Muslim attributes as 'quiet observant Muslims'. While they have some similarities in their self-identification, which is through multiple identities, they are different in their ways of being Muslim. The young Muslims in this group see Islam as their main identity marker. However, they tend to combine the term 'Australians' and 'Muslims'. They call themselves 'Australian-Muslims'. Moreover, they tend to describe themselves, first as the Australians, and then followed by the Indonesians and then Muslims. They see themselves Australians due to the fact that they have been exposed to Australian society since childhood. They also get along well with many 'Aussie-Aussie' friends. However, as they were born into Indonesian Muslim families, they cannot ignore that Indonesian and Islam are also big parts of their identity (ies). This fact leads them to call themselves Australian-Muslims of Indonesian background. Although those students regard Islam as one of the important sources of their identity as noted in Chapter Four, they do not take on all the religious rituals, the *ibadāt,* such as the *salāt* either when they are at home, in the mosque or beyond the two spaces. Some of them told me that they have a hectic schedule – their studies and homework, school activities and other activities. Due to this busy schedule, they take on only some of the markers of religious practices. They pray sometimes at home. They told me that they fast during the month of *Ramadhan.*

In addition, while two of them are attending the *Madrasah* held in the Indonesian mosque, three other students in this group do not attend the space. Some of them told me that they got bored when attending this religious space. They felt that they do not fit into this environment.

In the case of the attire, the three female Muslims in this group felt uncomfortable with wearing the religious attire, the *jilbab* as this dressing differentiates them from their teenage peers. Although they believe it as a religious requirement, they are not confident to wear it in public and they hardly wear it. They told me that their parents also do not pressure them to wear the veil. Their mothers and siblings also do not wear the veil.

The parents of the 5 young Muslims in this group while holding on to the Islamic rituals and principles also believe in having a dialogue with their children rather than 'forcing' them to conform. They provide opportunities for their children to engage with Islam through praying at home and taking them along to the mosque and religious activities. But they do not force their children to take on the markers of the 'good' Muslim. In fact, these parents take on a democratic style of Muslim parenting where there is a dialogue. This provides the five young Muslims in my study to take on different identity markers – that of Muslim, Australian and Indonesian in ways of being Muslim youth.

## *Being practising young Muslims, Australian and Indonesian*

I also had a group of six Muslim youth in my study who saw themselves as 'Indonesian-Muslims living in Australia'. Five out of the six young Muslims in this group were born overseas and some moved to Australia before the age of three, while two of them migrated to Australia at the age of five. Only one student in this group was born in Australia. The Muslim youth in this group told me that they did not see themselves as Australians because they argue that they do 'not even look like Australians'. They told me that they see themselves as Indonesian Muslims living in Australia.

These young Muslims took on most of the markers of a 'good' Muslim. They perform their *salāt* at home, in the school, and in the religious spaces. They have also been fasting in the month of *Ramadhan* from very young. They told me that they see themselves as being knowledgeable in Islam as a result of attending the *madrasah*. The two young girls in this group wear the headscarf when they go to the mosque and weekend school. They told me that they are not confident enough to express their Muslim identity in the wider community through veiling. They do not wear the headscarf due to the negative media coverage of veiled Muslim women. Like those students in Chapter Four, all six young Muslims in this group interact with their friends across cultures. They suggest that they get along well with all students, although some of them perceived Australians of Anglo backgrounds negatively. Some of them regard some of their 'Aussie-Aussie' friends as more 'arrogant' compared to other non-white students.

Most of them in this group are not very happy with their parents' regulations at home since they perceive them as too restrictive. This group of youth has also lost interest in attending their weekend school. They indicate that they get bored at attending the *madrasah* because they have been attending the place since they were in primary school. They are also not able to engage with some of the discussions in the mosque given the language issues.

### *Being a strong young Muslim, Australian and Indonesian*

In Chapter Six, I described a young Muslim girl, whom I referred to as a 'strong' Muslim. Like some of the students in the second group, Darni was born in Indonesia and moved to Australia when she was still three months old. She perceives herself as a 'strong' Indonesian Muslim who happens to live in Australia. Even though she grew up in Australia, she is aware that Indonesian is her nationality, since it is the nationality of her parents. Darni is different from other young Muslims in the study for several reasons. First, she neither shows her discontent with her parents' regulations nor expresses her disinterest in attending her *madrasah*. She seems to comply with her parents' requests to attend the Islamic class or the mosque. Second, she is assertive in terms of wearing the veil in the Australian society. She is consistent with covering her head contrasted with those in previous groups who show their lack of confidence with expressing their Muslim identity through wearing the veil. She explains that her persistence in wearing the veil is shaped by her parents' commitment at asking her to take on that particular clothing. In addition, she describes herself as a strong Muslim because of the fact that she is committed to all the religious rituals.

I found that 3 groups emerged from the narratives of the 12 young Muslim youth in my study. Having discussed the three groups of Muslim youth, I now discuss the differences and similarities in their ways of being Muslim at home and in the religious spaces and how parenting roles shape their Muslim identity.

## *Muslim Family and Ways of Being Muslim*

Indonesian Muslim families participating in this study live in many suburbs in Melbourne, Australia. Some live near the Indonesian Muslim community centre, while others live a bit further out. In spite of different residential areas, they usually gather in the Indonesian Muslim community centre located in Victoria. They rely heavily on the existence of the Indonesian Muslim community centres, which are used not only for performing the *ibadāt* such as the *salāt* and conducting Islamic sermons, but also for various types of religious and cultural programs.

Since family is the cornerstone of the Muslim society (1995) Becher, (2008), it is important to discuss the ways in which Indonesian Muslim families in Australia are educational and social sites for Muslim identity formation. As discussed in the previous three chapters, all Muslim youth in my study regardless of their observance of religious rituals perceived their home environment as positive. They said that they are thankful to be born into a Muslim family since through this they recognize Islam as an important part of their identity. In fact, they argue that it would be very difficult for them to be Muslim if they were not born to a Muslim family. Most of them generally get on well with their parents and are able to have dialogues with their parents on a number of issues. A few of them do have minor arguments in relation to attending the religious activities at the mosque and weekend schools. They understand that Islam stipulates its adherence to respect their parents. They also understand that Indonesian cultural values also discourage Muslim children from engaging in a harsh argument with their parents; they are expected to listen to and respond to their parents' requests in a good manner.

They all were born into Muslim families, through which they become Muslim. In spite of their 'ascribed' Muslim identity, as they grow older and learn more in-depth about Islam through attending *madrasah* and the teaching of their parents, most of them have come to a stage of 'chosen' identity (Peek 2005). Salma, Darni, Hanafi, Hafnizar, Yani and Ikhwan strongly claimed that Islam is their choice. In fact, Salma suggests that she has come to a stage where to her Islam is the true religion. Although most of them fall into the 'chosen identity', there are some different levels of religiosity. As noted earlier, some of them are indeed religious, while others are not very practising. These different levels of religious commitment are shaped by many factors: Islamic education, environment, and also ways of childrearing in the Muslim families. For this reason, diversity in these young Muslims' religiosity is understandable.

I found that Darni, Hafnizar and Hanafi's parents are very strict in term of transferring Islamic knowledge to them. For example, Eko, Hanafi and Hafnizar father imposes many regulations at home hoping that his children's religiosity will be well maintained. Eko also makes guidelines that his children do not go out much at night and many other kinds of regulations. These regulations as perceived by Eko are part of the process of *tarbiya*, which is to prevent his children from engaging with prohibited activities outside of home. At the same time, he also engages in the process of *ta'dib*, which is disciplining his children and shaping their attitudes. Likewise, Darni's father, Eri implements rules that enable him to control and watch his children's Muslim identity. Eri, for example, encourages Darni to put on the veil, and he also constantly reminds his children to pray and in fact takes a firm action to make them pray.

However, some young Muslims in this study show resistance in regard with their parents' strict regulation at home. In fact, this kind of regulation creates some 'tensions' between the children and the parents. Their parents' restriction at home and also their request to attend the *madrasah*, make some of these young Muslims feel unhappy. However, such tensions do not burst into ruthless arguments with their parents. Other young Muslims are found to enjoy more freedom in terms of their lived experience at home.

Some other parents in this study are found to have been more relaxed, in which they loosely implement religious regulations to their children. For example, Junaidi frankly admits that he faces some difficulties asking his daughter, Hera to pray and to attend Islamic weekend school. In fact, Hera who used to study in an Islamic private school moved to a public school. She told me during the interview that she did not enjoy the atmosphere of the Islamic school she enrolled in. She indicated that the school is too restricted when compared to her public school. Junaidi supported his daughter's decision to do so as he felt it was difficult to refuse her request. Some other parents such as Rizki and Tiarman let their daughters go out at night for movies and other teenage social activities. These different ways of parenting and educating children undoubtedly shape these young Muslims' ways of being Muslim in Australia.

All Muslim parents involved in my study indicate a concern for their roles in shaping their children's Muslim identity. They are worried about their children's choice of life partner, in that they are afraid that their children will choose their non-Muslim friends as their spouses. Most of them reiterate that they want their children to have Muslim spouses regardless of their ethnicities.

During the interviews, I found that most of the Indonesian young Muslims in my study belong to the so-called 'traditional' Muslim families. These Muslim families still ascribe fathers to hold the highest authority at home, and thus as noted by Adibi (2003), other family members are required to obey the commands of their fathers (Adibi 2003). Nilan, Donaldson and Howson (2007) contend that this leadership and protective roles of the father in the family is a symbol of masculinities (including that of Indonesian). Islam recognizes a hierarchical family structure, in which the family is led by a father, since in Islam, the father is known as the *qawwam* or the leader of the family (Beshir 2009), and yet mothers' role in childrearing is considered of important value as well in the Muslim families (Al-Mateen & Afzal 2004).

Although the fathers are assigned as those who hold higher authority, the mothers also hold very crucial roles in educating their children. The findings of my study indicate that these 12 young Muslims' mothers play a major role in guiding their Muslim identity. The parents in my study do not advocate for physical punishment as a way of disciplining their children. In fact, they believe in having dialogues with their children.

The parents of Indonesian young Muslims in my study continue to shape and guide their children's religiosity. In so doing, these parents teach their children about Islam at home and invite them to Indonesian Muslim gatherings held in Indonesian mosques and also in houses of some Indonesian Muslims. Muslim parents play their roles as *murabbi, muallim* and *muaddib.* In addition to such efforts, known as *ikhtiyār* in the Islamic literature, these Muslim parents also pray, asking for God's help, known as *do'a* in Islam in order that *Allāh* gives them strength to guide their children's Muslim identity. All parents interviewed indicated that *do'a* is important to them in providing a sense of calmness, optimism in life and spirituality. Byfield (2008) who studied the impact of religiosity on Black students' academic achievement found that prayer or *do'a* is significant in their lives. As the result of their *ikhtiyār* and *do'a* in shaping their children's Muslim identity, these Muslim parents have been successful in developing a sense of *Muslimness* in their children through the sharing of some basic knowledge about Islam and Islamic practices as well.

While they are thankful to their parents and feel senses of belonging toward the Islamic faith, some of the participants show a certain level of discontent with their parents' regulations as noted earlier. Although there are some emergent 'conflicts' in their relationship with parents, they do not show any direct confrontation. This suggests that their ways of being Muslim is constructed through the interplay of various agencies: between the fulfilment of their 'youthfulness' (Bayat 2010, p. 27) and '*Muslimness*' (Shah 2009, p. 530). On the one hand, they expect to gain more freedom in terms of going out and asserting their 'youthfulness' through electronic media, such as playing games, watching movies and also going out at night time with friends. On the other, they are aware of the Islamic rules and parents' regulations that they have to abide by. A study by Bayat (2010) also found that most Muslim youth both in the global North and South tend to combine between faith and 'youth lifestyles'. Asef Bayat put forwards:

> Most of these young people were religious. They often prayed, fasted, and expressed fear of God. Many heavy metal "Satanist" whom I interviewed considered themselves devout Muslims, but also enjoyed rock music, drinking alcohol, and romance. The mainstream young combined prayer, partying, pornography, faith and fun (Bayat 2010, p. 45)

Most of the young Indonesian-Muslims in my study negotiate ways of being between the two spectrums: on the one hand, they show their devotion to their religion and obedience to parents, on the other; they are concerned with 'claiming youthfulness' (Bayat 2010, p. 30), such as engaging in youth's activities, listening to western music and watching movies. Combining faith and fun is a typical way of being Muslim among young Muslims as argued by Bayat (2010).

In addition, this claim of youthfulness is often realized during their interaction beyond their home and mosque boundaries. As discussed in the last three chapters, these twelve young Muslims are similar, in terms of their interactions and activities beyond their home environment and the religious spaces. Their engagement in the broader spaces is similar even though their religious piety is different. For example, most of them engage in school sport teams, the music teams and also other kinds of students' organizations. Some of them are also active in attending birthday parties or other kinds of youth parties and social activities. In spite of involvement in these many kinds of youth's activities, the majority of them are consistent at fulfilling their religious duties, such as the *salāt* and are restraint from drinking alcohol. They negotiate multiple discourses in ways of being

Islam: that of Islam, their families, their community, and being a teenager in the broader community.

## *Religious Spaces of the Ummah and ways of Being Muslim*

Religious spaces are important venues for Muslim in their ways of exercising their religious duties. Prior to the establishment of the Indonesian Muslim community centre, Indonesian Muslims living in Victoria found some organizations that cater the needs of the Muslim community, especially Indonesian Muslims. The interview with the senior member of Indonesian Muslims reveals that in the 1980s the Indonesian Muslims established an organization that caters to cultural needs to preserve their cultural practices, known as PERWIRA. The other important organization, which functions as the venues for Islamic learning is also established known as *At-Taqwa*. Indonesian Muslim students studying in Victoria help organize this group, and one of the regular programs of this organization is conducting fortnight Islamic teaching, which is held from home to home[2].

In addition to helping organize the above two organizations, the Indonesian Muslim students studying in various Australian universities have established Muslim student organizations: Monash Indonesian Islamic Society-MIIS (Indonesian Muslim students at Monash); *Pengajian Brunswick* (Indonesian Muslim students in University of Melbourne); Victoria University Islamic Student Association-VUISA (Indonesian Muslim students at Victoria University); and Youth Indonesian Muslim Student Association-YIMSA (Undergraduate Indonesian Muslim students). These groups consistently run Islamic teaching (*muhadharah*) that cater to Muslim students in the respective universities, but the attendances in the program are not limited to students. Some Indonesian Muslims who hold permanent resident status also take advantage of these various *muhadharah*.[3]

When the population of Indonesian Muslim in Australia started to increase, the community members took it upon themselves to raise the financial support in order to have a community space. To organize their efforts and maintain their motivation, they established an umbrella organization, known as the Indonesian Muslim Community of Victoria (IMCV). This organization worked continuously to raise financial support to establish the Indonesian Muslims establish a centre. Their efforts yield a

---

[2] Personal communication with the senior members of the Indonesian Muslims in Victoria.
[3] The communication with the president of IMCV.

good result because the Indonesian Muslims bought a house in 1998, which then was transformed into a multi-purpose community centre located in Victoria.

The Indonesian Muslim community centre in Victoria was established in 1999, but only three years later, in 2002, the mosque was completely functional for praying, Indonesian community events, weekend *Qur'anic* teaching and other such other activities. Between 2000 and 2004, the mosque was specifically used for Indonesian Muslims' religious and social purposes. In 2005, the mosque was available for all Muslims, especially during the Friday prayer. Indonesian Muslim communities in Victoria recognise the benefit of the mosque's existence in their environment. Various religious teaching programs were established: Friday night *Qur'anic* lessons for adults and teenagers, Sunday morning Islamic teaching for adults and teenagers, Sunday Morning *Qur'anic* teaching for children, and other religious events. During these events, Muslim communities such as Indonesian students, permanent residents and Australian citizens (Indonesian Muslims) attend the mosque, and sometimes invite their children along.

In addition to the Indonesian mosque South-Eastern Melbourne, there is another Indonesian Muslim Islamic centre located in the Eastern part of Melbourne, known as *Surau Kita* (our mosque). The new established centre has activities such as the Saturday morning Islamic teaching. In addition to such centres, there are *At-taqwa* and various Muslim student organizations discussed earlier, Indonesian Muslim communities living in Victoria establish Islamic learning circles (*muhadharah*) catering religious needs of a certain Indonesian Muslim communities. At least ten learning circle groups have emerged within Indonesian Muslim groups in Victoria: *An-Nur, Al-Islah, Az-Zahra, SAS,* and *Minang Saiyo*. All these groups run typical programs, which are Islamic teaching for adults and the *Qur'ānic* class for children. These learning circles usually taking place fortnightly. Young Muslims in this study usually participate in *At-Taqwa* and *Minang Saiyo* Islamic group. All these Islamic learning groups are under the umbrella of the 'Indonesian Muslim Community of Victoria' (IMCV)[4].

Most Muslim families participating in my study are the regular attendees of the Indonesian mosque, while some others visit the mosque during special events. These families live within 30 to 45 minutes-drive from the mosque. The Indonesian Muslim families participating in the study joined in several programs at the mosque. For example, four families

---

[4] This information is obtained through personal and electronic communications with the President of IMCV.

were part of the *muhadharah* (Islamic learning circle) held every Sunday morning, while another four attend the one held every Friday night, and two families only occasionally visit the mosque during the special events such as the *Eid* (religious festivities) and wedding ceremonies. In spite of their attendance to the mosque during such *muhadharah*, rarely do they invite their children to join these programs. Some young Muslims in my study visit the mosque only occasionally during the *Eid* festivals, wedding ceremonies, and during the month of *Ramadhan*. During the *muhadharah* that takes place at different homes in the group, these Muslim families frequently invited their children to come along with them.

    This study found that most young Muslims in the study attend the *masjid* and the *madrasah*. Most of the youths in my study visited the mosque regularly for their weekend school. Most young Muslims in the study have been going to the *Qur'ānic* Class since they were in primary school. This length of period of attending the *madrasah* has reduced their interest in participating further in that particular space. In regard to attending the *masjid*, some of them argue that they do not understand the language used in the mosque during Islamic sermons. However, all of them are aware that such Islamic school allows them to interact with Indonesian Muslim friends. The space also enables them gain peaceful feeling.

    This expression is in line with a number of studies on Muslim community centres. Dwyer (1999a), for example, suggests that minority communities oftentimes share many commonalities, and thus a community centre is significant in helping minority community survives in the foreign states (Bouma, Daw and Munawar 2001; Humphrey 2001). Schumann (2007) asserts that community and religious centre for minority community is important; it is important because such a community gives an opportunity to minority groups to maintain their identity and avoid total assimilation with the mainstream culture. Works of some scholars on Muslims in the West suggests that Muslim minorities, as do other minority groups, attempt to establish community centres, which oftentimes functions as the mosque. Since Muslim community in Australia is widely diverse, later development of the minority community centre or mosque is based on ethnicity (Humphrey 2001). There are mosques in Victoria, for example belonging to a particular ethnicity: Preston Mosque (Lebanese); Broadmeadows and Noble Park mosque (Turkish); Fawkner Mosque (Iranian); Dandenong Mosque (Albanian); Westall Mosque (Indonesian), and other such Muslim community centres scattered across Victoria. However, Bouma, Daw and Munawar (2001) contend that these ethnic based mosques could be used by all Muslims regardless of their ethnic backgrounds.

Although it has been noted earlier, some Muslim youngsters in the study admit that their motivation to attend weekend school has waned, though most of them realize that the *madrasah* has played a significant role in shaping their identity. They are positive about the significant influence of weekend school on the construction and the maintenance of their religious identity. Studies by some other scholars also find that weekend school is an effective venue to guard Muslim students' religious identity (Schumann, 2007). Johns and Saeed (2002) and Yasmeen (2002) also reiterate that Sunday school played significant role in shaping and maintaining young Muslim religious identity. However, some Muslim youth in my study indicate that they are not very interested in attending their weekend school. Their reasons for their disenchantment with learning at the weekend school are varied. First, methods of teaching at the weekend school are not very effective; second, school curriculum is not very creative, and third, the lessons seem to be boring.

## *Multiple-Shifting Identities*

Young Muslims in this study tend to take on multiple and shifting identity markers. They are juggling many identity markers. Most of them feel that they are Indonesians, Australians, and Muslims at the same time. Indonesian-Muslim youths in my study told me that these three identity markers are inseparable because they believe that they have taken on some parts of these three different identities in their ways of being. What is interesting then, is the extent to which they take on the markers of the three different identities of Indonesian, Muslim and Australia. As discussed in Chapter Four, five of the youth: Hera, Imani, Suci, Billah and Zaki describe themselves as more Australian than Indonesian, while others see themselves otherwise and have chosen Australian to be their nationality. Students in Chapter Five, Salma, Fatma, Hanafi, Yani, Ikhwan, and Hafnizar and that in Chapter Six, Darni see themselves as Indonesian but they prefer to hold Australian passports.

All of them use multiple identities such as 'Australian-Indonesian' or 'Indonesian-Australian', to refer to their multiple identity markers (Sirin & Fine 2008). They call themselves Indonesian because their parents are of Indonesian descent, but they claim to have an Australian part in them due to the fact that they grow up in Australia and make friends with the 'Aussie-Aussie'. Children of minority background often times see themselves through multiple-shifting identities to signal that structurally they are assimilated to mainstream society (Sadat 2008). I see my participants as young Muslims as being structurally assimilated to the mainstream Australian society because of the fact they have grown up in Australia. Dwyer (2000) and Faas (2008) also identify similar ways of describing self through multiple identities. Some scholars suggest that Muslim identity is hybrid and mixed (Luke & Luke 1999; Schumann 2007). It is not stable and it is continuously constructed in the intersection between the values of host societies and their ethnic values (Dunn 2001; Keaton 2005; Mandaville 2001).

In spite of their preference to living in Australia permanently, the young Muslims in this study believe that 'Australians of Anglo background' do not see them as Australians. In fact, these young Muslims do not even see themselves as Australians although they are part of Australia. This self-assumption emerges because of the discourse of 'whiteness'. This shapes the notion of Australianness (Zevallos 2004), which suggests that Australians are white people, and other non-white people are not regarded as Australians by others. Others see Australians through stereotypes: personal, emotional and physical attributes such as through the terms: 'dumb', 'drinking', 'untidy', 'laidback' and other negative attributes. However, positive attributes of Australians such as those who are accepting and tolerant of differences also emerge. These multiple constructions of Australian identity derive from the settings in which the young Muslims reside, and from the experiences, they are exposed to within those many life settings. Dawson (2007) contends that identity construction is influenced by the past, the immediate and also the broader social context. It is also shaped by ethnic experience as suggested by Faas (2008).

Although others do not see them as Australians, Indonesian-Muslim youth seem to suggest that they are not discriminated against. They told me that they see their lives in Australia as being peaceful. Their interactions with their non-Muslim friends seem to be smooth. For example, beyond the boundary of their home and religious space, they engage in various activities with their friends from school. Some go out at night time with their friends, especially on the weekend, and they also sometimes attend their friends' parties. This information indicates that young Muslims in this study do not encounter major prejudice or racism from their mainstream Australian friends.

In spite of these multiple identities, they tend to maintain their Indonesian and Muslim identity, since their parents are Indonesian-Muslims. The other factor that makes them regard themselves as Indonesians is the fact that they are still engaging in Indonesian cultural practices including eating Indonesian food. They also explain that they usually attend Indonesian cultural events such as food festivals. Their interactions with the Indonesian Muslim community by attending the fortnight Islamic learning circles held in the mosque or in the homes of Indonesian families also shape Muslim identity. In addition, all family practices are typical of an Indonesian Muslim family.

## Summary

The study has unpacked the ways in which the 12 young Indonesian Muslims construct their Muslim identity. All of them see Islam, Indonesian and Australian as their important identity markers. The youths in my study told me that they are educated by parents to behave with the Islamic values, and thus consider Islam as an important component of their identity. Being born into Indonesian Muslim families is regarded as a blessing by the participants in all groups because from this they gain their Muslim identity. The findings also suggest that their parents' democratic teaching styles are also important, as they believe that through such teaching styles, they attempt to hold firm on the Islamic values. However, some disagreements also occur within the family life. As they live with their family, they are required to meet the expectations of their parents. They also live within the boundary of Muslim minority community, in which they attend the *madrasah* and also other kinds of Islamic learning circles. However, the study reveals that these young Muslims perceive their *Qur`ānic class* differently. Although they believe that it helps them to shape their Muslim identity, some of them have begun to lose their interest in coming to the weekend school, while some claim that they are committed to attending the spaces.

In addition to the two settings, they live within the wider secular Australian society and thus they are required to adapt to the expectations of this wider society. At the same time, they also attend school, in which they interact with many people from multiple backgrounds, be they Muslims, non-Muslims, Indonesians or non-Indonesians. These multiple settings play significant roles in shaping these young Muslims' ways of self-construction and constructing others (Cornell & Hartmann 2007).

In spite of living in multiple settings and holding multiple identity markers, these young Indonesian Muslims are not trapped within conflicting identities. They, in fact, are able to position themselves within the three contexts, in which they negotiate their ways of being at home, Muslim community centres, and also the broader Australian context. In her study of young Muslims in Britain, Basit (2009) found similar findings.

The young British Muslims in her study know when they become Britons and are also aware of their sense of belonging to the Muslim *Ummah*.

In this study, I also unpacked this group of Indonesian-Muslim youths' understanding on being Muslim in Australian society. The young Indonesian Muslims find life in Australia somewhat challenging as Muslims and suggest that there is some degree of suspicion in the society given the negative media reports on Muslims. Many scholars have identified some prejudicial sentiments that take place in the wider Australian society toward Muslims. Scholars such as Ho (2007); Humphrey (2001); Husain and O'Brien (2000); Kabir (2006); Mansouri (2005); Poynting and Mason (2007); and Yasmeen (2005b) have shown that Muslims are seen as inferior and as distinct to the West. In addition, Bloul (2008); Imtoual (2006); Kabir (2006); and Muedini (2009) note the role of media in the negative portrayal of the Muslim community. The negative projection of Muslims in Australian media increases a sense of *Islamophobia* within Australian society. My participants' assertion of the challenges encountered in the Australian society is in line with some existing findings regarding levels of prejudicial sentiments toward Islam and Muslims.

Young Muslims in the West, such as my Australian Indonesian-Muslim research participants, engage with the Islam faith, as well as discourses operating in the broader society (beyond their immediate family and Muslim community) in their ways of being.

# CHAPTER EIGHT

# CONCLUSION

In my study, I have drawn on the works of Muslim scholars who research Muslims in the West (Basit, 1997, 2009; Mondal 2008, Ramadan 1999, 2004; Sirin & Fine 2008; Yasmeen 2008; and Zine 2008). Tariq Ramadan (1999, 2004), who devotes himself to studying Muslims in the West argues that Muslims in the West should be proud and knowledgeable of their Muslim heritage and Islamic faith, but at the same time engage with the broader society within which they are located and play an active role as a responsible citizen. For Ramadan, Muslims living in a particular country must consider themselves as part of that country. For example, Muslims who live in Britain ought to consider themselves British Muslims instead of Muslims living in Britain, the term British Muslims indicating that British identity is seen as a central part of the identity of young Muslims. Ramadan's arguments are also reflected in the works of Basit (2009), Mondal (2008), Sirin and Fine (2008), Yasmeen (2008) and Zine (2008). These scholars explain that young Muslims living in the western countries are able to negotiate their multiple identities successfully. They can be British, Americans, Canadians, Australians, and Pakistani, Turkish, Indonesian and Muslims at the same time. Their identities are multiple and shifting and contextual.

The works of these scholars also indicate that Muslims living in non-Muslim countries (such as Australia, England, United States) encounter different challenges to those living in Muslim-majority countries, such as Indonesia, Malaysia or Pakistan. Most studies on Muslim identity reveal that young Muslims living in non-Muslim countries, such as the United Kingdom, the United States do feel a sense of belonging in these countries. They do see themselves as being part of the broader society. The work by Basit (2009), for example, found that young Muslims in her study seem to enjoy their lives as British Muslims in Britain. They enjoy the freedom within their British community and at the same times feel proud to be part of the Muslim community. The study also reveals that they are aware that some of the freedoms enjoyed by their fellow British girls are in conflict with their Islamic values. Basit states:

There was very little evidence of this perceived conflict during the interview. If there was a conflict, the girls, surprisingly, appeared to cope with it extremely well at such a young age. They showed no signs of neurosis and seemed to view their situation quite objectively. Most did not want the same amplitude of freedom that their English contemporaries had (Basit 1997, p. 431).

In her later work 'White British; dual heritage; British Muslim', she reiterates similar points arguing that young Muslims possess multiple identities. In her own words:

They are comfortable with the British component of their identity, yet have other hybrid identities that they are proud of (Basit 2009, p. 741).

Basit's work has revealed that for young Muslims, "their religious identity is paramount and they view religion as a code of conduct, which enables them to judge the parameters in which they operate" (Basit 2009, p. 739). However, they are proud to be British citizens. This similar point has also been found in other studies reviewed in Chapter Two, such as those conducted by Mondal (2008) and by Sirin and Fine (2008).

My study, on Muslim youth's ways of being Muslim within their home environments and the religious spaces of the *ummah* (Muslim communities), adds to the growing literature on the process of Muslim identity construction and negotiation in the West. This book has identified the ways in which young Muslims of Indonesian background construct and negotiate their Muslim identity in Australia. The Islamic teaching circulating within their families and the Muslim environment intersect with the broader secular settings to shape young Muslim identity. The study reveals that their ways of being Muslim are different from one setting to the other. For example, they adopt all markers of 'good' Muslims in one setting, such as within the home environment and the religious spaces. When they are beyond these two settings, they tend to take on other identity markers.

The study also finds that besides taking Islam as the central source of their identity, their parents' ethnic background is also paramount in shaping their ways of being Muslim in Australia. The young Muslims indicated that their parents' ethnic identity, their parents' religious background, and their parents' national identity have shaped their ways of being Muslim. While some of them like to be called Australians, most of them referred to themselves as Indonesian-Muslims because of their heritage. This also suggests that heritage plays an important role in the construction of one's identity.

I started this research with the following research questions: How do the Indonesian Muslim family dynamics shape young Muslims' identity and how do they negotiate their ways of being Muslim within their home environment? In what ways do programs and activities of Muslim community centres shape Muslim youth's ways of being Muslim? To answer these questions, I worked with conceptual frameworks on Muslim identity, which I discussed in Chapter Two. I first referred to the discourse of religious texts to unpack various characteristics of Muslim identity. The religious texts have provided *essentialized* understandings of Muslim identities. Religious texts, the *Qur`ān* and the *Hadith* are two important sources to understand Muslims' attributes. However, Islam also recognizes that social settings are influential in the formation of Muslim identity. It is for that reason that Islam encourages parents to provide the best environment for their children to nurture their children's Muslim identity.

Yasmeen (2008) provides some useful categories in understanding Muslim identity, ranging from the orthodox to the moderate. Some of the Indonesian Muslim youth in my study take some characteristics of the orthodox Muslim and some of the moderate Muslim. They believe that being Muslim lies in faith and spirituality as suggested by Ramadan (1999), but at the same time, they also see multiple ways of being Muslim, which reside not merely within the boundaries of ritual performances (Masquelier 2010). In his study of Muslim youth in Nigeria, Masquelier (2010) reveals that young Muslims' ways of expressing their Muslim identity is somewhat different from those of their parents. As suggested in Chapter Two, while young Muslims are faithful to Islam, their ways of being Muslim are not always related to the fulfilment of the *ibadāt*. Some young Muslims in the study believe in Islam but do not always express their ways of being Muslim through fulfilling religious duties, and yet they still consider themselves Muslims. They are Muslims because it is the way they perceive themselves.

This conception of Muslim identity is in line with the works of an anthropologist, Gabriele Marranci. He argues that Muslim identity is constructed through the ways in which people see themselves, and not through the ways in which they are perceived by others (Marranci 2008). While their main identity marker of the youth in my study is Islam, they take Indonesian and Australian as marking their identities as well. Some, however, choose Australian as their main identity marker followed by the Indonesian identity, while yet others take Indonesian as their main identity marker followed by the Australian identity marker. In addition, as explained by Mondal (2008), some young Muslims return to Islam when their identity is confronted. Likewise, in my study some young Indonesian

Muslims were found to learn more about Islam when their identity was confronted within the broader Australian contexts.

## *Studying Young Muslims*

This book consists of eight interrelated chapters. In Chapter One, I provided the rationale for conducting this research. As mentioned elsewhere, the study was undertaken to understand the ways in which young Muslims who were born and/or grow up in Australia construct and negotiate their Muslim identity. As a Muslim myself I am aware of the multiplicity of the ways of being Muslim. I found that there are some differences in my ways of being Muslim from those who were born and live in a non-Muslim country like Australia. These distinct ways of being Muslim are in part due to the different social settings, different ways of teaching Islam, and also different ways of perceiving Islam. In this chapter I also stated the research questions, the significance of the study and briefly described Muslims in Australia. This chapter provided an overview of the theoretical framework and research methodology.

Having identified the research purposes and designed the research questions, I drew on several theories in Chapter Two that enabled me to answer the research questions. First, I refer to discourses of the religious texts on Muslim identity. The texts perceive Muslims as those who have faith in *Allāh*. Muslims are seen as those who observe the religious obligations as prescribed by the *Qur`ān* and the *Hadith*. The *imān*, the *ibadāt* and the *akhlāq* are three important components of the *Qur`ān*, which define a good Muslim. In addition, I conceptualize Muslim identity as revealed through the studies of Muslim scholars. I also reiterated that, as found in many studies, ways of being Muslim were multiple. Some observe the religious rituals but some become Muslims through their Muslim heritage. Studies on being Muslim indicate that although Muslims are not very observant on religious rituals, they are proud to declare themselves Muslims. I also visited definitions of Muslim families, Muslim communities, and educational concepts as defined by the religious texts.

To develop my understanding of Muslim families in the West, I draw on several works of Muslim scholars who conceptualize Muslim families and their ways of negotiating multiple identity markers. I found that there are different ways of being Muslim in the West. Some Muslim families in the West are not able to fully comply with their religious obligations. As a result, some of them negotiate their ways of being Muslim in different ways (see Dizboni, 2008). The chapter also revealed that Muslim families bring with them their cultural values when they migrate to Australia. In spite of these obvious differences, they all have a common intention, which is transferring religious values to their children. In addition, the chapter saw that Muslim communities in the West hold on to some sense of collective Muslim identity. Their ethnic cultures shape their ways of establishing and running their community and the community centres. In addition, studies also found that Muslim girls living within their minority community experience internal surveillance. The chapter indicated that Muslim communities in non-Muslim countries strive to utilize their religious centres to carry out educational functions. All Islamic centres across non-Muslim countries play similar roles: for ritual functions, educational functions, and cultural functions. The final section of Chapter Two reiterated that both family and the religious spaces serve as social, religious and educational sites for the development of young Muslims.

I found three ways of being Indonesian Muslim youths in Australia through my data analysis. However, before discussing these three different groups of Muslims, in Chapter three I provided a discussion on markers of essentialized understanding of three identities, Muslim, Indonesian and Australian. In the eyes of my participants, markers of an essentialised Muslim identity include belief in God, rituals, and moral character, wearing the headscarf and peaceable interaction with others. Markers of essentialized Australian identity include being laidback and arrogant, white and blonde, living long in Australia and the idea of 'a fair go'. Essentialized Indonesian identity includes markers such as eating Indonesian food, Indonesian heritage and customs and traditions.

In Chapters Four, five, and Six; I presented the analysis of the young Muslims' ways of being Muslim. I grouped them into three groups based on their identity practices and levels of religious observance. Students in Chapter Four are seen as those who balance their ways of being Muslim and western. They seemed to be more relaxed compared to the other young Muslims. Students in Chapter Five were seen as practising Muslims. They also chose Indonesian and Muslim as their two essential identity markers. Nevertheless, Most of those in Chapter Five also take Australian as their important identity markers since most of them have grown up in Australia. In addition, Chapter Six contains an analysis about a young Muslim who shows rather different ways of being a Muslim. I called her 'the strong Muslim'. I treat her as a special case because she appears to be different from her colleagues in terms of her physical appearance. She showed her comfort with wearing the *jilbab* across the settings. She was also different from her friends in terms of her perceptions of home and the religious spaces. She did not show any discomfort with her parents' home regulations. In addition, she also explained that she enjoyed coming to *madrasah* every Sunday, since it was a source of happiness for her, in that there she could interact with other young Indonesian Muslims. She also suggested that these two religious spaces allowed her to be more obedient to *Allāh*.

Chapter Seven provides a discussion of the differences and similarities between the three groups of Indonesian-Muslim youths. This chapter also examines these twelve young Muslims' ways of being Muslim at home and within the religious spaces of the *ummah*. In the final section of Chapter Eight, I discuss their multiple-shifting ways of being Muslim.

## *The Key Findings*

I have stated earlier that the aim of the study was to explore ways in which Indonesian young Muslims construct and negotiate their Muslim identity within their home environment and the religious spaces within the *ummah*. I examined how they perceived Islam and how they described their Muslim identity. I also investigated their perception of their home environment; the Muslim community centre, and their perceptions of their multiple identity markers. In this section, I draw on four key findings that provide comprehensive ideas on the twelve young Muslims of the Indonesian backgrounds.

The first key finding concerns their chosen identity markers. All young Muslims in the study indicated that Islam was their identity marker. Although they showed their preference for other identity markers, such as ethnicity (Indonesian) and nationality (Australian), they took Islam as their main identity marker and it seemed to come first and then be followed by their other identity markers. Although their level of religious piety was different in some degree, when asked about their identity, the first marker that emerged from their narrations was invariably 'Islam and Muslim'. They saw themselves as Muslims regardless of their various ways of asserting their Muslim identity.

Second, the study also revealed that they negotiated between their ways of being young, being Muslim, being Indonesian and being Australian. These young Muslims showed the interplay of these identity markers that shaped their ways of being Muslim. For example, as Muslims, they are required by the teaching of Islam to comply with their parents' regulations and to respect them. I found that the parents encouraged some of them to attend the religious spaces: the mosque and the *madrasah*. However, at the same time, some of them (see Chapters Four and Five) showed their grave concern when their children engaged in youthful activities (such as going out at night, playing games on the computer) and quitted their *Qur`ānic* class, refusing to learn about Islam. Some young Muslims (see Chapter Four) tended to engage in activities commonly performed by some Australian youth, such as going to parties and drinking alcohol.

The third key finding of this study was in relation to their ways of perceiving their identity. I found that the 12 young Indonesian Muslims have multiple and shifting identities: All of them said that they were Indonesian-Muslims, Australian-Muslims and Indonesian-Australian Muslims or Indonesian-Muslims living in Australia. They juggled these three identity markers. However, they did not show any conflict between these multiple identities. They tended to accept Indonesian and Muslim as their identity markers when they were at home and in the religious spaces, and some of them tended to see themselves as being more prominently Australian upon attending their school environments and interacting with students of various religious and ethnic backgrounds.

Last but not least, the research identified their different ways of being Muslim. Some Muslim youths were committed to fulfilling their religious duties across the three settings, some were committed to performing them only in some settings, while others chose not to place a high value on their religious duties across settings. Nevertheless, all of them regarded religious clothes, such as the veil, as a specific religious marker, though most of them were not comfortable taking it on.

## Reflecting on the Research Journey

This recent research has been very interesting for me personally because it has enabled me to understand how my fellow young Muslims construct their ways of being Muslim in Australia, a western nation which is different from my home country, Indonesia. It is interesting because I can reflect on my own ways of being Muslim within multiple settings. As explained in Chapter One, I was born in a Muslim family. My parents are devoted Muslims. Since my childhood, I have been immersed in Islamic teaching and practices both in my home and in Islamic schools. My lived experiences have shaped my ways of being Muslim. I see myself as being both an orthodox and a moderate Muslim. My first journey to Australia was from January 2002 to June 2003, and then I returned to Australia in 2007. During my stays, I have been involved in various religious and cultural programs run in the Indonesian Muslim community centres. My engagement with Indonesian Muslim communities in Victoria encouraged me to conduct this study.

To gain some important information about Muslim youth, I started to engage with the literature on Islam and Muslims, and these readings have given me insights about young Muslims who were born and/or grow up in western worlds such as in the USA, Britain, Canada, and Australia. I also engaged with research discussing the lived experiences of Muslim youth in the West, such as the study by Irfan Yusuf, 'Once were radicals' (2009). The readings of this body of literature enabled me to gain some understanding about Muslims and their youth living in Muslim-minority countries. They engage in building multiple identities and their ways of being Muslim are more complex than those living in the Muslim-majority countries (see Herrera & Bayat, 2010b). The other fact that I noted during my reading of the literature is that there is a lack of study on young Muslims of Indonesian background in the West. My study addresses the gap in this body of work on Muslims in the West.

In March 2009, I started collecting data for this study. I had become acquainted with most of the Indonesian Muslims who made regular visits to the mosque. However, during my research journey, I then realized that my interaction with Muslim parents would perhaps detract from my efforts to study young Muslims of Indonesian background objectively. In addition, because of being born into a Muslim family and having lived in the largest Muslim community in the world, I realized that I might be trapped within a jungle of assumptions in examining the young Indonesian Muslims' ways of being Muslim. I was aware that my growing up in the Indonesian community would influence my assumptions regarding the notion of 'good' Muslim and this perception could influence my attempt to analyse my participants' ways of being Muslim. I made an effort to be aware of this – the ways in which I understand Islam as an orthodox-moderate Indonesian Muslim and how that was shaping the research process and my interactions with my research participants. Understanding my participants' ways of being Muslim cannot be examined merely by looking at their physical appearance (e.g., wearing the head scarf, attire and behaviour); researchers need to go beyond physical markers.

Therefore, to enable me to understand my participants' ways of being Muslim, I had to see beyond their physical markers and listen to their voices. The in-depth interviews provided me with the opportunity to understand their voices rather than use my own understandings and impose those onto their identity practices. In addition, I used the young people's personal journal to elucidate my participants' inner voices. I also observed my participants' presence in the Indonesian Muslim mosque.

Cornell and Hartmann (2007) argue that in order to understand identity practices, one has to understand the process of identity construction, and one has to examine how this process plays out in multiple settings. The multiple settings of the family and religious spaces (in addition to the broader context) are important in shaping young Muslim identity (Cornell & Hartmann 2007). These young Muslims lived at home. Their home environments and their parents' ways of raising the children shaped these youth's ways of being Muslim and also their negotiations in the Muslim community and religious centre, and beyond the two sites. It is difficult to understand the participants' ways of being Muslim comprehensively without examining their multiple lived experiences in multiple settings.

## *Implications*

This study has unravelled the importance of religion as the main source of identity markers for Muslims in this study. As we have seen in the previous chapters, the young Muslims in this study take Islam as an important part of their identity. Regardless of their level of religious commitment, they all see themselves first and foremost as Muslims. The study also affirms that in the process of Muslim identity construction, their parents' ways of teaching them Islam and their ways of bringing them up played significant roles in shaping their ways of being Muslim. I have noted earlier that some parents were very strict in their parenting styles, while some others tended to be relaxed. These different ways of parenting resulted in different kinds of Muslims. Chapters Five and Six discuss how parents who are more persistent and consistent in taking actions in their attempts at shaping their children's Muslim identity are more able to encourage their children to comply with their religious duties.

The study also adds to previous research on similar issues on ways of being Muslim. Some of the participants are committed to practising Islam across settings, while some others may show different attitudes. This indicates that their ways of being Muslim are not fixed but continuously constructed and shifting depending on contexts. Ways of perceiving themselves are also found to be multiple and shifting. They take multiple identity markers and tend to combine multiple identities at once.

Even though the Muslim youth in my study feel gratitude for being born and growing up in Muslim families, the study also found that there are some clashes of values between parents and their children. While the parents invited them to attend the mosque and the *madrasah*, some of them tended to refuse their parents' requests. However, the study does not suggest that harsh arguments occur in their interaction with parents. This affirms previous knowledge that some tensions and clashes occur between Muslim parents and their children in the global arena. This is because parents tend to take the values of their ethnic cultures and introduce them to their children, while their children have been much exposed to the different values of their host societies.

## *Recommendations*

This study has been conducted with the intention to understand Muslim youth's ways of being Muslim. The design of the study has been constructed in such a way to allow me to gain a rich understanding of these twelve young Muslims' voices regarding their lived experience in Australia as Muslims. Through my attempts to enable myself to comprehensively portray their ways of being Muslim, I seek to understand their experience in their multiple settings. Methods of data collection have been chosen to best meet my expectations.

There is much more to understand about Muslims and their children in Western countries. Therefore, further studies on this issue need to be carried out. This study has identified twelve young Muslims' ways of being Muslim (they are 14 to 17 years old), and the parents of those Muslims are those who regularly attend the mosque. The findings of this study will open some future research directions. In the future, studies on young Muslims of non-practising parents will enrich information on Muslim youth's ways of being Muslim. In addition, a study on young Muslims of post-secondary schools will also open a new understanding of the dynamics of young Muslims' ways of being Muslim.

This study has revealed the process of Muslim identity construction of Indonesian Muslim youth. Other studies comparing Muslim youth of Indonesian background with those from different ethnic background will also provide important information on the different ways of being Muslim in the West.

## Summary

In this chapter, I have summarized the conceptual framework I used in this study. I reiterated that in studying Muslims, it is important to refer back to the teachings of Islam and the conceptions of Muslim identity as prescribed in the discourse of religious texts. The *Qur`ān* and the *Hadith* are two prime sources in understanding Muslims and their ways of being Muslim.

This chapter has also identified the key findings of the study and made suggestions for future studies. It is important to suggest future research directions on Muslim identity, since ways of being Muslim are complex, especially for those living in Western countries. My reflections on the research journey and the research implications can perhaps be used as initial ideas for future studies.

I end this book with the awareness of the multiplicity in ways of being Muslim. This in a way challenges my pre-conception of Muslim identity. I once perceived that Muslims are only those who assiduously fulfil their religious duties. This study has allowed me to broaden my own understandings that while the religious texts define Muslim identity, multiple social settings (such as family, religious spaces and the broader society) also shape Muslim identities. There are multiple and shifting ways of being Indonesian-Muslim youths in Australia.

# GLOSSARY

| | |
|---|---|
| *Akhirāt* | An Islamic term derived from Arabic, meaning the life after this world. Believing in the existence of the *Akhirāt* is one of the pillars of faith |
| *Akhlāq* | An Arabic term meaning morality, virtue and conduct |
| *Akhlāq Al Makhmudāh* | Good or noble conduct. It also derives from an Arabic term |
| *Allāh* | The Muslims' God. Muslims refer to God as *Allāh*, an Arabic term |
| *Amāl Salih* | Good deeds – the deeds encouraged by Islam |
| Aussie-Aussie | An Australian slang term, which means Australians of Anglo background |
| Australianness | The sense, quality and state of being Australian |
| *Ayāt* | The verse of the *Qur`ān*, an Arabic word |
| *Birr* | Good acts with no limitation |
| *Dakwā* | The encouragement to do good deeds; preaching Islam |
| *Do'a* | An Arabic word, which means requesting and asking from *Allāh*. Muslims usually make *do'a* after performing prayers |
| *Eid* | Muslim religious festivals. Two festivals are celebrated by Muslims around the world each year |
| *Fiqh* | Islamic jurisprudence and the explanation of the Islamic law |
| *Hadith/Sunna* | Prophetic traditions; His statements and His deeds |
| *Hajj* | Going on pilgrimage to Mecca; this is one of the pillars of Islam |
| *Halal* | Lawful, legal and permissible to engage with in Islam |

| | |
|---|---|
| Halfie researcher | Researchers who have mixed backgrounds as the result of migration |
| Heritage Muslim | Those who become Muslim through birth but are not fully practising Muslims |
| *Hikma* | An Arabic word referring to wisdom |
| *Ibadāt An-Nawāfil* | Voluntary rituals. Muslims are rewarded by *Allāh* for doing them but are not punished for omitting these rituals |
| *Ibadāt Makhdāh* | Religious obligation; obligatory rituals |
| *Ilm* | Knowledge, which is derived from an Arabic word |
| *Ikhtiyār* | The efforts to gain and to do something |
| *Imān* | Faith or the belief in *Allāh* |
| Indonenesianness | Sense, quality and the state of being Indonesian |
| Insider | The members of a specific group |
| Insignificant others | Those of minority status, i.e. Muslim minorities in the West |
| Islam | The religion preached by the Prophet Muhammad (PbuH) |
| *Istiqhfār* | Acts to seek God's forgiveness |
| *Izzet* | Dignity |
| *Jilbab* | Headscarf or women's head cover |
| *Khalifāt Allāh fi al-ardy* | God's vicegerent in the world |
| *Madrasah* | Formal and informal Islamic school. In this context, it refers to Islamic weekend school, consisting of *Qur`ānic* learning and teaching of other kinds of Islamic knowledge |
| *Masjid* | The mosque, the Muslim religious venue |
| *Muammalāt* | Social interaction. It is also a transaction |
| *Muallim* | Those who teach something, also known as teachers |
| *Muaddib* | Those who engage in nurturing students, also known as educators |
| *Muhadharāh* | Islamic speech or sermon |
| *Murabbi* | Those who grow and shape students, also known as mentor |
| Muslimness | Sense, state and quality of being Muslim |
| Outsider | The non-members of a specific group |
| *Qawwam* | Providers or protectors of the family |
| *Qur`ān* | The Muslim Holy Book |

| | |
|---|---|
| *Ramadhan* | One of the months in Islam, in which Muslims are obliged to fast |
| *Sahadāt* | The declaration of faith |
| *Salāt* | Prayers that are obligatory for Muslims five times a day. One of the principles of the Islamic pillars |
| *Salāt Taraweh* | A special voluntary prayer conducted in congregation during the night of the month of *Ramadhan* |
| *Sawm* | Refers to fasting, which is obligatory for Muslims in the Month of Ramadan based on the Islamic calendar. One of the principles of the Islamic pillars |
| *Sahabāt* | The companions of the prophet |
| *Shari`ā* | Islamic law |
| *Sirah Nabawiyah* | The history of the Prophet Muhammad (PbuH) |
| *Surā* | The chapters of the *Qur`ān* |
| *Syahih* | The trustworthy narration of the prophetic tradition (the *Hadith*) |
| *Ta'lim* | To transfer knowledge to students |
| *Ta'dib* | To refine and to discipline students' attitudes |
| *Tafseer* | The interpretation of the *surā* and the *ayāt* of the *Qur`ān* |
| *Tarbiyāh* | To grow and to increase students' knowledge and morality |
| *Taqlid* | Blind acceptance of the truth |
| *Ulum Al-Qur`ān* | The science of and knowledge about the *Qur`ān* |
| *Ummah* | The community of believers known as the Muslim community |
| *Yaqin* | Certainty or the truth |
| *Zakāt* | Alms-giving, the obligation of charity given by all Muslims at the rate of 2.5 per cent of their wealth |

# BIBLIOGRAPHY

Abbas, T. (2005). British South Asian Muslims: State and multicultural society. In T. Abbas (Ed.), *Muslim Britain: Communities under pressure*. London, New York: Zed Books.

Abid, L. J. (2006). Muslims in Austria: Integration through participation in Austrian society. *Journal of Muslim Minority Affairs, 26*(2), 263-278.

ABS (2007). *Perspectives on migrants*. from http://www.abs.gov.au.

Adibi, H. (2003). *Identity and cultural change: The case of Iranian youth in Australia*. Paper presented at the The Social Change in the 21st century Conference, Queensland University of Technology.

Akhtar, M. (2007a). The identity conflict for Muslims in the West. In M. Aktar (Ed.), *Muslim family in a dilemma: Quest for Western identity*. Lanham, Boulder, New York, Toronto, Plymouth: University Press of America, Inc.

Akhtar, M. (Ed.). (2007b). *Muslim family in a dilemma: Quest for a Western identity*. Lanham, Boulder, New York, Toronto, Plymouth, UK: University Press of America, Inc.

Al-Attas, S. M. N. (1977). Preliminary thoughts on the nature of knowledge and the definition and aims of education. In S. M. N. Al-Attas (Ed.), *Aims and objectives of Islamic education*. Jeddah: Hodder and Stoughton: King Abdul Aziz University.

Al-Mateen, C. S., & Afzal, A. (2004). The Muslim child, adolescent, and family. *Child Adolesc Psychiatric Clin N Am, 13*, 183-200.

Al-Mubarakfury, S. S. (2006). *Sirah Nabawiyah*. Jakarta: Pustaka Al-Kautsar.

Alavi, H. R. (2008). Nearness to God: A perspective on Islamic education. *Religious Education: The Official Journal of the Religious Education Association, 103*(1), 5-21.

Alghorani, M. A. (2003). *Identity, acculturation, and adjusment of high school Muslim students in Islamic schools in the U.S.A.* Unpublished Dissertation, University of Texas at Austin, Austin, Texas.

Ali, S. (2005). Why here? why now? young Muslim women wearing hijab. *The Muslim World, 95*(4), 515-530.

Alridge, D. P. (2003). The dilemmas, challenges, and duality of an African-American educational historian. *Educational Researcher, 32*(9), 25-34.

Aly, W. (2007). *People like us: how arrogance is dividing Islam and the West*. Sydney: Pan Macmillan.

Ansari, H. (2004). Process of institutionalisation of Islam in England and Wales, 1830s-1930s. In J. Malik (Ed.), *Muslims in Europe: from margin to the centre*. New Brunswick, London: Transaction Publishers.

Anwar, M. (2005). Muslims in Britain; Issues, policy and practice. In T. Abbas (Ed.), *Muslim Britain: community under pressure*. London, New York: Zed Books.

Anwar, M. (2008). Muslims in Western states: The British experience and the way forward. *Journal of Muslim Minority Affairs, 28*(1), 125-137.

Ata, A. W. (2009). *Us and Them: Muslim-Christian relations and cultural harmony in Australia*. Sydney: Australian Academic Press.

Atkinson, P., & Delamont, S. (2006). Rescuing narrative from qualitative research. *Narrative Inquiry, 16*(1), 164-172.

Azmi, S. (1997). Canadian social service provision and the Muslim community in metropolitan Toronto. *Journal of Muslim Minority Affairs, 17*(1), 153-166.

Babbie, E. (2005). *The basics of social research* (3rd ed.). Belmont: Thomson Wadsworth.

Babbie, E. (2008). *The basic of social research* (4 ed.). Belmont: Thomson Wadsworth.

Barazangi, N. H. (1989). Arab Muslim identity transmission: Parents and youth. *Arab Studies Quarterly*, 65-82.

Basit, T. N. (1995). *Educational, social and career aspiration*. University of Cambridge, Cambridge.

Basit, T. N. (1997). 'I want more freedom, but not much': British Muslim girls and the dynamism of family values. *Gender and Education, 9*(4), 425-439.

Basit, T. N. (2009). White British; dual heritage; British Muslim: young Britons' conceptualisation of identity and citizenship. *British Educational Research Journal, 35*(5), 723-743.

Bayat, A. (2010). Muslim youth and the claim of youthfulness. In L. Herrera & A. Bayat (Eds.), *Being young and Muslim: New cultural politics in the global South and North*. Oxford, New York: Oxford University Press.

Bayat, A., & Herrera, L. (2010). Introduction: Being young and Muslim in neoliberal times In L. Herrera & A. Bayat (Eds.), *Being young and Muslim: New cultural politics in teh global South and North*. Oxford: Oxford University Press.

Bayoumi, M. (2010). Being young, Muslim, and American in Brooklyn. In L. Herrera & A. Bayat (Eds.), *Being young and Muslim: New cultural politics in the global south and north*. Oxford, New York: Oxford University Press.

Becher, H. (2008). *Family practices in South Asian Muslim families: parenting n a multi-faith Britain*. New York: Palgrave Macmillan.

Berg, B. L. (2004). *Qualitative research methods for the social science* (5th ed.). Boston: Pearson.

Beshir, M. R. (2009). *Family leadership: Qawamah, an obligation to fulfill, not an excuse to abuse*. Beltsville: Amana Publication.

Best, J. W., & Kahn, J. V. (2003). *Research in education* (9th ed.). Boston: A Pearson Education Company.

Bloul, R. A. D. (2008). Anti-discrimination laws, Islamophobia, and ethnicization of Muslim identities in Europe and Australia. *Journal of Muslim Minority Affairs, 28*(1), 7-25.

Boeije, H. (2010). *Analysis in qualitative research*. Los Angeles, London, New Delhi, Singapore, Washington DC: Sage Publication, Ltd.

Bogdan, R. C., & Biklen, S. K. (2007). *Qualitative research for education: An introduction to theories and methods* (5th ed.). Boston: Pearson Education, Inc.

Bone, P. (2003). Bridging the differences. *The Age,* pp. 1-7. from www.theage.com.au/articles/2003/01/03/1041566221402.html.

Bouma, G. D. (1994). *Mosques and Muslim settlement in Australia*. Canberra: Australian Government Publishing Service.

Bryman, A. (2004). *Social research methods* (2nd ed.). Oxford: Oxford University Press.

Byng, M. D. (2008). Complex inequalities: the case of Muslim Americans after 9/11. *American Behavioral Scientist, 51*, 659-674.

Chaudhry, L. N. (1997). Researching 'my people,' researching myself: fragments of a rfelxive tale. *International Journal of Qualitative Studies in Education, 10*(4), 441-453.

Clark, E. H. (2007). *"I'm a produc of everythinh I've been through": A Narrative study of cultural identity construction of Bosnian Muslim female refugee students.* The florida State University.

Cleland, B. (2001). The history of Muslims in Australia. In A. Saeed & S. Akbarzadeh (Eds.), *Muslim communities in Australia*. Sydney: UNSW Press.

Cole, D., & Ahmadi, S. (2003). Perspectives and experiences of Muslim women who veil on college campuses. *MUSE, 44*(1), 47-65.

Collet, B. A. (2007). Islam, national identity and public secondary education: Perspectives from the Somali diaspora in Toronto, Canada. *Race Ethnicity and Education, 10*(2), 131-153.

Cook, B. J. (1999). Islamic versus western conceptions of education: refelections on Egypt. *International Review of Education, 45*(3/4), 339-357.

Cornell, S., & Hartmann, D. (2007). *Ethnicity and race: Ethnicity and race: Making identity in a changing world* (2nd ed.). Thousand Oaks, London, New Delhi: Pine Forge Press.

Creswell, J. W. (2007). *Qualittaive inquiry & research design: Choosing among five approaches* (2nd ed.). London: Sage Publication, Ltd.

Curtis, E. E. (2009). *Muslims in America: A short history.* Oxford, New York: Oxford University Press.

Dawson, M. C. (2007). Identity formation among learners at a South African high school: assessing the interaction between context and identity. *Race Ethnicity and Education, 10*(4), 457-472.

Dean, H., & Khan, Z. (1997). Muslim perspectives on welfare. *Journal of Social Policy, 26*(2), 193-209.

Dizboni, A. G. (2008). Muslim discourses in Canada and Quebec. *ARSR, 21*(1), 17-47.

Doogue, D., & Kirkwood, P. (2005). *Tomorrow's Islam: Uniting age-old beliefs and a modern world.* Sydnet: ABC Books.

Douglass, S. L., & Shaikh, M. A. (2004). Defining Islamic education: differentiation and applications. *Current Issues in Comparative Education, 7*(1), 5-18.

Duderija, A. (2008). Factors determining religious identity construction among Western-born Muslims: toward a theoretical framework. *Journal of Muslim Minority Affairs, 28*(3), 371-400.

Duderija, A. (2010a). Identity construction among western (born) Muslims: Religious traditions and social orientation. In S. Yasmeen (Ed.), *Muslims in Australia: The dynamics of exclusion and inclusion.* Melbourne: Melbourne University Press.

Duderija, A. (2010b). Progressive Muslims-defining and elineating identities and ways of being a Muslim. *Journal of Muslim Minority Affairs, 30*(1), 127-136.

Dunn, K. (2001). Representations of Islam in the politics of mosque development in Sydney. *Tijdschrift voor Economische en Sociale Geografie, 92*(3), 291-308.

Dunn, K. (2004). Islam in Sydney: contesting the discourse of absence. *Australian Geographer, 35*(3), 333-353.

Dunne, M., Pryor, J., & Yates, P. (2005). *Becoming a researcher: a research companion for the social sciences.* New York: Open University Press.

Dwyer, C. (1999a). Contradictions of community: questions of identity for young British Muslim women. *Environment and Planning, 31*, 53-68.

Dwyer, C. (1999b). Veiled meanings: Young British Muslim women and teh negotiation of differences [1]. *Gender, Place & Education: A Journal of Feminist Geography, 6*(1), 5-26.

Dwyer, C. (2000). Negotiating diasporic identities: Young South Asian Muslim women. *Women's Studies International Forum, 23*(4), 475-486.

Ekram, & Beshir, M. R. (2009). *Meeting the challenge of parenting in the west: an Islamic perspective* (4th ed.). Beltsville: Amana Publication.

Elliott, J. (2005). *Using narrative in social research: Qualitative and quantitative approaches.* London, Thousan Oaks, New Delhi: Sage Publications.

Esposito, J. L. (2010). *The future of Islam.* Oxford, New York: Oxford University Press.

Faas, D. (2008). Constructing identities: the ethno-national and nationalistic identities of white and Turkish students in two English secondary schools. *British Journal of Sociology of Education, 29*(1), 37-48.

Fadil, N. (2005). Individualizing faith, individualizing identity: Islam and young Muslim women in Belgium. In J. Cesari & S. McLaughlin (Eds.), *European Muslims and the secular state.* Aldershot, Burlington: Ashgate Publishing Limited.

Ganter, R. (2008). Muslim Australians: The deep histories of contact. *Journal of Australian Studies, 32*(4), 481-492.

Gendrot, S. B. (2007). France upside down over a headscarf? *Sociology of Religion, 68*(3), 289-304.

Georgakopoulou, A. (2006). Thinking big with small stories in narrative and identity analysis. *Narrative Inquiry, 16*(1), 122-130.

Gergen, M. M., & Gergen, K. J. (2006). Narratives in action. *Narrative Inquiry, 16*(1), 112-121.

Glesne, C. (2006). *Becoming qualitative researchers: An introduction* (3rd ed.). Boston: Pearson Education.

Guessoum, N. (2008). The Qur'an, science, and the (related) contemporary Muslim discourse. *Zygon, 43*(2), 411-431.

Halstead, M. (1995a). Toward a unified view of Islamic education. *Islam and Christian-Muslim relations, 6*(1), 25-43.

Halstead, M. (1995b). Voluntary apartheid? problems of schooling for religious and other minorities in democratice society. *Journal of Philosophy of Education, 29*(2), 257-272.

Halstead, M. (2004). An Islamic concept of education. *Comparative Education, 40*(4), 517-529.

Hamdani, D. (2007). *The quest for Indonesian Islam: contestation and consensus corcerning veiling.* Australian National University, Canberra.

Hassan, R. (2002). *Faithlines: Muslim conceptions of Islam and society.* Oxford, New York: Oxford University Press.

Hassan, R. (2006). Globalization's challenge to the Islamic *ummah. AJSS, 34*(2), 311-323.

Hassan, R. (2007). On being religious: Patterns of religious commitment in Muslim societies. *The Muslim World, 97*(3), 437-478.

Hassan, R. (2008). *Inside Muslim minds.* Carlton: Melbourne University Press.

Hassan, R., Corkindale, C., & Sutherland, J. (2008). The reality of religious labels: A study of Muslim religiosity. *ARSR, 21*(2), 188-199.

Henwood, K. l. (1996). Qualitative inquiry: perspectives, methods, and psychology. In J. T. E. Richardson (Ed.), *Handbook of qualitative research method for pyschology and the social sciences.* Leicester: BPS Books.

Herrera, L., & Bayat, A. (2010a). Knowing Muslim youth. In L. Herrera & A. Bayat (Eds.), *Being young and Muslim: New cultural politics in the global South and North.* Oxford, New York: Oxford University Press.

Herrera, L., & Bayat, A. (Eds.). (2010b). *Being young and Muslim: New cultural politics in the global south and north.* Oxford, New York: Oxford University Press.

Heyl, B. S. (2001). Ethnographic interviewing. In P. Atkinson, A. Coffey, S. Delamont, J. Lofland & L. Lofland (Eds.), *Handbook of ethnography.* London, Thousand Oaks, New Delhi: SAGE Publications.

Hilgendorf, E. (2003). Islamic education: History and tendency. *Peabody Journal of Education, 78*(2), 63-75.

Ho, C. (2007). Muslim women's new defenders: Women's rights, nationalism, and Islamophobia in contemporary Australia. *Women's Studies International Forum, 30*, 290-298.

Hodkinson, P. (2005). 'Insider research' in the study of youth culture. *Journal of Youth Studies, 8*(2), 131-149.

Humphrey, M. (1998). *Islam, multiculturalism and transnationalism: from the Lebanese Diaspora.* New York: The Centre for Lebanese Studies, Oxford and I.B. Tauris & Co Ltd.

Humphrey, M. (2001). An Australian Islam? Religion in the multicultural city. In A. Saeed & S. Akbarzadeh (Eds.), *Muslim communities in Australia*. Sydney: UNSW Press.

Husain, F., & O'Brien, M. (2000). Muslim communities in Europe: Reconstruction and transformation. *Current Sociology, 48*(4), 1-13.

Hussain, A. (2004). Islamic education: why is there a need for it. *Journal of Beliefs & Values, 25*(3), 317-323.

Imam, S. A. (2009). Separation of what and state: The life experiencs of Muslims with public schools in Midwest. In O. Sensoy & C. D. Stonebanks (Eds.), *Muslim voices in school: Narratives of identity and pluralism*. Rotterdam, Boston, Taipei: Sense Publishers.

Imtoual, A. S. (2006). *'Taking things personally': young Muslim women in South Australia discuss identity, religious racism and media representation*. UNiversity of Adelaide, Adelaide.

Irfan, S. (2008). Childrearing practices among South Asian Muslims in Britain: The cultural context of physical punishment. *Journal of Muslim Minority Affairs, 28*(1), 147-161.

Johns, A. H., & Saeed, A. (2002). Muslims in Australia: The building of a community. In Y. Y. Haddad & J. I. Smith (Eds.), *Muslim minorities in the West*. Walnut Greek, Lanham, New York, Oxford: Altamira Press.

Johnson, B., & Christensen, L. (2004). *Educational research: Quantitative, qualitative, and mixed approaches* (2nd ed.). Boston: Pearson Education, Inc.

Jones, J. S. (2010). Origins and ancestors: a brief history of ethnography. In J. S. Jones & S. Watt (Eds.), *Ethnography in social science practice*. London and New York: Routledge.

Joseph, C. (2009). Postcoloniality and ethnography: negotiating gender, ethnicity and power. *Race Ethnicity and Education, 12*(1), 11-25.

Kabir, N. A. (2004). *Muslims in Australia: Immigration, race relations, and cultural history*. London, New York, Bahrain: Kegan Paul.

Kabir, N. A. (2005). Muslims in Australia: Immigration, race relations and cultural history. *Sydney papers, 17*(2), 62-72.

Kabir, N. A. (2006). Representation of Islam and Moslims in Australian Media, 2001-2005. *Journal of Muslim Minority Affairs, 26*(3), 313-328.

Kabir, N. A. (2007). Muslims in Australia: The double edge of terrorism. *Journal of Ethnic and Migration Studies, 33*(8), 1277-1297.

Kabir, N. A. (2008a). *A study of Australian Muslim youth identity*. Paper presented at the NCEIS Conference, University of Melbourne.

Kabir, N. A. (2008b). To be or not to be an Australian: Focus on Muslim youth. *National Identities, 10*(4), 399-419.

Kabir, N. A. (2010). *Young British Muslims: Identity, culture, politics and the media*. Edinburg: Edinburgh University Press Ltd.

Kadi, W., & Billeh, V. (Eds.). (2007). *Islam and Education: Myths and truths*. Chicago: The University of Chicago.

Kaya, I. (2003). *Shifting Turkish American identity formations in the United States*. The Florida State University, Tallahase.

Kaya, I. (2004). Turkish-American immigration history and identity formations. *Journal of Muslim Minority Affairs, 24*(2), 295 - 308.

Keaton, T. (2005). Arrogant assimilastion: National identity politics and African-origin Muslim girls in the other France. *Anthropology and Education Quarterly, 36*(4), 405-423.

Keely, A. A. (2006). Beginning Christian -Muslim dialogue in Western Sydney: Context and practice. *Islam and Christian-Muslim relations, 17*(4), 471-482.

Khan, T. (2009). *Emerging Muslim identity in India's globalized and mediated Society: An ethnographic investigation of the halting modernities of the Muslim youth of Jamia Enclave, New Delhi*. Ohio University, Athens.

Kibria, N. (2007). The 'new Islam' and Bangladeshi youth in Britain and the US. *Ethnic and Racial Studies, 31*(2), 243-266.

Killian, C. (2007). From a community of believers to an Islam of the heart: "conspicuous" symbols, Muslim practices, and the privatization of religion in France. *Sociology of Religion, 68*(3), 305-320.

Kraus, W. (2006). The narrative negotiaton of identity and belonging *Narrative Inquiry, 16*(1), 103-111.

Krause, N., & Ellison, C. G. (2007). Parental religious socialization practices and self-esteem in late life. *Review of Religious Research, 49*(2), 109-127.

Küçükcan, T. (2004). The making of Turkish-Muslim diaspora in Britain: religious collective identity in a multicultural public sphere *Journal of Muslim Minority Affairs, 24*(2), 243 - 258.

Kusat, A. (2001). The influence of minority feelings on the formation of religious concept and individual identity: The case of Bulgarian Muslims. *Journal of Muslim Minority Affairs, 21*(2), 363-372.

Lathion, S. (2008). Muslims in Switzerland: Is citizenship really incompatible with Muslim identity? *Journal of Muslim Minority Affairs, 28*(1), 53-60.

Lewis, P. (2007). *Young, British and Muslim*. London: Continuum.

Litchman, M. (2010). *Qualitative research in Education: A user's guide*. Los Angeles, London, New Delhi, Singapore, Washington, DC: Sage.

Lotfi, A. (2001). Creating Muslim space in the USA: Masjid and Islamic centers. *Islam and Christian-Muslim relations, 12*(2), 235-254.

Luke, C., & Luke, A. (1999). Theorizing interracial families and hybrid identity: An Australian perspective. *Educational Theory, 49*(2), 223-249.

Mandaville, P. (2001). Reimaging Islam in diaspora: The politics of mediated community. *Gazette, 63*(2-3), 169-186.

Mansouri, F. (2005). Citizenship, identity and belonging in contemporary Australia. In S. Akbarzadeh & S. Yasmeen (Eds.), *Islam and the West: Reflections from Australia*. Sydney: UNSW Press Ltd.

Mansouri, F., & Kamp, A. (2007). Structural deficiency or cultural racism: the educational and social experiences of Arab-Australian youth. *Australian Journal of Social Issues, 42*(1), 87-102.

Mansouri, F., & Wood, S. P. (2008). *Identity, education and belonging: Arab and Muslim youth in contemporary Australia*. Melbourne: Melbourne University Press.

Marranci, G. (2003). "We speak English": language and identity processes in Northern Ireland's Muslim community. *Etnologies, 25*(2), 59-75.

Marranci, G. (2007). Migration and construction of Muslim women's identity in Northern Ireland. In C. Aitchison, P. Hopkins & M.-P. Kwan (Eds.), *Geographies of Muslim identities: Diaspora, gender and belonging*. Hampshire, Burlington: Ashgate Publishing Limited.

Marranci, G. (2008). *The anthropology of Islam*. Oxford, New York: BERG.

Masquelier, A. (2010). Securing futures: youth, generation, and Muslim identities in Niger. In L. Herrera & A. Bayat (Eds.), *Being young and Muslim: New cultural politics in the global south and north*. Oxford: Oxford University Press.

McAulife, C. (2007). Visible minorities: Constructing and deconstructing the 'Muslim Iranian' diaspora. In C. Aitchison, P. Hopkins & M.-P. Kwan (Eds.), *Geographies of Muslim identities: Diaspora, gender and belonging*. Hampshire, Burlington: Ashgate Publishing Limited

McGown, B. R. (1999). *Muslim in the diapora: The Somali communities of London and Toronto*. Toranto, Buffalo, London: University of Toronto Press.

Meer, N. (2007). Muslim schools in Britain: challenging mobilisations or logical development. *Asia Pacific Journal of Education, 27*(1), 55-71.

Mernissi, F. (1991). *The veil and the male elite: A feminist interpretation of women's rights in Islam*. Cambridge: Perseus Books.

Merriam, S. B. (2009). *Qualitative research: a guide to design and implementation*. San Francisco Jossey-Bass. A Wiley Imprint.

Merry, M. S. (2005a). Cultural coherence and the schooling for identity maintenance. *Journal of Philosophy of Education, 39*(3), 477-497.

Merry, M. S. (2005b). Social exclusion of Muslim youth in Flemish-and French-speaking Belgian schools. *Comparative Education Review, 49*(1), 1-22.

Merton, R. K. (1972). Insiders and outsiders: a chapter in the Sociology of knowledge. *The American Journal of Sociology, 78*(1), 9-47.

Mills, S. (2003). *Michel Foucault*. London and New York: Routledge.

Mir, M. (2007). The Qur'an, the word of God. In V. J. Cornell (Ed.), *Voices of Islam*. Westport, Conecticut, London: Praeger Perspectives.

Mishra, S., & Shirazi, F. (2010). Hybrid identities: American Muslim women speak. *Gender, Place & Culture, 17*(2), 191-209.

Moghissi, H. (Ed.). (2006). *Muslim diaspora: Gender, culture and identity*. Abington, New York: Routledge.

Mondal, A. A. (2008). *Young British Muslim voices*. Oxford, Westport, Connecticut: Greenwood World Publishing.

Monsour, A. (2002). Whitewashed: the Libanese in Queensland, 1880-1947. In G. hage (Ed.), *Arab-Australians: Citizenship and belonging today*. Carlton South: Melbourne University Press.

Mosselson, J. (2010). Subjectivity and reflexivity: locating the self in research on dislocation. *International Journal of Qualitative Studies in Education, 23*(4), 479-494.

Muedini, F. (2009). Muslim American college youth: Attitudes and responses five years 9/11. *The Muslim World, 99*, 39-59.

Muhaimin (2006). *Nuansa baru pendidikan Islam: mengurai benang kusut dunia pendidikan*. Jakarta: PT RajaGrafindo Persada.

Mulyana, D. (1995). *Twenty-five Indonesians in Melbourne: The study of social construction and transformation of ethnic identity*. Monash University Clayton.

Mulyana, D. (2000). *Islam dan orang Indonesia di Australia*. Jakarta: Logos.

Naylor, S., & Ryan, J. R. (2002). The mosque in the suburbs: negotiating religion and ethnicity in South London. *Social and Cultural Geography, 3*(1), 39-59.

Nielsen, J. S. (2000). Fluid identities: Muslims and westerns eroupe's nation states. *Cambridge Review of International affairs, 13*(2), 212-227.

Nilan, P., Donaldson, M., & Howson, R. (2007). Indonesian Muslim masculinities in Australia. *Asian Social Science, 3*(9), 1-27.

Peek, L. (2005). Becoming Muslim: The development of a religious identity. *Sociology of Religion, 66*(3), 215-242.

Pepper, C., & Wildy, H. (2009). Using narrative as a research strategy. *Qualitative Research Journal, 9*(2), 18-26.

Peterson, E. E., & Langellier, K. M. (2006). The performance turn in narrative studies. *Narrative Inquiry, 16*(1), 173-180.

Philips, T., & Smith, P. (2000). What is 'Australian'? knowldge and amonga gallery of contemporary Australian. *Australian Journal of Poltical Science, 35*(2), 203-224.

Poole, M. (2007). Socialization and the new genetics. In J. Germov & M. Poole (Eds.), *Public sociology: An introduction to Australian society*. Crows Nest: Allen and Unwin.

Poynting, S., & Mason, V. (2007). The resistible rise of Islamophobia: Anti-Muslim racism in the UK and Australia before 11 September 2001. *Journal of Sociology, 43*(1), 61-68.

Qadeer, M. A. (2006). *Pakistan: Social and cultural transformations in a Muslim nation*. London and New York: Routledge.

Qardawi, Y. (2008). *Fiqh of Muslim minorities: Contentious issues and recommended solutions*. Cairo: New Vision.

Raby, R. (2001). On the move: Young people making identity. *Discourse: Studies in the cultural politics of education, 22*(3), 383-390.

Raedt, T. D. (2004). Muslims in Belgium: a case study of emerging identities. *Journal of Muslim Minority Affairs, 24*(1), 9-30.

Ramadan, T. (1999). *To be a European Muslim*. Leicester: The Islamic Foundation.

Ramadan, T. (2001). *Islam, the West and challenges of modernity*. Leicester: The Islamic Foundation.

Ramadan, T. (2002). Europeanization of Islam or Islamization of Europe? In S. T. Hunter (Ed.), *Islam, Europe's second religion: the new social, cultural, and political landscape*. Westport, Connecticut, London: PRAEGER.

Ramadan, T. (2004). *Western Muslims and the future of Islam*. New York: Oxford University Press, Inc.

Read, J., G., & Bartkowski, J., P. (2000). To veil or not to veil? A case study of identity negotiation ammong women in Austin, Texas. *Gender and Society, 14*(3), 395-417.

Rippin, A. (2005). *Muslims: Their religious beliefs and practices* (3rd ed.). London and New York: Routledge.

Sadat, M. H. (2008). Hyphenating Afghaniyat (Afghan-ness) in the Afghan Diaspora. *Journal of Muslim Minority Affairs, 28*(3), 329-342.

Saeed, A. (2003). *Islam in Australia*. Crown Nest: Allen & Unwin.

Saeed, A. (2006a). *Interpreting the Qur'an: towards a contemporary approach*. London and New York: Routledge.

Saeed, A. (2006b). *Islamic thought: an introduction*. London and New York: Routledge.

Saeed, A. (2008). *The Qur'an: an introduction*. London and New York: Routledge.

Saeed, A., & Akbarzadeh, S. (2001). Searching for identity: Muslims in Australia. In A. Saeed & S. Akbarzadeh (Eds.), *Muslim communities in Australia*. Sydney: University of New South Wales Press Ltd.

Saikal, A. (2005). Islam and the West: containing the rage? In S. Akbarzadeh & S. Yasmeen (Eds.), *Islam and the West: reflections from Australia*. Sydney: UNSW Press.

Saktanber, A. (2007). Cultural dilemmas of Muslim youth: Negotiating Muslim identities and being young Turkey. *Turkish Studies, 8*(3), 417-434.

Samers, M., E. (2003). Diaspora unbound: Muslim identity and erratic regulation of Islam in France. *Iternational Journal of Population Geography, 9*, 351-364.

Sarroub, L. K. (2005). *All American Yemeni girls: Being Muslim in a public school*. Philadephia: University of Pennsylvania Press.

Sarroub, L. K. (Ed.) (2007) Women and Islamic Cultures (Vols. V). Leiden: Brill NV.

Sarroub, L. K. (2010). Discontinuities and differences among Muslim Arab-Americans: Making it at home and school. In M. L. Dantas & P. C. Manyak (Eds.), *Home-school conncetion in a multicultural society: Learning from and with culturally and linguistically diverse families*. New York, London: Routledge.

Schmidt, G. (2004). Islamic identity formation among young Muslims: the case of Denmark, Sweden and the United States. *Journal of Muslim Minority Affairs, 24*(1), 31-45.

Schumann, C. (2007). A Muslim 'diaspora' in the United States. *The Muslim World, 97*(1), 11-32.

Shah, S. (1998). Flash-backs-and-forth:re-searching the roots. In K. Haw (Ed.), *Educating Muslim girls: Shifting discourses*. Buckingham, Philadelphia: Open University Press.

Shah, S. (2009). Muslim learners in English schools: a challenge for school leaders. *Oxford Review of Education, 35*(4), 523-540.

Shih, C.-Y. (2000). Between the mosque and the state: The identity strategies of the Litong Muslims. *Religion, State & Society, 28*(2), 197-211.

Sirin, S. R., & Fine, M. (2008). *Muslim American youth: Understanding hyphenated identities through multiple methods*. New York and London: New York University Press.

Spalek, B., & Imtoul, A. (2007). Muslim communities and counter-terror responses:"hard" approaches to community engagement in teh UK and Australia. *Journal of Muslim Minority Affairs, 27*(2), 185-202.

Stevens, C. (1993). Afghan camel drivers: Founders of Islam in Australia. In M. L. Jones (Ed.), *An Australian pilgrimage: Muslims in Australia from the seventeenth century to the present.* Melbourne: Victoria Press.

Stewart, S. M., Bond, M. H., Ho, L. M., Zaman, R. M., Dar, R., & Anwar, M. (2000). Perceptions of parents and adolescent outcomes in Pakistan. *British Journal of Developmental Psychology, 18*, 335-352.

Stokes, C. E., & Regnerus, M. D. (2009). When faith divides family: religious discord and adolescent reports of parent-child relations. *Social Science Research, 38*, 155-167.

Subedi, B. (2006). Theorizing a 'halfie' researcher's identity in transnational fieldwork. *International Journal of Qualitative Studies in Education 19*(5), 573-593.

Tabar, P., Noble, G., & Poynting, S. (2003). 'The rise and falter of teh field of ethnic politics in Australia: the case of Lebanese community leadership'. *Journal of Intercultural Studies, 24*(3), 267-287.

Tuncer, A. (2000). *The influence of Islam on Indonesian women resident in Melbourne.* La Trobe University, Faculty of Humanities and Social Sciences.

Vertovec, S. (1998). Young Muslims in Keighley, West Yorkshire: Cultural identity. In S. Vertovec & a. Rogers (Eds.), *Muslim European youth: reproducing ethnicity, religion, culture.* Aldershot: Ashgate Publishing Ltd.

Walford, G. (2007). Classification and framing of interviews in ethnographic interviewing. *Ethnography and education, 2*(2), 145-157.

Werbner, P. (2004). Theorising complex diasporas: Purity and hybridity in the South Asian public sphere in Britain. *Journal of Ethnic and Migration Studies, 30*(5), 895-911.

Woodlock, R. (2010a). The *masjid* is for men: competing voices in the debate about Australian Muslim women's access to mosques. *Islam and Christian-Muslim relations, 21*(1), 51-60.

Woodlock, R. (2010b). Praying where they don't belong: Female Muslim converts and access to mosques in Melbourne, Australia. *Journal of Muslim Minority Affairs, 30*(2), 265-278.

Yasmeen, S. (2002). Muslim women as citizens in Australia: Perth as a case study. In Y. Y. Haddad & J. I. Smith (Eds.), *Muslim minorities in the West: Visible and invisible.* Walnut Creek, Lanham, New York, Oxford: Altamira Press.

Yasmeen, S. (2005a). "Dealing with Islam" in Australia: After the London bombings. *The Sydney Paper*,

Yasmeen, S. (2005b). Islam and the west: Some reflections. In S. Akbarzadeh & S. Yasmee (Eds.), *Islam and the West: Reflection from Australia*. Sydney: UNSW Press Ltd.

Yasmeen, S. (2008). Understanding Muslim identities: From perceived relative exclusion to inclusion. Unpublished Report. Center for Muslim Studies and Societies, University of Western Australia.

Yasmeen, S. (Ed.). (2010). *Muslims in Australia: the dynamics of exclusion and inclusion*. Melbourne: University of Melbourne Press.

Yusuf, I. (2009). *Once were radicals: my years as a teenage Islamofascist*. Crows Nest: Allen & Unwin.

Zevallos, Z. (2003). 'That's my Australian side': The ethnicity, gender and sexuality of young Australian women of South and Central American origin. *The AUstralian Sociological Association, 39*(1), 81-89.

Zevallos, Z. (2004). *'You have to be anglo and not look like me': identity constructions of second generation migrant-Australian women*. Swinburne University, Hawthorn.

Zevallos, Z. (2005). 'It is like we're their culturfe': Second-generation migrant women discuss Australian culture. *People and Place, 13*(2), 41-49.

Zine, J. (1997). *Muslim students in public schools: Education and the politics of religious identity*. University of Toronto, Toronto.

Zine, J. (2001). Muslim youth in Canadian schools: Education and the politics of religious identity. *Anthropology and Education Quarterly, 32*(4), 339-426.

Zine, J. (2006). Unveiled sentiments: Gendered Islamophobia and experiences of veiling among Muslim girls in a Canadian Islamic school. *Equity & Excellence in Education, 39*(3), 239-252.

Zine, J. (2007). Safe havens or religious getthos? Narratives of Islamic schooling in Canada. *Race Ethnicity and Education, 10*(1), 71-02.

Zine, J. (2008). *Canadian Islamic school: Unravelling the politics of faith, gender, knowledge, and identity*. Toronto, Buffalo, London: University of Toronto Press.